PREFACE.

THE following lectures on St. Paul's Epistle to the Romans were delivered by Colet in the University of Oxford, though not, as it would appear, in any official capacity, about the year 1497. Some extracts from them were given a short time ago by Mr. Seebohm, in his *Oxford Reformers;* but, with this exception, the manuscript containing them has lain undisturbed on the shelves of the Cambridge University Library. In seeking to make them heard once more, and by a more varied, if not more numerous, auditory, I trust that no such malediction need be feared, as our great poet invoked on the disturbers of his rest. For Colet himself seems, in one place (p. 57), to have had a presage of some such result; and, if this were not enough, the desire of Erasmus, expressed in the words prefixed as a motto to this work, would be a sufficient justification.

The Latin text is taken from the manuscript volume before referred to, numbered Gg. iv. 26. The Epitome, or Summary of Contents, prefixed to the first Chapter, is from the Parker MS. (No. 355), in the Library of Corpus Christi College. Had this latter MS. been complete, I should have preferred it to the other; but unfortunately it contains only a portion of these Lectures, bound up with a like defective portion of Colet's Letters on Genesis. The interesting Letter to the Abbot of Winchcombe has already appeared in print; otherwise it would have formed an appropriate sequel to the present work.

In preparing the Latin for publication, I have had a somewhat difficult course to steer. Colet's style was long ago remarked upon by Erasmus, as not altogether faultless; and in this instance there is the additional disadvantage, that the present text appears to have been only partially corrected by the author. Indeed, the brevity of treatment in the earlier chapters, as compared with the later ones, almost leads to the conclusion, that we have in the former an abstract only of what Colet really delivered. Excepting, however, in the case of a palpable slip of the pen, I have not ventured on any corrections. The translation will show what I thought was intended to be written. Neither have I judged it prudent to alter the spelling, beyond writing uniformly æ, instead of e, for the feminine termination, and using j and v, according to modern custom, for i and u. This is in accordance with the plan followed in editing Colet's former treatises. When we find, in a single sentence of Bishop Longland, printed during Colet's lifetime, such fluctuations of spelling as " aule suæ presentia," this will not seem a great liberty to take.

In a review of the *Treatises on the Hierarchies*,

IOANNIS COLETI ENARRATIO IN EPISTOLAM
S. PAULI AD ROMANOS.

AN EXPOSITION OF ST. PAUL'S EPISTLE TO THE ROMANS,

DELIVERED AS LECTURES IN THE UNIVERSITY OF OXFORD
ABOUT THE YEAR 1497,

BY JOHN COLET, M.A.
AFTERWARDS DEAN OF ST. PAUL'S.

NOW FIRST PUBLISHED, WITH A TRANSLATION,
INTRODUCTION, AND NOTES,

BY J. H. LUPTON, M.A.
SUR-MASTER OF ST. PAUL'S SCHOOL, AND LATE FELLOW OF
ST. JOHN'S COLLEGE, CAMBRIDGE.

Wipf and Stock Publishers
199 W 8th Ave, Suite 3
Eugene, OR 97401

An Exposition of St. Paul's Epistle to the Romans
By Colet, John
ISBN 13: 978-1-55635-577-6
ISBN 10: 1-55635-577-7
Publication date 8/13/2007
Previously published by Bell and Daldy , 1873

published in 1869, some regret was expressed that the work had not been preceded by a Life of the Author. And certainly, when we observe what misconceptions of his character are still entertained in many quarters, there does seem a need of some authentic account. But I hold to the opinion, that it is too soon to write the Life of any one, till his works have been made known. To this first, and preparatory, chapter in such a Biography, my present task has been a contribution. If I may borrow the closing words of Dean Colet himself, "How I have done this, I confess I do not know. But the best will to do it I have had."

I have now only to express my best thanks to the Senate of the University of Cambridge, for permission to make free use of the manuscript containing these Lectures; and to the Librarian, Mr. Bradshaw, for his courtesy in aiding me to procure the loan of it. I have also to thank the Librarian of Corpus Christi College, the Rev. S. S. Lewis, F.S.A., for his kindness in affording me ready access to the Parker manuscript above mentioned. My previous obligations to Mr. Seebohm are increased, on this occasion, by the loan of his transcript of the manuscript Gg. iv. 26, which has enabled me to check my own, and also of his copy of the interesting manuscript described in the Appendix, which has served to illustrate several points in the present Lectures. I am indebted, lastly, to the Rev. W. Sparrow Simpson, D.D., Librarian of St. Paul's and Lambeth, for many valuable communications. The Coletine

Statutes, now for the first time printed in their entirety, in Dr. Simpson's elaborate edition of the Statutes of St. Paul's Cathedral, have helped to throw further light on the character of this remarkable man.

St. Paul's School,
Easter, 1873.

CONTENTS.

INTRODUCTION.

		PAGE
§ 1.—On the Times in which Colet lived	. . .	xi
§ 2.—University Studies in 1486	. . . .	xiv
§ 3.—Divinity Lectures at Oxford in 1497	. . .	xx
§ 4.—On the Official Sanction given to these Lectures		xxv
§ 5.—Platonic Character of Colet's Lectures	. .	xxvi
§ 6.—Influence of the Writings of Ficino and Mirandola		xxix
§ 7.—Comparison with other Contemporary Lectures	.	xxxv
§ 8.—In what sense Colet was a Reformer	. .	xxxviii

LECTURES.

Summary of Contents 1
Chapter I.—St. Paul's Commission—State of Jewish and Gentile world 3
   ,, II.—Way of acceptance with God . . . 4
   ,, III.—No Superiority to Jews over Gentiles—Foreordained way of Salvation for both . . 5
   ,, IV.—Circumcision—Abraham's faith, and its reward 7
   ,, V.—Power of Grace, that is, of God's love . . 9
   ,, VI.—No further Atonement for Sin—The Jews slow to accept the true one—Weakness of their Law—Weakness of man's corrupt nature 13
   ,, VII.—Jewish Law, continued—No power in it to remove sin—This done by the death of Christ alone 20
   ,, VIII.—Comfort in this for the faithful—Their duty to requite such love of God—Love superior to knowledge 25
   ,, IX., X.—St. Paul's Affection for his People—Their wilfulness unable to defeat the counsel of God—Predestination—Man's pride disqualifies him for understanding the purposes of God 33

CONTENTS.

	PAGE
Chapter XI.—Ultimate conversion of the Jews—Balance rightly held between them and the Gentiles	54
” XII.—Argument resumed—Consequences that follow from what has been said—Duty of reformation—Sacrifices now required—Unity of new life, in the individual, and in the Church—The Body and its Members—Causes, and remedy, of disease	58
” XIII.—Practical application to the state of the Christians in Rome—Evil not to be returned for evil	91
” XIV.—Duties of Christians towards one another—Of the stronger towards the weaker—Questions of *meats*, observance of *days*, and the like—Charity the solver of difficulties—Evils of a contentious spirit	103
” XV.—Concord to be sought—Neither Jew nor Gentile forgotten by Christ—St. Paul's labours in this spirit; his travels; his dangers	123
” XVI.—Farewell greetings—Conclusion	131
ENARRATIO	133
INDEX	233

ERRATA.

Page 1, line 12. *After* two, *insert the words* since they esteemed themselves highly, on account of the Law given them by God.

Page 119 *n, for* Burnet's *read* Kennett's.

INTRODUCTION.

§ 1.—On the Times in which Colet lived.

THERE have been few men whose lives have bridged over more stirring periods of the world's history than that of John Colet.

Born in 1466,[1] he was a child just learning his letters, when the first book appeared that was printed by an Englishman. While he may have been carrying his satchel, now a boy of eight years old, to St. Anthony's school in the City, the first printing-press ever seen in this country was being set up by Caxton at Westminster.

If we follow him to Oxford, after a few more years have rolled away, and see him entered on the splendid foundation of William of Waynflete,[2] it is hard to realize, without an effort, the greatness of the events that were then going on abroad. While he was patiently completing his seven years of probation for the degree of Master of Arts, the struggle of more than as many centuries between Christianity and Mahometanism was being decided. The tide of Moorish invasion, long fluctuating, was at length finally rolled back. Spain had entered on her brilliant, if unenduring, career of glory; and when Columbus saw the banners of Ferdinand

---

[1] This is the date commonly given; derived, I suppose, from the inscription on his monument, "vixit annos 53," since he died Sep. 16th, 1519. But Erasmus, who was born Oct. 28th, 1467, says that Colet was two or three months younger than himself—"me minor duobus aut tribus mensibus."

[2] Wood, the only authority we have for this point, judges this to be the most probable, though there is no certain evidence; and fixes the date at about 1483. Though but recently founded, no College surpassed this of St. Mary Magdalen in the munificence of its endowments, or the distinguished scholars it was beginning to produce. *Athenæ Oxon.* i. 22, and *Hist. et Antiqq.* (1674), ii. p. 189.

and Isabella planted on the towers of the Alhambra,[1] he may be said to have watched the passing away of an old world, before setting forth to discover a new.

Let us carry our glance for a moment still further to the south. We in these days may smile at the idea of danger in a voyage to the Cape: but the achievement that inspired Camoens to write the noblest passage in his Lusiad, must not be despised by us; and that achievement, the first sighting of Cape Stormy, was accomplished while Colet was at Oxford.[2] More than all this, that great event in the world's history, the discovery of America, was then taking place. Before the title of "Magister noster" had yet lost its freshness to Colet's ears, Columbus had sailed back into the harbour of Palos, with tidings of his discovery of the West Indian islands. And by the time that he returned from his tour in France and Italy, or within a little after, the mainland of North America had been reached by the Cabots of Bristol; Vasco di Gama had doubled the Cape; and the East Indies, as well as the West, lay open to the adventurers of Europe.

Nor, if such were the changes taking place without, were any less stirring scenes being enacted within the narrower limits of his own country. Colet saw the final defeat of the Lancastrians at Barnet, and at the "bloody meadow" of Tewkesbury. He saw the line of York come to an end in the battle of Bosworth-field. Scenes that impressed themselves most vividly on the mind of Shakespeare, and through him are imprinted for ever on the memory of our race, were the current topics of the day in his lifetime. The murder of the young princes in the Tower, the public penance of Jane Shore, the death of Richard the Third:—such formed the news that would break in upon his studies at Oxford; while tidings of "dark Flodden" would reach him afterwards in his Deanery of St. Paul's.

It is true that the full grandeur of these events was not

---

[1] Helps: *Life of Columbus* (1869), p. 93.
[2] The Cape of Good Hope was not *doubled* till afterwards; but it was sighted by Bartholomew Diaz in 1486. Helps, *ut sup.* p. 37.

appreciated by those who lived in the midst of them. A scholar like Baptista Mantuanus, writing a treatise on Patience for the consolation of a sick friend, in the very year that Columbus entered the mouth of the Orinoco, alludes indeed to the great discoveries that were being made, but with none of the interest or enthusiasm we should expect. He uses the fact, only as it bears on that declaration of Scripture:—*Their sound has gone forth into all lands, and their words unto the ends of the world.*[1] But this was not wholly through ignorance or indifference. We may rather take the incident just quoted as revealing to us the cast of mind, then most prevalent among thoughtful men. If less attention, than we should have looked for, was given to the importance of new discoveries as affecting the material prosperity of nations, it was because, in the inner world of men's spirits, revolutions were taking place, a reflection of those without, but the more absorbing of the two.

There is little need to enter at large on so familiar a subject as this. Equally unprofitable would it be, to attempt to compare the changes in the inner and outer world, or speculate on their relative importance. Suffice it to say, that the vicissitudes seen by Colet in the one, were as mighty, in their own domain, as those he witnessed in the other. Luther was born the year after he entered Oxford. And though he lived not to see that "tragedy of Luther" (as Erasmus so often calls it[2]) played out, he yet saw the first act, the epitome of the whole. His lot was cast, in short, in one of those periods of rare recurrence in history, that form the evening and the morning of a new order of things.

It is from no desire to exaggerate the importance of the part taken by Colet in these events, that they have been thus briefly recapitulated. But on his mind, as on the

---

[1] *De Patientia,* iii. 12.—Mantuani *Opera* (1576), iv. p. 136.
[2] The phrase *tragœdias excitare* meant, of course, no more than "to make a stir;" but for some reason it has become the fashion to render thus literally the words of Erasmus.

minds of others, what was daily passing could not but leave its reflection. It was a maxim of his, and one cited by Erasmus[1] in terms of very unusual commendation, that "such as our daily talk is, such are we." To have lived in the days when printing in this country had its birth, when a new world was being discovered, when the name of Luther began to be noised abroad, when Italy, in second youth, was again at the head of civilization, as in the days of Augustus; to have watched all this with observant eyes, and heard it furnishing the conversation of the hour; was in itself an education of the highest kind. It is well therefore to bear these things in mind, as we come to estimate the value of Colet's own work. It may easily be that we are disposed to rate it too high, and if so, time will soon rectify the balance. But at present our aim, in thus tracing the historical birth and parentage of his Lectures at Oxford, is nothing less than this; namely, to show that he brought to his University the tidings of a Newfoundland, in religion and learning, as real as that discovered in the physical world by Sebastian Cabot.[2] In other words, that to Colet first, more than to any other Englishman after the revival of letters, we owe the introduction of Platonism into this country; and, far more than that, the introduction of pure, scriptural teaching, in the days when Professors of Divinity still lectured on Duns Scotus, and when Luther and Tyndale were still boys at school.

In evidence of this, let us try to recall, for a moment, the state of learning in our Universities four centuries ago.

§ 2.—UNIVERSITY STUDIES IN 1486.

Erasmus, writing from the Bishop of Rochester's palace

---

[1] Erasmus quotes it in his *Adagia*, under the proverb *Corrumpunt mores bonos*, etc., with this very striking praise:—"Proinde nullum adhuc apophthegma philosophorum memini legere, quod mihi videtur cum illo conferendum, quod Ioannes Coletus meus, vir pariter et eruditus et incorruptus, subinde dictitare consuevit: *Tales nos esse, qualia sunt quotidiana colloquia;* tales evadere, qualia frequenter audimus." The last words I take to be Erasmus's paraphrase of it.

[2] In the self-same year, June 24th, 1497.

UNIVERSITY STUDIES IN 1486.

in 1516, has left us, in a few lines, a description of the studies pursued at Cambridge thirty years before, that is, while Colet was an undergraduate at the sister University. As the course followed in the two places was far more identical then than it is now, his description may be taken as almost equally applicable to Oxford. "Nothing was taught in the schools of Cambridge," he says, "except *Alexander*, the *Parva Logicalia* (as they call them), with the old-established Readings on *Aristotle*, and the *Questions* of Scotus."[1]

When we recollect that Erasmus had himself recently been Greek Professor at Cambridge, and that Bishop Fisher, from whose house he wrote, was for many years its Chancellor, we shall feel that the statement comes with the highest authority. Let us examine it therefore a little more minutely, and see what can be learnt by a closer acquaintance with the works named in this list.

The first author named, Alexander de Villa Dei, or Dolensis, so called as being a native of Dol in Brittany, was one who had for many generations been supreme in the region of Grammar. His treatise was in rhyming hexameters; each verse of which was made the text of laborious comments, and each line of these comments itself often painfully annotated, as the "stuft margins" of many an extant copy show. One single specimen may suffice. The first line of his *Doctrinale*, familiar as "Arma virumque" to schoolboys now, was

"Scribere clericulis paro doctrinale novellis."

Opposite this, in the Ulme edition of 1487, is printed the gloss, "Intentio Alexandri." And in one copy[2] of that edition, filled by some assiduous student with metrical

---

[1] "Ante annos ferme triginta, nihil tradebatur in schola Cantabrigiensi, præter Alexandrum, Parva Logicalia (ut vocant), et vetera illa Aristotelis dictata, Scoticasque quæstiones."—*Epist. Lib.* ii. 10, ed. 1642.

[2] Brit. Mus. Library, marked 12933 l.—It is impossible to give, by any single extract, an adequate idea of the labour that seems to have been spent upon these books.

comments, are written in the margin the following lines, in which we may see displayed the *formal, material, efficient,* and *final* cause of the work :—

> " *Scribere* formalem dat causam : materialem
> *Doctrinale :* item *paro* denotat efficientem :
> Causam *clericulis* dat finalemque *novellis.*".

The supremacy of Alexander was seriously impaired by the *Lac Puerorum* of Sir Thomas More's schoolmaster, John Holt; and in the *Epistolæ Obscurorum Virorum,* as might be expected, the wits of Hutten's party often make merry at his expense.[1]

This might be a tempting occasion to speak of Colet's title to be considered a true reformer of Grammar. But as our object is to show how thoroughly new was the philosophy introduced by him from Italy, we will turn to the next two subjects mentioned by Erasmus. As Grammar chiefly occupied the first year of an undergraduate's *quadriennium,*[2] and Philosophy the fourth, so the two intervening years were filled up by those studies in dialectic which he is here evidently referring to, in his mention of the " *Little Logicals,* as they term them," and the " old established *Readings* on Aristotle."

What was the exact compendium described under the former of these titles, I have not been able to ascertain.[3] But whatever it was, it is often mentioned by contemporary

---

[1] As for example, " Copula ista cum tuo Alexandro, qui fuit asinus Parrhisiensis, sicut adhuc sunt plures."—Ed. 1557, leaf Q 4. Some burlesque verses follow in defence of him.

[2] See Peacock's *Observations on the Statutes* (1841), p. 8. A reference to App. p. xlv. *n.* of the same work will illustrate the use of the term *Dictata,* " Readings " or " Lectures," answering to the *Reportata* of the pupil.

[3] Kennett, though he copies the Latin correctly, renders the words " *Alexander's* Parva Logicalia." But Alexander wrote no such treatise, so far as I can discover; his only other extant work being an *Algorismus,* or metrical Arithmetic, printed in Halliwell's *Rara Mathematica.* Antonius Cornelius (Coronel) is stated by Possevin to have written a *Rosarium parvorum Logicalium;* but the only work of his that I can find, at all answering the description, is his *Expositio super Libros Posteriorum,* printed at Paris in 1510.

writers, and with no great respect. More [1] thought it was called "Little Logicals," because of the little logic it contained! Vives, tutor to Queen Mary, and one of the most learned men of his time, is equally severe upon it;[2] and in the *Epistolæ Obscurorum Virorum* an academic of the old school is introduced, lamenting the good old days, "when it was thought a scandal for a student to be seen walking in the street, without having Peter of Spain, or the *Little Logicals*, under his arm." [3]

In like manner, though it may not be easy to determine what were the exact Readings, or Dictations, from Aristotle, next mentioned, there is no difficulty in finding an abundance of text-books, from which such Readings may have been given, during the last twenty years of the fifteenth century. The number of them, in fact, is simply bewildering;[4] and the real difficulty in this case, as in that of Grammar, is to convey, by any brief citations, an idea of the enormous labour spent in cultivating a field so barren. To appreciate it at all, we must have the books themselves in our hands. The eye must travel over the detached lines of the Latin text of Aristotle, heading solid masses of commentary in smaller type; both alike assiduously annotated by the student.

---

[1] "Cæterum liber ille Parvorum Logicalium (quem ideo sic appellatum puto, quum parum habeat Logices) operæ pretium est videre, etc."—*Opera* (1563), p. 379.

[2] *De causis corrupt. Artium* (1636), iii. p. 213.

[3] *Ut supra*, leaf R. 8.

[4] As a rough test of the degree in which the printing-press was occupied by works connected with Aristotle and Plato respectively, during Colet's lifetime, I counted the number of articles under those two headings in the General Catalogue of the British Museum. Up to the year 1520, *four* works alone are thus entered under the head of Plato; while under the head of Aristotle's *Logic* alone, there appear thirty-six. The Indexes of Manuscripts in the Harleian and Cambridge University Libraries, tell the same tale. It may give some little notion of the extent to which Aristotle has, on the whole, absorbed men's thoughts more than Plato, to mention, that works entered under the former heading fill two whole volumes (184 leaves in all) of the Museum Catalogue; those under the head of Plato, less than nineteen leaves of one volume.

Let the reader take up one of the most popular of the text-books of this time,[1] by Petrus Tataretus; let him ponder well the *Questions, very subtile and useful*, it contains; let him observe the laborious apparatus devised for "finding the middle term in a syllogism," with its pictured illustration of the "Asses' Bridge," through whose treacherous timbers the unskilful would slip and fall; let him mark, lastly, how the painful learner has written whole poems of memorial lines in the margin, full of the barbarous terms of a *memoria technica*, "Bocardo," "ferio," "hebare," and the rest[2]:—and he will be disposed, I think, to sympathize with Erasmus in his joy at the change of studies that had come over Cambridge; a change like that which Budé speaks of as coming over the University of Paris.[3]

As regards the fourth subject mentioned in the above extract from Erasmus, the *Questions* of Duns Scotus, I shall have occasion to refer to them hereafter.

Such, then, is a faint outline of the studies pursued at Cambridge, in 1486. And the same portrait, with very little alteration, will serve for Oxford. Even Anthony à Wood, loyal as he is to his own Alma Mater, contends only that the darkness there was not quite so Cimmerian as on the banks of the Cam.[4] The study of Grammar, in particular, he describes as being at a very low ebb. While, as regards Logic, we may gather from Sir Thomas More, who went through the same course as Colet, and nearly at the same time, what the impression was that it left on an inquiring mind. Speaking of the Utopians, he says that "as they are almost in every thing equal to the ancient Philosophers, so they far exceed our modern Logicians; for

---

[1] *Expositio magistri Petri tatareti super textu logices, etc.* Friburg, 1494. The particular copy referred to is in the British Museum Library, No. 8461 ff.

[2] *Ut supra*, fol. 61. An explanation of these terms will be found in Du Hamel's *Philosophia* (1700), i. p. 27.

[3] See his letter to Erasmus, in Erasmi Epist. (1642), p. 18. He compares the Sorbonne, as it used to be, to the "Serbonian bog" of which Milton wrote.

[4] See his criticisms on Fuller's *Hist. of Cambridge, Hist.* p. 237.

they have never yet fallen upon the barbarous niceties, that our youth are forced to learn in those trifling logical schools that are among us."[1]

Through such "trifling logical schools" Colet had passed, whilst graduating in Arts at Oxford. That he loved not their "barbarous niceties," is plain, if only from the fact that, though devoted to theology, he had no desire to graduate in Divinity. Abroad, as well as at home, he would meet with ample evidence of the sorry results of such mental training. The story told by More,[2] of the disputatious Divine, whom he met at the table of an Italian merchant, and who could be silenced by nothing but texts of Scripture, extemporized by the host for the occasion, from such sources as the *seventeenth* of St. Mark, and the like— is matched by one told by Codrus Urceus,[3] of what befell him at Forli, when encountered by a pedantic doctor from Verona. Equipped with such mental arms as these, Christian teachers were little likely (as Erasmus sorrowfully complains) to convert the Turks, or achieve any other victories, except in fighting with shadows.[4]

And therefore, when Colet brought over from Italy the Platonism of Ficino, to replace such meagre grist as that which the mills of the academic intellect had been so long and wearily grinding; when Abbots and Heads of Houses thronged to hear him, and Erasmus, as he listened, could declare that he seemed to hear Plato,[5] he must be held to

---

[1] *Utopia*, Bp. Burnet's Translation, 1753, p. 90.

[2] In his Letter to Martin Dorpius:—" Forte aderat in cœna religiosus quidam Theologus, disputator egregius, qui recens e continente venerat, etc."—*Op. ut sup.* p. 390.

[3] *Sermones* (1502), leaf L. iii.

[4] Albertus Pius, Count of Carpi, the most temperate of Erasmus's opponents, makes the best defence he can for the logical form taken by theology. But he has to make some strong assertions; as for instance: "Dicere ausim quandoque in una quæstiuncula exacte tractata, non minus succi, non minus theologicæ doctrinæ, contineri quam in aliquo justo et integro priscorum doctorum volumine."— *Tres et viginti Libri* (1531), leaf 135.

[5] "Coletum meum cum audio, Platonem ipsum mihi videor audire."—*Epist.* v. 2.

have done something towards appeasing the intellectual, as well as spiritual, hunger of his time.

§ 3.—DIVINITY LECTURES AT OXFORD IN 1497.

The last decade of the fifteenth century has been before spoken of as a time of travail, of new hopes and enterprises springing up amid the closing troubles of a season of general misery. One, well able to judge, has described the century on the whole as "that melancholy period," which "Death may truly be said to have shared with Folly."[1] And Oxford, with its visitations of the plague, its royal visits, its new life stirring within, presents a microcosm in which we may see reflected the events of the greater world without. In 1493, for example, so strong was the general feeling of depression, from the repeated ravages of the plague, the poverty of students, and other causes, that the University authorities appear to have seriously debated the question, whether they should not remove from the banks of the Isis altogether.[2]

But presently an event occurred, that had a more permanent influence for good on the studies and reputation of Oxford, than any countenance which passing visits from Woodstock could bestow: an event that brings us more directly to the distinctive work of Colet. This was, the foundation, by the Lady Margaret, Countess of Richmond and Derby, of those Divinity Professorships, by which her name has since been chiefly remembered. In the year 1497, pending the completion of the legal settlements,[3] she appointed her own confessor to read a Divinity Lecture in

---

[1] Thomas Wright: *History of Caricature and the Grotesque in Art* (1865), p. 217.

[2] Wood, *ut supra*, p. 236.—The Magdalen men had removed to Brackley in Northamptonshire; the plague prevailing from the beginning of April to Midsummer-day in this year. Hence, possibly, one motive for Colet's journey on the Continent shortly after.

[3] See the Catalogue prefixed to Lady Margaret's *Funeral Sermon*, reprinted 1708. The first actual Professor at Oxford was John Roper, B.D., Fellow of Magdalen, appointed under the charter, Sept. 8th, 1502, at the same time as Bishop Fisher at Cambridge. The name of Erasmus stands fourth in the latter list.

DIVINITY LECTURES IN 1497.

the University; and in this year, accordingly, the first discourse of that long, and still unbroken, series was delivered, by one who held so responsible an office, Edmund Wylsford, B.D., Fellow of Oriel.

What subject, now, was chosen by the newly-appointed Lecturer, and how was the choice likely to influence Colet? For we must remember that he had returned from his tour in France and Italy the year before,[1] and had just begun the course of public life from which he never afterwards wavered.

He began to read, Wood tells us,[2] to a great concourse of hearers, on the *Quodlibets* of Duns Scotus.

It is probable, indeed, that his choice of a subject was considerably restricted. Being as yet only a Bachelor in Divinity, it was his distinctive privilege to be entitled to lecture on the *Sentences* of Peter Lombard.[3] And however lax the University rules on this point may have been, it is but natural to suppose, that the first occupant of so distinguished a post would be more than usually careful to keep within the strict letter of the law. But from whatever reason, whether purely from his own choice, or in obedience to the customs of his University, the new Lecturer took for his subject, not some book of the Old or New Testament, but the Quodlibetical Questions of Duns Scotus.

In this fact, as I think, lies some of the significance of the step taken by Colet, in publicly lecturing on the Epistles of St. Paul. As the probability is that he himself had begun in 1496, it cannot indeed be asserted that disappointment at the line taken by the new Lecturer was his immediate motive.

---

[1] For the evidence that Colet began his Lectures towards the end of 1496, see *The Oxford Reformers*, p. 1.

[2] "Incepit legendo Quodlibeta Doctoris Subtilis solemniter, cui occurrebat maxima audientium multitudo."—*Ut sup.* p. 237.

[3] Though it appears that, during one of his four years' probation for the degree of Doctor in Divinity, the Bachelor was required to read *cursorie* on some one book of Scripture.—See Peacock's *Observations*, App. A., p. xlvi. It was not till 1536 that the above mark of homage to Peter Lombard was abolished.

Still, it is hard to believe that the two events were entirely unconnected. Let us assume that Colet had begun his exposition of St. Paul some months before Wylsford read his inaugural discourse on Scotus. It is certain that so important an act as this of the Countess of Richmond would not be devised and carried into execution in a day. Cardinal Wolsey, by whose solicitation Wylsford had been appointed,[1] was Chancellor of Oxford; and it is likely enough that the intended appointment had been known, and the character of the new Lecturer discussed, in Oxford combination-rooms, before the Michaelmas Term of 1496.

Be this as it may, it is quite certain that Colet's opinion of such a subject as that chosen by the Queen's Confessor would confirm him in his own course, if already begun. Colet knew something of Duns Scotus "and the rest of that kidney,"[2] and viewed their admirers with no great respect. "The Scotists," says Erasmus,[3] "to whom of all men the vulgar attribute peculiar acumen, he used to say appeared to him slow and dull, and anything but clever: for to argue about the expressions and words of others, to object first to this and then to that, and to divide everything into a thousand niceties, was the part only of barren and poor talents." If there be a passage in all Colet's writings, in which his language trembles on the borders of invective (I had almost said, abuse), it is in his School Statutes, where he "abannyshes and excludes .... all barbary, all corruption, all Laten adulterate, which ignorant blinde foles brought into this worlde, and with the same hath dystayned and poysonyd the olde Laten speche."

For this "barbary and corruption" Duns Scotus has in no small degree to answer. "The Latinity of Duns,"

---

[1] Wood, *ut sup.* p. 237.

[2] "Aliosque hujus farinæ."—Erasmi *Epist.* Jodoco Jonæ, translated by J. G. Nichols, in the Appendix to his *Pilgrimages* (1849), p. 131.

[3] *Ut supra*, p. 143.—It would not increase Colet's liking for the Subtle Doctor in after years, that Fitz-James, Bishop of London, was a "superstitiosus atque invictus Scotista."

writes Dean Milman, "is a barbarous jargon. His subtle distinctions constantly demanded new words: he made them without scruple. It would require the most patient study, as well as a new Dictionary, to comprehend his terms."[1]

There was indeed a certain fitness in choosing the works of Duns Scotus for a new course of Divinity Lectures at Oxford; since it was in this University that the great schoolman, then a Fellow of Merton, had won his first laurels nearly two centuries before. But let any reader, after becoming imbued in some measure with Colet's spirit, by a study of what he has written, open one of the twelve bulky volumes[2] in which the works of Scotus are entombed; and he will be at no loss, I think, to understand his aversion from them. The *Quæstiones Quodlibetales*[3] fill the last of these; and, though only twenty-one in number, occupy, with their diffuse *scholia* and commentaries, more than 600 pages. I will not intimidate the reader by quoting more than the first of the *theses* as a specimen. It runs thus: *Utrum in Divinis essentialia sint immediatius essentiæ divinæ quam notionalia.* This is thrown into the form of a syllogism, with its major and minor, and argued *pro* and *con*. Then follow lengthy expositions, by commentators, of the terms employed:—how in ordinary matters *essential* is the opposite of *accidental*, but in theology has a different meaning;[4] how by *notional* is meant in this case what distinguishes one of the Divine Persons from another; how the idea of *immediately* (that is, with no *mean* interposing), may be illustrated by observing that the surface of any body is

---

[1] *Latin Christianity*, vi. p. 467.

[2] Folio, Lugduni, 1639.

[3] The title is derived from a custom originating in the University of Paris, when the degree of Doctor of Divinity was about to be conferred. The candidate had a number of questions propounded to him, on various subjects; and these he was expected to be able to sift and arrange mentally, so as to be ready with an answer on any one of the questions chosen by the propounder. Hence the term *quodlibet* ("any you please"), and the name *quodlibetica*, applied to the whole discussion.

[4] Compare Mirandola *De ente et uno; Op.* 1601, p. 176.

more *immediate* to it than its colour:—and much more to the same effect.¹

As we think of such mental food as this being prepared to satisfy the appetite of Divinity students at Oxford, and that too by the highest official provider of it, the dignity of Colet's undertaking seems to grow upon us.

I am not anxious to join in any thoughtless depreciation of the works of those whom we call the great schoolmen. The mere presence of those works must convict too many among us of indolence; he who, on intellectual grounds only, affects to disparage them, must be very careful lest he expose his ignorance also.² They stand as monuments of severe and laborious thought, in the days when no science of Mathematics, properly so called, had arisen as a substitute. We may pass the jest at their infinite wordiness; but the laugh is turned very sorely against ourselves, as we mark the confused, illogical manner in which controversies, and especially what are called religious controversies, are now too often carried on. The merest novice among the disciples of Walter Burley or Dulcifluus would be amazed, and with reason, at the way in which we mix up *datum* with *probandum*, starting without postulates, and blundering into conclusions.

But, while cheerfully according to Duns and his fellows the praise of real intellectual power, we are not equally bound to admit the religious value of their teaching. There is surely nothing more religious in taking a sentence from

---

¹ That it may not be thought a more abstruse topic than the average has been selected, I subjoin the second Thesis, and also the last :—" Utrum in Deo possint esse plures productiones ejusdem rationis " (an exceedingly subtle argument); and " Utrum ponens mundi æternitatem possit sustinere aliquem esse universaliter bene fortunatum." Many more such examples are given by Erasmus in his note on the *vaniloquium* (" vain jangling.") of 1 Tim. i. 6. His opinion of them will be sufficiently inferred from the word he has chosen to append his note to.

² " Within a short time, I have met with four living English writers who have read parts of Thomas Aquinas. . . . Still, I cannot bring myself to think that there are four more in this country who could say the same."—Hallam, *Middle Ages*, ch. ix.

Augustine, and drawing from it an endless series of logical propositions, than there would be in selecting a sentence from Hooker, at the present time, and making it the groundwork of mathematical problems. So that, if we are to use the term Divinity in its truest sense, we can hardly avoid the conclusion, that, whatever might be the ability of the Queen-Mother's confessor, in expounding the subtleties of Scotus, the real teacher of Divinity at Oxford in 1497 was John Colet.

§ 4.—ON THE OFFICIAL SANCTION GIVEN TO THESE LECTURES.

It would be a difficult, and perhaps, fruitless task, to endeavour to ascertain the degree in which Colet's proceeding was an irregular one, when, being as yet only a Master of Arts,[1] he began to lecture publicly on the Epistles of St. Paul. That he was kept in good countenance, is plain from what Erasmus says, that "there was in Oxford no doctor either of divinity or of law, no abbot nor any other dignitary, but what came to hear him, even bringing their note-books with them."[2] And it will be safer to point to the undisputed fact, that voluntary lectures, even delivered by laymen in churches, were now becoming not unusual.[3] In this way Sir Thomas More, while still a young man, lectured on Augustine's *City of God* in his parish church of St. Lawrence Jewry.[4] Grocyn, the most learned Greek scholar then to be found among our countrymen, gave similar lectures on the supposed works of Dionysius the Areopagite, in St. Paul's Cathedral, and (as Bishop Kennett is inclined to believe), at Oxford also. And

---

[1] "In theologica professione nullum omnino gradum nec assecutus erat, nec ambierat."—Erasmus *Jodoco Jonæ*.
[2] J. G. Nichols' *Translation, ut sup.* p. 132.
[3] See Bp. Kennett's *Collections*, vol. xcvi. (Lansdowne, No. 1030), f. 18.
[4] Milk Street, in which More was born, was formerly divided between the two parishes (now united) of St. Lawrence Jewry and St. Mary Magdalene. Hence I have ventured to call St. Lawrence's his parish church, though not certain which part of Milk Street could claim what Fuller calls "the brightest star that ever rose in that Milky Way."

in Cambridge we find George Stafford, a Fellow of Pembroke in 1515, afterwards continuing for four years to read a lecture on the Scriptures, "whereas former lecturers in divinity had always read on the Sentences."[1]

It is to be observed that the above instances are all of lectures subsequent to those of Colet's, and that they may therefore have been more or less suggested by his. But this is not the point insisted upon. It is not to any originality in beginning a voluntary course, that attention is here called; but to the nature of the subject chosen. It is in this that the strength of Colet's claim lies, to be considered a reformer, in the best sense of the term. For, after comparing his work in this field with that of others before him, one well able to judge has recorded his opinion, that "the inference is plain, that the Public Lecturers, both in the Universities and the Cathedral Churches, took the liberty of reading upon any book rather than upon the Holy Scriptures, till Dr. Colet reformed the practice, and both at Oxford and in St. Paul's brought in the sounder way of reading and expounding the Canonical Epistles of St. Paul."[2]

§ 5.—PLATONIC CHARACTER OF COLET'S LECTURES.

But it is time that we turned our attention from the circumstances connected with the delivery of these Lectures, to the nature of the Lectures themselves. It will need but a very slight inspection to show how tinctured they are with Platonism. Plato and Plotinus are quoted by name,[3] and there may be traced, in particular, the influence of a study of the *Timæus*. Blending with this, we find an admixture of Aristotelian thought, as in the constant reference made to *form*, not *ideas*, in relation to *matter*; in the mention of a *common sense*, and the like.[4]

---

[1] Cooper's *Athenæ Cantabr.* i. p. 39.
[2] Kennett, *ut sup.* f. 53.
[3] *Infra*, pp. 74 and 16.
[4] In his MS. comments on 1 Corinthians, he uses Aristotle's term *entelechia*, to illustrate the animating presence of God's Spirit in the Church:—"Cujus anima et (ut utar Aristotelis verbo Greco) *entelechia*, id est, actus perfectio et consummatio, Deus ipse . . . est."

That we may understand better how far this was the result of Colet's own mental training, and how far it does but represent the current notions of the time, it may be well briefly to notice in what direction the philosophy of the Church had been long tending.

From the earliest times the leaders of the Western Church had instinctively felt the teaching of Plato to be more congenial than that of his great rival. But they could not dispense with the weapons that Aristotelian dialectic put into their hands. Hence they had to bring about, if possible, some kind of harmony between the two; and at the same time to adjust the language of both to the doctrines of Christianity. The result was one that probably neither of the two masters would have been willing to accept. Whereas it was the very essence of Plato's philosophy, that it contained no system of doctrine,[1] they persisted in elaborating one from his writings. He had told of voyages to the Hesperides, and they reduced his journals to a compendium of geography. The method of Aristotle, in like manner, was turned to purposes very alien from his own; and used to discover, not the laws to be deduced from an investigation of the natural world, but such objects as the origin and nature of the soul, the attainment of the chief good, and the like.

Inferring, for example, from Plato, that the only real existences were the *ideas;* and from Aristotle, that an object existed, by virtue of its possessing *form;* they harmonized these tenets with each other and with their own theology, by concluding that the *forms* impressed upon matter were copies of the eternal *ideas;* and that those *ideas* had their abode in the Divine Mind.[2] Hence the relative terms *matter* and *form*, though Aristotelian in their origin, were absorbed into the current Platonism of theology, and became themselves in turn the parents of endless theories.[3]

---

[1] See this well brought out by Van Heusde, *Characterismi* (1839), p. 200.

[2] See the passage quoted below, p. 46 *n.*

[3] See the remarkable chapter on Thomas Aquinas by the late

It was owing to the same cause that the *Timæus*, which is " of all the writings of Plato the most obscure and repulsive to the modern reader,"¹ became the most popular of all his works. For in it, if anywhere, Plato had himself discoursed in the Aristotelian vein. In that dialogue he had for once forsaken his favourite topics of mental investigation, and rehearsed the part of a natural philosopher. And we need not be surprised to find it quoted by Colet,² when it was regarded at one time as a kind of uninspired record of the creation, and the author of it as an " Attic Moses."

But if Colet may seem, thus far, to use but the common language of the schools, there is this great difference to be observed. In the one, the philosophy of Plato had come to be a mere shadow. Its room was occupied by the more substantial, or at least more tangible, philosophy of Aristotle, with the vast brood that sheltered under his name.³ With the other, Platonism was a real and living power. As he took his divinity from the Bible, so he took his philosophy from no second-hand source. He read Plato and Plotinus for himself. In the schools, Platonism, which began by being the mistress, had gradually lost precedence; and Aristotelianism, the servant, had usurped its room.⁴ Nay,

---

Bishop of Hereford, reprinted from the *Encyclop. Metrop.* (1858), p. 80. Traces of these scholastic opinions may still be seen, as the same writer elsewhere points out, in our Office for the Private Baptism of Infants; where the Minister is directed to inquire: " With what *matter* was this child baptized ? With what *words* [corresponding to the scholastic *form*] was this child baptized ?"

¹ Professor Jowett's *Introduction to the Timæus*, p. 468.
² *Infra*, p. 74.
³ Erasmus gives two principal reasons for the inferiority of the theologians of his day to the ancient ones, in the ability to draw forth the spiritual and allegorical meaning of Holy Scripture: and one of them is, their preference for Aristotle, and consequent expulsion of Platonism from the schools:—" Altera, quod uno Aristotele contenti, Platonicos et Pythagoricos arcent a ludis."—*Enchiridion* (1523), leaf g 2.
⁴ Albertus Pius admits, and justifies, the change. After stating the merits of each, with reference to the wants of altered times, he gives the palm unhesitatingly to the " maximus ac prope divinus Aristoteles ;" and adds: " Hinc contigit ut præ cæteris illius doc-

more, this latter system of philosophy had undergone such ceaseless alteration and development; the original substance of it had in many cases been so lost sight of, or perverted, in the wilderness of commentaries through which it was drawn, that, like the famous dragon-tree of Teneriffe, it had moved far away from the soil that its roots once clasped.

Sir Thomas More, who had studied (as he tells us) both at Paris and Louvain, and had therefore gone to the fountain-head for instruction in the dialectic of his time, does not scruple to call Jacobus Faber "the restorer of true dialectic and true philosophy, the Aristotelian above all."[1] And he tells a story, as none could do better than himself, of a most learned dialectician, who had protested to him, that "Aristotle wrote in but a scurvy fashion. In that age, mere boys were so solidly grounded in their *Little Logicals*, that could Aristotle have risen from his grave, and had an argument with them, he would be sworn they would shut him up in fine style, not only in sophistry, but in his own logic too."[2]

Without pursuing this topic further, I trust it may now be apparent to the reader, that while Colet's Lectures reflect in some degree, as they must needs have done, the current phraseology of the schools; yet his philosophy is taken from no such remote and deteriorated streams. Between Colet and Plato there interposed but one only;—one, without whose help it would have been hard indeed for an Englishman then to study Plato,—the interpreter Ficino.

§ 6.—Influence of the Writings of Ficino and Mirandola.

Just in time to be of use to Colet, when beginning his studies at Oxford, had appeared the first edition of Plato's

---

trinam homines complexi fuerint, et ad deserviendum theologiæ illam traduxerint."—*Tres et viginti Libri in Erasmum*, 1531, leaf 134.

[1] In his Letter to Martin Dorpius:—Mori *Opera* (1563), p. 376.

[2] Ib. p. 379:—"Illi bene concluderent eum, non solum in Sophistria, sed etiam in Logica sua." More says he cannot do justice to such flowers of diction, without quoting the exact words.

works, now at length made fully accessible to Western scholars by the Latin translation of Ficino.[1] Before he left England, this was followed by the first edition of Plotinus, also in a Latin dress.[2] During his course at the university, as Erasmus informs us, "he had steadily digested the works of Plato and Plotinus."[3]

Accordingly when, in or about 1493, he set out to visit France and Italy, the reputation of the Florentine scholar must have been familiar to him; and it is not unlikely that one motive of his journey was, to visit, and gather fresh knowledge from, the greatest living exponent of Plato.

So much has been said on a former occasion[4] about the personal history of Ficino, and his fellow-worker Mirandola, that it would be out of place to repeat it here. But as Colet quotes both these writers in the course of his Exposition,[5] and owes much more to them than any mere quotations can represent, it may be as well to glance briefly at one work of each (those, namely, to which he appears most directly indebted); that we may understand both what he had set before him for imitation, and also how he varied from, as well as followed, his pattern.

The *Theologia Platonica* of Marsiglio Ficino appeared at Florence in 1482. In dedicating it to Lorenzo de' Medici, the author speaks of it as having been undertaken from a conviction that no philosophy, so well as the Platonic, could teach men the knowledge and worship of God, and the truth of the immortality of the soul.

From the great length of the treatise, it is utterly impossible to do justice to it in a few meagre extracts. He begins by analyzing the constitution of man, to discover the ruling principle. He rises from *matter* to *quality*, and from that to the *rational soul*, or *third essence*, which is itself subordinated to angels, and inferior to the *intellectual*

---

[1] Printed at Florence, with no date attached, but about 1482.—Harles, ii. 161.
[2] In 1492. *Ib.* ii. 442.   [3] Nichols, *ut supra*, p. 131.
[4] *Hierarchies* (1869), Introd. p. xxii.
[5] Page 5 *n*, and p. 29.

INFLUENCE OF FICINO.

soul, breathed into man by God himself. The former, or *rational* soul, is in some degree a sharer, at dissolution, with the fortunes of matter : it is the latter that is properly immortal. In due course he discusses the objections found in rival schools of philosophy ; and among these, the argument of Lucretius against the soul's immortality, drawn from the observed fact, that, at the approach of death, the mental powers grow gradually more and more dim. This he neutralizes by observing, that the same thing happens at the approach of sleep ; from which nevertheless the spirit wakes refreshed.[1] In discussing the probability of miracles, he argues with great acuteness from the physical influences known to be exerted by one living body upon another, in communicating infection, and the like, to the spiritual influences of mind upon mind, or upon matter.[2] The common objection against miracles, as being disturbances of a law of Nature, is also met by an argument that it has been an element in that fore-ordained law, that in due season the want of a so-called miracle should arise ; and that thus predisposing causes have led up to it.[3] In what he writes concerning a resurrection, there is a strange mixing up of citations from Plato, with the evidence of alleged miracles wrought by the relics of St. Peter at Volaterra. But he presently rises to a higher theme, reasoning that, as the body is here a participator with the soul in its good or evil deeds, so it is fitting that hereafter it should share its rewards or punishments. Towards the close of the work, there are some powerful passages on the sufferings of the wicked after death, wrought especially by the agency of *phantasia,* or imagination. Just as a sufferer from disease may be lulled into a transient unconsciousness, by the use of opiates, only to feel the more racking pains when their effect has passed away; so the one who has gone drowsily

---

[1] *Opera,* 1576, i. p. 217.
[2] *Ib.* p. 300. " Cur minus subjiciatur corpus tuum alterius animo, quam alterius corpori ? " In this passage he falls into some of the astrological conceits that the very word *influence* may serve to remind us of.
[3] *Ib.* p. 304.

through this stage of existence, or has sunk into the heavy slumber of sensuality, will have but the more bitter awaking hereafter. A novel force is thus imparted to the words of Christ: "What I say unto you, I say unto all, Watch."[1] This is followed by some reflections on the sublime vision of Er, in the Tenth Book of the *Republic;* and, with a few words more, the work is brought to a close.

Even from this scanty specimen, it is hoped, the reader may discern that Ficino deserved something of the praise bestowed upon him by Colet;[2] and that the disparaging criticisms of some modern writers are not altogether merited.[3]

Still, it must be confessed that there is an extraordinary mixture of dross with this precious metal. His astrological notions may be in some measure excused. They prevailed in his time and country; and to Mirandola belongs the praise of first successfully attacking them. Less excusable to us will appear his indiscriminate appeal to authorities. Averrois and Plato, Zoroaster and St. Paul, Avicenna and Aristotle, are but a sample of the multitudinous names, that all seem equally to serve his turn for a citation. Less excusable, too, his strange blending of the creations of ancient mythology with the truths of revealed religion; so that Cocytus and Phlegethon are introduced as in no way incongruous with our thoughts of a life hereafter, and the words of Holy Scripture are parodied by their application to Plotinus.[4]

The *Heptaplus*, or seven-fold Exposition of the first chapter of Genesis, by Pico della Mirandola, was published in 1489, and dedicated, like the preceding work, to Lorenzo. Through the exertions of Salviato, in introducing it to the notice of the learned, and from other causes, it soon attained a remarkable popularity.[5] Colet takes it as the

---

[1] *Ib.* p. 422.   [2] *Infra,* p. 32.
[3] See Harford's *Life of Michael Angelo* (1857), i. p. 70.
[4] *Opera, ut sup.* ii. p. 1548; where a lecture on Plotinus is prefaced by an adaptation to him of St. Mark i. 11.
[5] Greswell, *Memoirs of Politianus,* 2nd edition, p. 285.

basis of his comments on the early part of Genesis in his
"Letters to Radulphus;"[1] and several allusions to it may
be traced in the present work. It is interesting, therefore,
to see how far the English scholar was drawn into the vortex
of the brilliant Italian; and how far he could borrow from
him, yet preserve his independence.

The plan of Mirandola's Exposition is a very singular
one. After justifying his search for allegorical meanings
in the writings of Moses, by the example of the parables of
the New Testament, with their esoteric interpretation, he lays
down the following principles:—As Moses is relating the
creation of the *world*, that word must be taken in its widest
acceptation. Now the ancients were familiar with *three*
worlds: first, the super-celestial (called by theologians the
angelic, by philosophers the intellectual); secondly, the
celestial; and thirdly, the sublunary, which we inhabit.[2]
These three worlds were symbolized in the construction of
the tabernacle. What exists in any one of them, exists in
all, but under different conditions. Thus, the elementary
fire of earth appears in heaven as the shining sun, and in
the heaven of heavens as the fire of seraphic intelligence.
Hence, what is predicated of any one of these, may be predicated in varying proportions of them all; and Moses, in
his single history, is recording the simultaneous creation of
all the three.

But further, since man is himself the microcosm, reflect-
ing in his own being the whole external universe,[3] therefore
the Bible record is an account of the origin of him, as a
fourth world. As the natural heaven and earth, the two
extremes, are connected by light, as a mean; so man's immaterial soul and material body, his heaven and earth, are

---

[1] "Verum primum totam universitatem, quod Platonicus Mirandula in Exaemero facit, parciamus in mundos quatuor, etc." He
then proceeds to make the same division as is referred to in the
text.—Parker MS. 355, p. 202.

[2] *Opera* (1601), p. 3.

[3] In keeping with this, the words of St. Mark xvi. 15, " preach the
gospel to *every creature* " (*omni creaturæ*), were interpreted to mean
that man was himself the "whole creation."—*Ib.* p. 5.

connected by those *spirits,* of which Colet speaks.¹ It will thus be seen at once how the opening words of Genesis are explained under this fourth head.

The fifth and sixth worlds are accounted for, rather artificially, by treating the preceding four over again separately and collectively; that is, as they offer points of specific difference or agreement. The last world is the Sabbatic; and the seventh, or last, of these methods of interpretation, is that by which all is referred to Christ as its ultimate object. One single instance of this last method may suffice. According to it, the "fourth day," on which the sun was set to give light upon the earth, was a figure of the four thousand years that were to elapse before the " Sun of righteousness" should arise.²

It may be concluded, from this hasty survey of Mirandola's work, how extremely fanciful his views were, and how baseless, and therefore valueless, his reasoning was often likely to be. Yet there is at times great beauty in his language, and in the analogies he draws. Thus, in his exposition of the words *Let the waters under the heaven be gathered together, and let the dry land appear,* he writes:—
"Let us learn from the *land,* that we too shall not bring forth the fruit wherewith we travail, unless we first keep away and repel from us the onpour of perishable matter in its ceaseless flux, and drive back from our abode the eddying torrent of pleasures, that rush in upon us like a flood.

"From the *waters* let us learn, that they were not deemed fit for producing fish, till they were *gathered together* to the entirety of their own element. Neither shall we be able to bring to the light any offspring worthy of our own nature, if we be distracted and drawn asunder to conflicting ends, and do not, with collected strength, aim wholly at a single object."³

The genuine piety of Mirandola (and there breathes through much that he has written a very genuine piety), Colet embraced with all his heart. Some of his more

---

¹ *Infra,* p. 73. ² *Opera,* p. 36.
³ *Ib.* p. 30. See also *infra,* p. 100, *n* 3.

striking thoughts and expressions he retained to the last. Witness the language used by him in his Convocation Sermon,[1] when describing the injury done to the clergy by their secular pursuits:—"Through spiritual weakness, bondage, and fear, *being made weak with the waters of this world,* they dare neither do, nor say, anything but such things as they know to be pleasing to their Prince's ears." He drew, in truth, from Ficino, and from that "man of an incontinent wit,"[2] Mirandola, to the same good effect as his friend More did from the latter alone.[3] It may be a just decision, that observes in the one little more than "follies and infirmities," "astrological conceits," and "theological aberrations;"[4] and that dictates an epitaph of oblivion for the other.[5] But it is no mean glory for these brilliant, if erratic, scholars of Italy, to have fed the intellectual life of Englishmen like Colet and Sir Thomas More.

§ 7.—COMPARISON WITH OTHER CONTEMPORARY LECTURES.

It may help to illustrate the real nature and value of the present Lectures, if we compare them with some that were delivered by others during the lifetime of the author. Care must no doubt be taken to find a just parallel, or the comparison will prove illusory. But in John Longland, Bishop of Lincoln, it would seem that we have one, whom it is fair,

---

[1] Edited by Thos. Smith (1661) p. 12.
[2] So he is called by one who in many things resembled him, Dr. John Donne:—*Essays in Divinity* (Jessop's edition), p. 31.
[3] See the extracts given in Seebohm's *Oxford Reformers*, pp. 151-157. More's *Life of Picus* was modernized in 1723 by a Mr. Jesup, and a comparison added between Pico della Mirandola and Pascal.
[4] Harford, *ut supra*, i. p. 70.
[5] "His name, then celebrated in the remotest corners of the earth, is now almost forgotten; and his works, then studied, admired, and applauded, are now mouldering in obscurity."—*Johnson's Works*, ii. p. 273; quoted in *The Life of Donne, by an Antiquary*, p. 10, *n*. The reference is plain to Mirandola's epitaph:—
"Joannes jacet hic Mirandula: cætera norunt
Et Tagus et Ganges, forsan et Antipodes."
Mirandola died Nov. 17th, 1494, aged 33; Ficino, Oct. 1st, 1499, aged 66.

for many reasons, to contrast with Colet. Both were educated at the same college. Both filled the same office of preacher before the Court during Lent.[1] Richard Kyderminster, Abbot of Winchcombe, was a common friend and correspondent of both of them; a man of kindred spirit with Colet at least, as is shown by the very praise bestowed upon him by Longland. For Kyderminster had not only been a reformer of his Order, but had set an example of true sincerity and humility, by resigning his office, and becoming a simple monk once more."[2] Lastly, Colet and Longland have been associated together (most unjustly so, as I believe) as persecutors of heretics.[3]

What has been said will at any rate suffice to show, that between Colet and the Bishop of Lincoln of his day, there was sufficient similarity of circumstances, to make a comparison between them instructive. And certainly the comparison of their writings *is* instructive; though in this limited space it is impossible to pursue it at any length. But it may be said, in brief, that the discourses of Longland are as inferior to Colet's in point of learning and originality of thought, as in point of true Christian charity. Where the one quotes Plato and Plotinus, the other cites the

---

[1] Frowick came between them :—" Coleto Froickoque jam ante relatis in numerum sanctorum patrum." This occurs in a Dedication of his *Quinque Sermones* to the Abbot of Winchcombe, printed by Pynson with date 1517: but of course the Dedication must be later.

[2] *Quinque Sermones*, as above, leaf 86.

[3] "It is painful to see that to such proceedings, not only Wareham, but Tonstal, afterwards Bishop of London, and even such a man as Dean Colet, were parties."—R. Vaughan, *Revolutions in English History* (1861), ii. p. 107, n. This is based, I presume, on the single mention of Colet as one of a commission of "Persecutors and Judges," under whom certain martyrs suffered in Canterbury Diocese in 1511 (Foxe, *Acts and Monuments*, 8vo. edition, v. p. 648). But if Colet were really named on such a commission, the best evidence that he was not likely to have been more than a nominal and official member, is found in the fact, that men were charged with heresy for attending his sermons. It was a charge brought against a person *in Longland's own diocese*, in 1521, that he had gone "divers Sundays . . . to London, to hear Dr. Colet."—Foxe, iv. p. 230.

Glossa ordinaria, the Master of the Sentences, or Aquinas. While the one loves to speak of that grace of God, which alone can melt the heart, and burn up sins as flame does the stubble, the other is found setting forth, in all its nakedness, the doctrine of purgatory.[1] And lastly, while Colet is raising his voice against the corruptions of the Church in his day, and pleading in words, as he had done in acts, the cause of true learning, Longland does but slight that *grammar*, which taught men how to draw forth the literal sense of Scripture, and is never so vigorous as when inveighing against the arch-heretic Luther.[2]

Like one of his predecessors in the see of Lincoln, Richard Fleming, the founder of Lincoln College, it would seem as if Longland grew more averse from a reformation, the nearer its prospect of being realized. For he who thus protested against the value of grammar, when urged by the new school of Scripture students, was himself a patron of grammarians; and it was to him that Robertson dedicated his works in that branch of learning. But like Fleming, who began by supporting the doctrines of Wickliffe, and ended by disinterring the Reformer's ashes, to throw them into the Swift; like Robertson, who "was a friend to the Reformers, as far as concerned discipline, but drew back when they began to pare to the quick;"[3] like Sir Thomas More himself, Longland dreaded the movement that more vigorous minds were now urging on.

Colet's death in 1519 was so far a timely one, that it saved him from the necessity of being obliged to pronounce

---

[1] "Qui si sine venialibus e vivis excederes, excelsa cœli palatia subito possideres. Verum hiis obnoxius, in certum tempus ignibus purgatoriis examinandus injiceris; non levioribus ibi cruciandus pœnis, quam si ad tempus in inferno degeres."—*Ib.* leaf 60. For Colet's silence on the subject of Purgatory, see the *Hierarchies*, p. 145 *n.*

[2] "Tuam, O Luthere, Luthere, tuam hæresim intelligo; tuam, homo mendacissime; tuam, impostor hominum perditissime; tuam, minister infidissime Deo pariter ac orbi Christiano, *etc.*" This occurs at f. 42 of his *Tres Conciones*, in a sermon preached at Westminster somewhat later than the previous ones, Nov. 27th, 1527.

[3] See *Wakefield Worthies* (1864), pp. 31 and 51.

distinctly for, or against, Luther. His course was thus suffered to be one of singular consistency to the last; and none could apply to him the reproachful words of Deianira,

> "Cœpisti melius quam desinis; ultima primis
> Cedunt: dissimiles hic vir et ille puer."[1]

§ 8. IN WHAT SENSE COLET WAS A REFORMER.

The words of the Roman poet just quoted will remind us of that great disruption, that seemed to break in two the course of life of so many of Colet's contemporaries. It becomes an interesting endeavour to trace from the present Lectures (to which alone the inquiry must now be confined) some indications of the line of action he might have taken had his life been protracted a few years longer. Is it likely that he would have sided with Luther, or stood aloof from him, as Erasmus did, or even become an active opponent, like Sir Thomas More?

The answer must be in great measure conjectural, owing, in part, to the early date of these writings. But, though they anticipate, by twenty years, the decisive measures taken by Luther, I think we may trace in them certain well-defined principles, to which Colet never ceased to adhere, and from which we may in some measure conclude what his course would have been, had a crisis been forced upon him.

In the first place, we do not observe that strong Augustinian tendency which was predominant in Luther. In treating of the deep and absorbing questions of predestination and free-will, as any commentator on this Epistle could not avoid doing, he gives it its due proportion in the Apostle's argument, but no more. He does not make it the central topic, to which all else is but an introduction or an appendix; but regards it in its proper bearing on the state of the Jewish people. It is to abate their pride, and "loose them from their moorings," that St. Paul,

---

[1] Ovid; *Heroid.* x. 23. The lines are cited by Jortin as exactly descriptive of Sir Thomas More.

according to him, declares God to choose and elect whom He will.¹ Agreeably with this, he includes what has been called *national* predestination, in interpreting the Apostle's words; showing how God's fore-ordained decree points not only to "things eternal, for the election of men to the possession of eternal happiness," but also to "earthly matters, for the attainment of some earthly and temporal happiness."²

Again, while admitting St. Paul's teaching to be, that in the work of salvation "all things are done for men by the promise and free election of God, they themselves contributing nothing towards that election,"³ he is careful, on the other hand, to uphold the free agency of man, whose will is "secretly accompanied" by the will and providence of God, not in any way forcibly coerced by it.⁴ As for the doctrine of reprobation, or anything approaching the tenets afterwards pushed to their dreadful conclusions at the Synod of Dort, it need scarcely be said that there is no trace of them to be found here. While grace is the cause, and the only cause, of man's salvation, his guilt, and not God's decree, is the cause of his condemnation.⁵

In all this, sober and scriptural as it will sound to us now, we do not discern that strong bias which the mind of the Augustinian friar of Erfurt had received; a bias necessary, perhaps, for him, to strengthen him in his vehement protest against the scholastic doctrines of human merit.⁶

---

¹ See pages 4, 16, 38-40.   ² Page 37.
³ Page 40.   ⁴ Page 38.   ⁵ Page 48.
⁶ Erasmus has left on record what Colet's esteem for Augustine was; but unfortunately his expression (a thing very unusual with him) has proved ambiguous. The words are; "Priscis illis potissimum delectabatur, Dionysio, Origene, Cypriano, Ambrosio, Hieronymo; atque, inter veteres, *nulli erat iniquior,* quam Augustino." By *iniquior* has generally been understood "more unfavourable to;" and such is certainly its meaning in the only other passage where it occurs in the same Letter. But the late Mr. J. G. Nichols, in his *Pilgrimages to St. Mary of Walsingham, &c.,* 1849, p. 131, is of opinion that "Erasmus clearly meant to imply that Colet read Augustine *more* than the other Fathers;" and I have the high authority of Dr. Kynaston for saying that the word is capable of such an interpretation, answering in fact to our "more partial to." Colet quotes Augustine in terms of approval, p. 36.

But further, there is apparent in Colet an almost excessive love of order and method.¹ Corruptions in the Church strike him most forcibly as *disorders*, as symptoms of a decline from the true *form* that ought to pervade it. Hence, while severe and intrepid in the highest degree in his rebuke of them, it is doubtful how far he would have felt Luther to be a congenial fellow-worker. Nothing, surely, can exceed the fearless honesty with which Colet denounces contentions about tithes, rapacity disguised under the pretence of zeal for the Church's patrimony, and the like.² To have uttered such words before the doctors and abbots of Oxford, showed a spirit of kindred boldness to that which animated the Saxon reformer at Augsburg and Leipsic.

But *reform*, with Colet, had a different meaning from that which it bore with Luther. It was a term instinct with the spirit of the philosophy he had embraced.³ The Church, to his mind, would be *re-formed*, if every individual member of it had power given to draw in and limit itself to its proper office; if there were no deviation, no encroachment on the functions of another member; if, in short, all were to work together once more, as members of a body, now restored to health, and animated by its proper *form*.⁴ To attain this result by violence, or correct evils by measures productive of fresh evils, would have been out of harmony with Colet's notions. There are few subjects on which he speaks more emphatically, than on the folly of attempting to repel evil by evil, or subdue any opposing principle except by its opposite.⁵

---

¹ See, for example, pp. 72 and 81. In his Cathedral Statutes this is very strongly marked. See also his Treatise on the *Hierarchies*, Introd. p. xliv.

² Pages 118, 121. ³ See p. xxvii.; and also below, p. 43.

⁴ See pp. 71, 82-3.—*Conformation* and *Reformation* were the topics of Colet's great sermon before the assembled clergy in 1512.

⁵ See p. 93.—Such language as Luther applied to his fellow-worker Bucer, for inserting some comments in his translation of the fourth volume of Luther's Postils, would have been abhorrent to Colet:—" Lapsus est in monstrum illud blasphemum Sacramentarii Spiritus, et donum illud facundiæ et intelligentiæ contaminatur, imo

Granting, then, that Luther was an agent needed in the disordered condition of those times; that, in the ordinary course of Providence, great revolutions, beneficial on the whole, are attended by some counterbalancing evils; and that no remedies, less violent than his, would have availed for the distempered state of the Church: still, I think we may see reasons for doubting whether Colet would have thrown in his lot with him. And in making this admission, we need not stigmatize such conduct as weakness.

There has been, I cannot but think, too great a readiness to disparage, as wavering or time-serving, the course followed by those who laboured anxiously for a reformation, but drew back, as it seemed, when Luther began to take the lead. Such obloquy has often been heaped upon Erasmus; of late years, as much as ever.[1]

And though Colet was made of sterner stuff than Erasmus, their principles were in many respects so much in harmony, that, whatever course was pursued by the one, we may judge the other likely to have pursued also, under similar circumstances.

But, admitting that Colet might have taken a position towards the German reformers, not far differing from that of Erasmus, I demur to the justice of imputing it, in his case as well as in the other, to fear or a spirit of time-serving. Colet had his own theory of a reformation; a

---

perditur pestilenti illo veneno, etc."—See the Letter to Hervagius, prefixed to the fourth volume of his Postils (Argentorati, 1527), Leaf C 6.

[1] It may seem presumptuous to question the opinions of such a writer as Froude. But I feel a strong conviction that he does not do justice to Erasmus, in the contrast drawn between him and Luther. "Truth," we are told, "was not the first necessity to Erasmus. He would prefer truth, if he could have it. If not, he could get on moderately well upon falsehood. Luther could not."—*Short Studies on Great Subjects*, i. p. 93. Froude admits, afterwards, that Erasmus "through all storms . . . stuck bravely to *his own proper work;* editing classics, editing the Fathers, writing Paraphrases; still doing for Europe what no other man could have done."—Page 122. If this *was* his proper work, may not Erasmus have been conscious of the fact?

theory shadowed forth in the following pages, expressed most fearlessly in his great Sermon before Convocation, and maintained consistently to the last. Whether it was one potent enough to bring about a reform, had no Luther arisen, is quite another matter. To borrow an illustration from an art, which often furnished Colet himself with one, we have to estimate the intrinsic merits of two methods of healing: one of which has in fact expelled a virulent disease, and raised the patient from a bed of sickness, but at the cost of bitter suffering, and of having the seeds of future disorders implanted in his frame: while the other had not the opportunity of being tried, and thus has missed the test of experience.[1]

We have enjoyed the benefits of the one method; and far be it from me to underrate them. No loss of unity, no injury done to reverential feelings, is worth putting in the balance for a moment, against that greatest of blessings, free access to the fountain-head of revealed truth. But yet it is no small matter to be laid to the charge of the Lutheran Reformation, that it was the fosterer of that " egotistic, self-complacent, and subjective spirit," as one truly calls it,[2] which alienated some of the noblest minds in our country then, and is still seen busily working, in the thousand sectarian contentions that distract our Church. Were Colet alive now, he might still address to us some of the stirring expostulations his pages contain; nor would the language need much altering. With his intense love of order, with the sublime vision of the Celestial Hierarchy so present to his thoughts, that the reflection of it is perceptible even in

---

[1] I think there is a growing conviction that this is the true state of the case. Thus, in a recent article by the authoress of *Cameos from English History*, we read that "the plans for a calm and authoritative reformation of the Church, such as men like Colet and Erasmus would have brought about, were postponed at first by the wars and ambitions of kings, then stifled by the wickedness of the Papal Court, and only partially effected, at the expense of an explosion, whose rents still remain deep and wide."

[2] Hardwick: *History of the Christian Church during the Reformation*, 1856, p. 10.

his most familiar letters, it is certain that much in our practices would have seemed to him "miserably deformed."

May the reforming work begun by him at Oxford in 1497, still go on to its completion! May his voice, so long silent, be listened to again; as he bids us turn from "multiplicity" to unity, from self-will to a desire for the common good, from a hankering after earthly things to a longing for the heavenly; that we may pass, with him, through those three stages of the upward road, "purification, illumination, and perfection."

LECTURES ON *ROMANS*.

SUMMARY OF CONTENTS.

IN the Epistle written by St. Paul the Apostle to the Romans, he counsels peace and concord to those who in that city bore the name of Christ.

There were among them three disputes. The first was that between the Jews and Gentiles; the second between Christians and Heathens; the third was in the Christian community itself, between those who were strong in the faith and those who were weak.

The Gentiles and the Jews were mutually accusing one another; each party in turn proudly claiming precedence over the other. But the presumption of the Jews was the greater and more overweening of the two. Accordingly, when St. Paul interposes to allay this fierce contention, he uses many arguments to beat down the haughtiness of the Gentiles, but still it is to the Jews that he chiefly turns, and directs against their faction the main force and point of his discourse. For the Jew was stiff-necked, ever struggling against the yoke of humility.

Both parties, Jew and Gentile, St. Paul endeavours to raise to a higher level, to lift them above all distinction of Jew and Gentile, and to lodge them both immoveably in Jesus Christ alone. For he alone is sufficient; he is all things; in him alone is the salvation and justification of mankind.

After declaring the Church to consist of these (namely, Jew and Gentile) alike, the Apostle then describes of what nature the Christian Church is, and what are its duties and actions.

It was hotly disputed by many, in what way the Christians at Rome were to conduct themselves towards the heathen, in whose midst they then were, and under whose authority they were living; that is to say, how far they were to submit to injuries from them, and to what extent they were to pay the tribute exacted.

Under this head, St. Paul prudently inculcates peace and obedience.

The third dissension and strife that was in the Christian Church, was between the stronger in the faith and the weaker.[1] In this, scrupulous persons, of weak conscience, were shocked at the boldness of their stronger brethren; while the latter, confiding in the decision of their own conscience, looked down upon the weak. And the matter in debate was the eating of meats; how far it was lawful to proceed in different kinds of food. By the Jewish ceremonial law many things were forbidden. From the *idolothyta*,[2] for example (that is, things offered in sacrifice unto idols) many shrank with abhorrence. But yet there were some who acted boldly in this matter as they considered lawful, and ate on every occasion what they pleased, thoughtlessly and inconsiderately, with no small scandal and offence to the weak.

In this place, therefore, St. Paul enjoins that kindly account must be taken of the weak; that the mind and resolution of the feebler one must not be startled by any venturesomeness of act even in what was lawful; that offence must be avoided, edification sought, and peace maintained by a settlement of their disputes.

In the first of these he counsels humility, in the second patience, in the third charity.

After giving a reason for writing to the Romans, and promising after a time to visit them, he concludes his Epistle with remembrances and salutations.

---

[1] In the Latin, the sentence is apparently incomplete.
[2] Explained in the old *Mammotrectus*: "Ydolotitum, id est, ydolis immolatum" (ed. 1470).

CHAPTER I.

IN the first place St. Paul salutes the Church in Rome. And in this salutation he says that he has been taken by grace into the apostleship, that in the name of Jesus Christ he may go forth as an ambassador to all nations, both of the Jews and of all others whomsoever; to proclaim to them obedience to the faith, and belief in God; to wit, in the new dispensation and dealing of God touching his Son, for the sanctification and salvation of mankind. Which Son of God, himself God and man, drew his descent from Abraham after the flesh; but after the spirit of sanctification, whereby he sanctifies men, he was fore-ordained and manifested upon earth to be the mighty Son of God, quickening the dead again from their sins by his own resurrection.

And among those that have been quickened and drawn back from their sins, he says that they also are to whom he is writing at Rome; to the intent that they may now henceforward be Jesus Christ's, and belong to him alone. On which account he wishes them grace and peace and union *from God their Father, and the Lord Jesus Christ.*   i. 7.

In the next place, he rejoices over the faith of the Romans, that was published throughout the whole world, and longs to visit them, to be a partner in their faith, and teach them. For he says that he is *not ashamed of the gospel, which is the power of God* to them that believe, and a   i. 16. revealing of man's justification through faith; inasmuch as it is in the gospel that faith is taught. For *the just liveth by*   i. 17. *faith* and by the true worship of God. But if either Gentiles or Jews neglected God, and worshipped idols, as without doubt they did worship them, they were assuredly ungodly and abominable in their deed, seeing that they might have clearly recognized God in his creatures. Wherefore all such, whether Gentiles or Jews, being wholly deserted and forsaken of God, fell into pitiable ignorance and a wicked mind, and finally into every kind of guilt.

CHAPTER II.

HENCE St. Paul concludes that none of them, whether Jew or Gentile, ought to accuse another; but that each one should acknowledge his own sin, and hasten to repent of his own wickedness, and not abuse the forbearance of God. For He of his mercy has thus far deferred his just vengeance, that in the meantime men may repent. He also, of his equity and justice, *will render to every man according to his deeds:* to the good, and them that follow truth, eternal life; but to the wicked, and them that cleave to falsehood, everlasting death, whether they be Jews or Gentiles. For God is not a chooser and accepter of persons; nor, as the Jews supposed, does he hold them, on account of the Law given specially to them, far more pleasing to himself than the rest of the nations. But in every nation he regards and praises men's own proper deeds. And if the Gentiles, without having the Law given them, lived well, it harmed them not to have not the Law. So likewise if the Jews lived ill under the Law, then for them to have the Law profited nothing. The real state and praise of man consists wholly in action; and if the acts that one has wrought be good and righteous, even though he has had no law given him, he is still accounted by God to have lived righteously according to law.

But in this place it must be remarked, that St. Paul means not that the Gentiles, or any Gentile man, had lived rightly without the Law; since beyond doubt his opinion is that no one lives rightly or can be righteous, save by faith in Christ. But, that he may break down that vain hope which the Jews had in the Law of Moses, according to what it presented outwardly, in the husk, not according to what it contained inwardly and in the kernel of it; and that he may show that the good life of man, proceeding from a holy mind, is alone pleasing to God,—he asserts that even the Gentiles, who were without law given to them, if only they had lived rightly, were as well-pleasing and acceptable to

ii. 6.

God as were the Jews. For these had the Law given them that they might be prepared for virtue, and might exhibit a circumcision of the heart and purification of the mind; in which alone man's justification consists. And as the Jews were ignorant of this, they in no wise excelled the Gentiles; so far that is, as pertains to justification.

CHAPTER III.

IF, however, they did in aught excel them, it was in this alone, that they had entrusted and committed to them the oracles of God.[1] And what though all understood them not? their folly did not frustrate the wisdom of God. For He knew what he gave, and wherefore, and what was to be the final issue; and the foolishness and wickedness of the Jews he discerned and foresaw. Not that their folly and error and iniquity happened for this very cause, that God might appear wise and true and righteous;[2] as men lightly imagine, when they hear that God's knowledge cannot be frustrated, and that what God has foreseen in the future, does alone at length surely come to pass. Whence St. Paul, assuming this very objection, says, *I speak as a man.* But God is not therefore to be thought true, *because* men sin; nor are we to suppose that men sin, *because* His discernment is true. But each proceeds from its own proper

iii. 5.

---

[1] In the margin opposite this passage, in the Latin, is written: "Hic dicit Origenes, considerandum esse quia non dixerit literas esse creditas, sed *eloquia Dei.*: ergo præter litteralem legem aliud quid traditum fuit Judeis, quod hic vocat Paulus *eloquia Dei.*—Hæc Mirandola."

This is quoted almost verbatim from the *Apologia* of Mirandola (ed. 1516, leaf f. 7), and involves a comment from Origen on Rom. iii. 2. Colet refers to the same passage in his *Treatises on the Hierarchies*, p. 112.

[2] "If I foreknew,
Foreknowledge had no influence on their fault,
Which had no less proved certain unforeknown."
Par. Lost, ii. 117.

cause; sin from men themselves, God's foreknowledge from God himself. And these concur together and go side by side, in such a way that, whatever man commits is of necessity foreknown, and also whatever is foreknown as about to be in the number of sins, is of necessity committed. But yet this is in such wise, that neither are God's foreknowledge and truth the cause of sin being committed;[1] nor is a sin, though foreknown, in any degree the cause of God's foreknowledge appearing true. Hence St. Paul concludes:

Rom. iii. 6. *For then how shall God judge the world?* if either the falsehood of man made God true, or the truth of God made man false. For then there would be room for men to say: *Let*
Rom. iii. 8. *us do evil, that good may come;* whose damnation the
Ps. lxvii. 4. Apostle says is just. But God will judge this world, and condemn the wicked righteously. Hence it follows that neither is the truth of God's knowledge the cause of sin, nor sin the cause of God's being seen to have had true knowledge.

And so the Jews, not understanding the divine declarations, and on that account not giving credence to them, did not yet frustrate the purpose of God; nor yet, by reason of their unbelief did they render the foreknowledge of God true. But out of their own mouths they were acknowledged to be false and sinful, and in like case with others that were Gentiles, whether for just condemnation or for gracious salvation. For, as it is in the Psalm of David, *There is*
Ps. xiv. 3.; *none that doeth good, no not one.* And, as St. Paul says,
Rom. iii. 22. there is no difference between nations, as touching grace.

---

[1] This is stated in nearly the same words by Jerome in his comment on Jer. xxvi. 3 : "Non enim ex eo quod Deus scit futurum aliquid, idcirco futurum est : sed quia futurum est, Deus novit, quasi præscius futurorum."—Origen, in many places, asserts the same thing. Thus, in his Commentary on *Romans* viii. 29, 30 (ed. 1837, ii. p. 130), "Non ergo quia prophetæ prædixerunt, idcirco prodidit Judas ; sed quia futurus esset proditor, ea, quæ ille ex propositi sui nequitia gesturus erat, prædixerunt prophetæ ; cum utique Judas in potestate habuisset, ut esset similis Petro et Joanni, si voluisset."— Augustine (*De Civit.* v. 10) might have been in Colet's mind : "Neque enim ideo peccat homo, quia Deus illum peccaturum præscivit."

The Jews therefore have no ground for confidence in their observance of laws, in their customs and rites; for these things do not take away, but pass sentence on, sin. For that system of rites and ceremonies neither purifies the soul nor justifies any one; nor, indeed, without grace could those commands and prohibitions have been observed.

Wherefore St. Paul teaches that this one thing remains whereby men can be justified; namely, for them to trust in God, and acknowledge the dispensation and grace of God, which in due time was offered to all mankind through his Son Jesus Christ. For by his death and dissolution comes man's redemption from the power of the devil, and reconciliation with God. Whoever owns and believes and observes this mystery of salvation, no matter of what race of men he be, St. Paul pronounces that he will be saved; and also that he must firmly believe this, in order to his salvation. Accordingly, making Jews equal with Gentiles, and showing both peoples to be on a level in guilt and wickedness, the Apostle draws all together to one faith in Christ Jesus, whereto he implies that the law of the Jews did point.

CHAPTER IV.

FOR what else was the meaning of Abraham's circumcision, and cutting off the foreskin, than a cutting off from the mind of all distrust, that the faith of man may appear naked and undisguised before God? This faith existed in Abraham, to his great praise and justification, before the rite of circumcision was adopted, as a sign of the mind's being circumcised, and believing in God without any distrust. And so great was it in Abraham, that, if only God had promised anything, even though it seemed impossible to men, he trusted in it undoubtingly, and looked for its coming to pass. For which cause he was both accounted righteous before God, and marked out to be the heir of the world along with his seed; that is, his *faithful* seed and offspring. And the promise of this inheritance to the faithful may picture to us Abraham's great faith, and the *expression*, so to speak, of his mind; that we may judge of his posterity according to their imitation of his faith.[1] For theirs assuredly is the inheritance, and the world—even God himself, who is the true world.

He of His grace imparts himself to those who believe and trust in Him, who have also been taken and drawn away by Him from unbelief, that they may trust in Him alone, and believe that by no other means whatever can they be justified than by the divine grace. For the Law, in which the Jews hoped, points out sin, defines boundaries, threatens transgressors; but it takes not away the fault, nor draws man out of his strait, nor graciously cherishes and sustains him, which very thing divine grace does, with both strength and sweetness, so that man may be able to trust in God alone. And this grace touched, and drew, and justified Abraham, and gave him a promise that men innumerable, yea, even to the number of the stars, should be equally and in like manner justified. Such were to be counted as his sons; in part, as I said but now, by virtue of a certain likeness, and in part, and chiefly, because the parent and second ancestor of the faith, Jesus Christ, was thence to draw his descent after the flesh. He was the Son, and the promised seed. To his issue the divine promises given to Abraham had regard.

Now the issue and offspring, as it were, of Christ, is faith, and the multitude of the faithful, from whatever place and people they may have been called by God; who, as St. Paul saith, *calleth those things which be not as though they were.* But the Jews, being ignorant of this dispensation, understood not the object of their own Law, but, keeping to the servile work prescribed by their Law, claimed the reward of happiness on the ground of being workers. They perceived not that Abraham had testimony borne to his righteousness before the works and ceremonies of the Law were ordained; that it might be clearly taught that justifi-

---

[1] From their showing a family likeness, as we might say, to Abraham, in having the same character of mind.

cation belongs not to those who do works under the Law, but to those who imitate the faith of Abraham; such as readily believe God and the divine dispensation, as our father Abraham once believed, even though God's promises far exceeded human reason.

So also at this time, he who trusts in God, believing that he has both the power and the will, and that his dealings with his Son have been such as they have been (namely, that he was both incarnate, and died, and was raised again, for the redemption of the human race and its reconciliation to God):—he, I say, who firmly believes and constantly keeps this unspeakable mystery and sacrament,[1] has therein alone enough for his justification and salvation.

CHAPTER V.

WHEREFORE St. Paul concludes that, being justified by faith, and trusting in God alone, men are reconciled to God through Jesus Christ, and restored to grace, that they may stand before God, and themselves remain sons of God, and look for the certain glory of the sons of God; for the obtaining whereof all things are meanwhile to be endured with patience, that the steadfastness of our hope may be set forth; a hope that will not be deceived. For it is of the great love and grace of God toward us that we have been reconciled. Otherwise his Son would not have died for us, even when we were ungodly and at enmity with God. Now if, when estranged from him, he loved us, how much more, being reconciled, does he love us, and, being loved, will he save us? Wherefore we ought to be of a strong and stable hope and joy, and to trust undoubtingly in God through Jesus Christ; through whom alone is man's reconciliation with God. For it was from the first man himself, and from his want of faith, ungodliness, and

---

[1] For this use of the word, see Colet's Treatise *On the Sacraments*, p. 33.

guilt, that there came the destruction of the whole human race; so that neither by the law of nature, nor yet by the law of Moses, could it be restored to life.

Now if there was such force in sin, and that too the sin of one man, for destruction, then ought there to be a much greater force and power in grace, for quickening men, and restoring them to an entire and sure salvation. And that this is so, one may discern even from hence: namely that, whatever grew from one sin, for destruction (and there *did* grow sin manifold and infinite), when the tale thereof was all made up, and the virulence of the disease, as it were, at fever height, then at the same time all-powerful grace, by its prevailing and marvellous force, dispelled it, and destroyed all the sin. For it was mightier to take away the evil when completed, than [the evil was] to begin. Thus it happens that men, being laid hold of by the love and grace of God, and drawn to God, will, if they have hope, be more strongly and firmly sustained and preserved unto life by that same prevailing grace, than they had been thrust down and kept under by sin unto death. Sin is indeed a violent and aggressive thing; but the glorious power of sweet and pleasant grace, that works softly and marvellously, and with a secret and wonderful effect, nothing can resist. Wherefore we must believe that grace, which reconciles to God, has far more power in the world than sin, which estranges from God.[1] And hence, that the righteousness and obedience of Christ has far more power to recall to God men who are to be recalled, than the sin and disobedience of Adam had to call them away from God. For without doubt virtue is a much more life-giving thing than sin is deadening, and the Author of virtue far more powerful than the cause of sin. Yet sin nevertheless had such power, that it could neither be subdued by the law of nature nor the law of Moses. Nay rather, being increased by these laws, sin wrought to man's greater destruction. For

---

[1] Origen says the same of the word of God: "Nullus profecto malus affectus est animi, quo verbum Dei non sit potentius."—*Contra Cels.* (Spencer's ed. p. 425).

by the rising of the light, first of the natural, then of the Mosaic law, transgressions that aforetime were not detected or marked, did then most plainly appear; and men, acknowledging their own wretchedness and wanderings, but being powerless of themselves to return to the right way, did, in a measure, knowingly sin.

Wherefore St. Paul says, *The law entered, that sin might abound:* that is, after the introduction of the Law, men sinned far more grievously; not indeed from the Law bringing that to pass, but because men of themselves, such was their own weakness without grace, were unable to do otherwise than sin. And so, as sin grew and gathered strength, it was needful, for the healing of mankind, that saving grace should then much more increase and abound; that men, being justified by it, might be able through Jesus to attain eternal life. v. 20.

Now we must here remark, that this grace is nothing else than the love of God towards men; towards those, namely, whom it is his will to love, and by loving to inspire with his Holy Spirit. That Spirit is very love, even the love of God; and, as our Saviour speaks in St. John the Evangelist, it *bloweth where it listeth*.[1] And they who are loved and inspired by God are called, to the end that, having received love, they should in turn love God that loves them, and should long for, and await him, in love. This awaiting and this hope come of love. Our love towards him is in truth because he first loved us. As St. John writes in his Second Epistle[2]: *Not that we first loved God, but that he loved us,* even though worthy of no love, as being ungodly and unjust, rightly destined to everlasting destruction. But certain ones, whom He knew and whom He would, did God love; by loving, called; by calling, justified; by justifying, glorified. Joh. iii. 8.
1 Jn. iv. 10.

This gracious love in God, and charity towards men, is

---

[1] The force of this quotation is partly lost from the words in the English version, "wind" and "bloweth" not being cognate words to "spirit;" as in the Latin, *spiritus* ubi vult *spirat*.

[2] An error of memory for the First Epistle.

itself their calling and justification and glorifying; nor do we mean anything else by so many terms than one thing, namely, God's love towards those whom it is his will to love.[1] In like manner, when we say that by *grace* men are drawn, are called, are justified, are glorified; we signify nothing else than that men return the love of a loving God. In this love and return of love consists the justification of man. And this reciprocal love in us is joined with hope, and needs to be steadfast, as that which will not be made ashamed. For we are beloved by God, that we should in
v. 5. turn love and hope in him; *because*, in the words of St. Paul, the charity and *love of God is shed abroad in our hearts*. That is to say, because we are beloved, we love God again, through the Holy Spirit which is given us; or, in other words, through the love received, which is bestowed upon us from the divine love, we love God, trust in God, hope for God.

---

[1] This may sound at first very alien from the precise definitions of the schoolmen, and may recall to our minds the dislike Colet once expressed of Aquinas. It is natural also to compare it, as Mr. Seebohm has done (*Oxf. Ref.*, 2nd ed., p. 37), with the language of Savonarola, in his tract *On the love of Jesus Christ*, published in 1492. But *quo semel est imbuta recens, servabit odorem Testa diu*. It was not so easy to escape from the dominion of school-thought. And Colet in this passage does not so much differ from scholastic theories of *grace*, as grasp their real meaning and spirit, and present in one view the sum and substance of them. Grace "*is* justification, if the progress of grace be considered in its effect on the sinner. It is predestination, if it be contemplated in God himself, as the effect of his eternal love. It is salvation, if the antecedent agency of the Son of God be the point from which the process is viewed."— Hampden's *Bampton Lect.*, 1833, p. 190. And Bishop Hampden shows how the schoolmen's conception of grace arose from, or at least was greatly modified by, the Aristotelian doctrine of the struggle of all things in nature to attain to the *ultimate form* of beauty and perfection (p. 193). Hence it may now be thought that Colet's teaching rather concentrated, than opposed, the teaching of the schools. And in the same light may be read what Savonarola wrote in the treatise just mentioned: "Man, in fact, rises continually from humanity to something divine when he is animated by this love, which is the sweetest of all affections, penetrates the soul, acquires a mastery over the body, and causes the faithful to walk on earth, rapt, as it were, in the spirit."—Villari's *Hist.*, tr. by Horner, i. 109.

From this love, which is our justification, the Apostle strongly exhorts us not to be led away; admonishing us that all adversities and afflictions must be borne, and that we should rejoice in them, that our golden love towards God may be approved, and our faith and hope may be shown to be steadfast; a hope which the love and grace of God will not disappoint, seeing that it was the love and grace of God that awakened it in man.

But let us return to St. Paul: though in these remarks we have not wandered very far away from him.

CHAPTER VI.

ST. PAUL now proceeds in his Epistle skilfully to show, that they who by grace have been set free from their sins, must not sin again;—as perhaps some would slanderously affirm, taking occasion from the words added by St. Paul above, when speaking of the weakness of the Law and the deserts of sin; namely, *But where sin abounded, grace did much more abound.* Lest, I repeat, they should captiously argue from that passage and say, *Let us continue in sin, that grace may abound,* the Apostle puts in a saving clause, proving by a profound argument, that men, loosed from the bonds of sin by the love and grace of God, have nothing more to do with sins for ever. For, so far as sin is concerned, they have utterly perished; to appear henceforth no more at all in that way of living. They are indeed, so to speak, *planted together* with Christ, and dead, and *buried with him,* that they may also rise again, and be born anew, and live again with Christ; who was willing to die for the salvation of men, that they should consider themselves to have died along with him.

Now he was willing to die, that by his glorious death the transgressions of men might be blotted out, for which they themselves would have perished; and that those who were called, having ceased to act a sinful part, and having altogether done away with their accustomed habit of sinning,

v. 20.

vi. 1.

vi. 5.

might not appear for the future such as they had been, but be, as it were, dead with Christ. These have in a manner *crucified the old man*, even that former sinful life; to the end that, just as if dead and buried, they should henceforward have no place or recognition among sins, and in a sinful part,¹ but be renewed to a fresh state and condition; and, rising with Christ in his resurrection to newness of life, should display themselves always and unceasingly new, and far different from their early state. For there is a danger that, if they choose to hold any intercourse with it, they may seem neither to have died with Christ, nor to have risen again with him. But if they be risen again as though from the dead, and from their life of death to a quickening life, they must assuredly stand heedfully and abide in it; lest, if they shall sin again, another saving death be not found, whereby their sins may be abolished. For Christ will not die a second time; *nor will death any more have dominion over him.* He died for our sins once, that, for them who follow Christ, their sins might perish. But if they revive, where will the death be whereby they may be taken away? since Christ will not again die.

Rom. vi. 9.

In this passage St. Paul seems to have an under meaning, that it is by the death of Christ alone that men's sins can be blotted out; and that for such men as have laid aside their sins, if they shall again relapse into them, there is no hope of healing; seeing that the medicine which takes away sin, even the death of Christ, will not be repeated. But all St. Paul's sayings must be cautiously examined, before any opinion touching his meaning be given. For he would never have decided that the fornicator, whom in his first Epistle to the Corinthians he delivered up to Satan, should be recalled to the Church, had he left no room for repentance to them that sin after baptism. Wherefore we must consider that the Apostle spake in this place with the greater severity, and urged as an argument the fact that Christ would not die a second time, that he might the

1 Cor. v. 5.

---

¹ That is, as actors on the stage, when they have laid aside the dress by which they could at once be recognized in any character.

better keep back from sin those to whom he wrote; by inducing a suspicion of incurable disease, if they should sin again; that they might take the more heed not to sin. Because, just as a disease does not beget the medicine, but has one applied to it according to the will of the physician; so sin does not beget nor call for the grace; but once for all, according to the will of God, has medicinal grace been given in the death of Christ for healing the disease of sin.

And this being once for all performed for the destruction of sin, they who, by following Christ, have killed sin in themselves, must not bring it to pass that they should recall sin, as it were, from the dead, so that it be needful for the death of Christ to be again resorted to, as an effacer of their sin.[1] But having now risen out of the waves of sin to virtue, and out of death to life, they must make it their most earnest business to continue living in virtue and righteousness, that they may be able to obtain eternal life, and to stand in the grace and love of God, by which they were laid hold of. They should fear that, if they fall away from God, there may be the very greatest danger that they cannot return to his love and grace. For it is likely that God will be the slower to love again such as make light of his love. But, unless beloved, you cannot love again; that is, you cannot follow, unless called, nor ascend, unless drawn. And if you have often slighted a loving God, then of a truth it is to be feared lest, wholly bereft of his love, and with all hope taken away, you should perish everlastingly, and pass in misery to endless death, the bourne of sin and neglect of God. Wherefore they who

---

[1] It will be seen that Colet interprets this passage (vi. 10), not so much as conveying an assurance of the believer's full emancipation from sin, and everlasting life with Christ, as containing a warning against repetition of wilful sin, like that in Heb. x. 26, "there remaineth no more sacrifice for sins," &c. Possibly Colet's way of understanding the text had been suggested by Origen: "Unde miror quosdam contra hanc evidentissimam Pauli sententiam velle asserere, quod in futuris iterum seculis vel eadem vel similia pati necesse sit Christum, ut liberari possint etiam hi, quos in præsenti vita dispensationis ejus medicina sanare non potuit."—Quoted in the *Annotationes* at the end of Spencer's *Orig. c. Celsum* (1677), p. 94.

are drawn to him by grace, and moved by a loving God to love again, must abide in a constant requital of love; that without ceasing they may be beloved by a loving God, and by this divine love and grace be saved, and live in endless felicity. For, as St. Paul says, *the grace*[1] *of God is eternal life;* and this is all powerful to sustain and save, if you trust in it. Which thing not even the Law could do; for it rather exposed and aggravated the disorder than took it away. Therefore, esteeming all things else, and all other medicines, of less account, the man who would be safe and sound must rest in the grace and love of God alone.

vi. 23.

But because the Jews clung to the Law of Moses so tenaciously that they could scarcely be torn away from it by any means, St. Paul first brings forward some such considerations as the following, that he may loose them from their moorings,[2] and induce them to think that there is now no danger in leaving the law, so to speak, altogether behind. Nay, he would show that this must of necessity be done, if they wish to belong to the new order of things they now profess under Christ and under grace.

And herein, that the Apostle's language may be better understood, we must observe that—man consisting of a *soul* (which St. Paul calls the *inner man*) and a *sentient body* (which may be termed, in Plotinus's[3] words, the *animal part*

---

[1] The word in the Vulgate being *gratia.* The Greek combines the meaning of this and our "gift."

[2] Ov. *Met.* xiv. 444.

[3] *Enn.* i. *Lib.* i. of Porphyry's arrangement in Teubner's Edn., Lips., 1856, vol. ii., pp. 427-8. It has been mentioned in the introduction that Ficino was the first to make Plotinus known to Western scholars by his Latin translation, published at Florence in 1492. Independently of that, we may trace very plainly, in Colet's application of this passage, the influence of the Florentine scholar. For, in his comment on the ninth section of this book, Ficino gives at the outset a theological turn to it: "the inner man complaining of the outer, *I find a law in my members,*" and so on. He ends by comparing the complete man to Adam, and the degenerate, animal part of his nature, to Eve, formed from him while his soul was asleep and off its guard. Colet's good sense kept him clear of these extravagancies; but it will be apparent, from what presently follows, that he had Ficino's comment in his mind.

of man)—from Adam's transgression, who chose to be the slave of his beguiling senses, and revolted from God, this animal part of man in the whole human race (save only in a few, whom God rescued from that wretchedness and took to himself) has borne sway in man's estate, and so to speak in the human commonwealth. After its own folly and lust it has governed all things in man, and sunk all down to misery.

From its violence and tyranny the soul, that is, the poor inner man, being weak and powerless by reason of Adam's unhappy fall, has been incapable, with all its efforts, of releasing and liberating itself. It has indeed been capable of receiving admonition, and of being roused to some sense of its own misery and bondage, and when so roused, of feebly wishing to follow its admonisher for some little way onward. But to do this in reality, and follow closely any good admonitions and precepts, is what the infirmity of the soul has not endured.

Now the Law of Moses was an admonisher of the soul, and a giver of good and wholesome precepts; a Law, we must grant, that was good and holy, and, as St. Paul also terms it, *spiritual*; recalling us as it does some way back towards the spirit, and being a harbinger of the spirit that was to come. But this Law, while it admonished, did nothing further. By its admonitions, and the boundaries it defined, it pointed out transgressions; but strength, whereby a man might restrain himself from wandering and going crooked, it gave none. Hence it came to pass, that through the Law, and those good precepts, instead of there being no sins, there were more, and more grievous ones. For the precepts, by pointing out and displaying men's deviations when sinning, brought them both a consciousness and knowledge of their offence; so that, taking count of man's weakness and inability to obey laws, it had been better for them if they had never had the Law given.

As with sick persons, whom a dangerous disease has long been weakening, and whose life is despaired of, it profits not to apply a medicine to expel the disease, but does them much more harm, though the medicine be a most approved one, because through their weakness they cannot bear it; so also with the Jews, the Jewish Law profited them not; not because it was not in itself good, but because the Jews were bad, and, on account of their inveterate malady of disobedience, unfit to obey good precepts. And, as with sick persons,[1] whose bodily strength has been almost wholly exhausted by a long disease, if there be any hope of recovery, it must needs be only in giving and increasing strength, to the intent that an invigorated system may escape from the bonds of disease; so was it with the Jews, when their weakness had been detected by the laws, through which they could not be roused to heal and justify themselves. For the disorder did so gain strength more and more in succession from Adam, and the taint and foul contagion of the mischief did so deeply penetrate, that by human strength there could be no healing. In this state, I say, of so great infirmity, the only hope left for the Jews was this, that by grace their strength might be increased, and when increased and invigorated might quickly escape from its ills, and carry that *inner man* away from its bad and slavish condition to liberty and goodness. And furthermore, just as the physician, who has applied a good and suitable remedy, is not to be accused, nor deemed unskilful, albeit his remedy has not healed; nor the remedy to be despised, although it has not restored health, the man being radically incurable; but rather the physician is to be commended, and the remedy approved, which has disclosed the greatness and peril of the disorder; that, warned by it, the man may betake himself to a more skilful physician;—so assuredly, in the same manner, neither is God nor the Law

---

[1] The frequency of Colet's illustrations from the healing art will be observed. Without assuming any connection between the two facts, it may yet be remarked that it was during his occupation of the deanery of St. Paul's, that all who sought to practise as physicians or surgeons within the City of London, were for the first time required to obtain a licence, after examination by the Bishop of London, *or the Dean of St. Paul's*, with the aid of four doctors of physic. —See the Act (3 Hen. VIII.), quoted in Knight's *Life of Colet*, 2nd ed. p. 396

of Moses to be taxed, although by it man has not recovered his ancient goodness and righteousness; but thanks are to be given to God and the Law, for that, admonished through it, men fly for refuge to a more efficacious remedy, even to God himself, and to his grace. For thereby at length, being set free and restored to health, they may rest in saving grace alone, and think no more of the Law, now that the sinful character, to which it had regard, has been laid aside; nor deem that it concerns them, any more than the sick man we supposed, who has now by admirable skill been restored to health, deems that he has any concern with the remedy, which in his own case, by reason of his own weakness, he found to be powerless and ineffectual. For being released from the condition, on account of which the remedy was devised, he has nothing further to do with the remedy in question, since by other ways and means he has attained the object sought by it.

Even so the Jews, who could not be justified by the Law, being justified at length by the marvellous and wonder-working grace of God, have now no reason for dependence on the Law. Nay, rather they have the very strongest reason for not depending on the Law, and for discarding it altogether, seeing that they are now in such a state through grace, as to have no manner of need of the Law. But if they choose to maintain that they still have need of the Law, and still belong to it, then must they perforce confess that grace has been of no avail in them, and that they are yet in their sins. For it was to admonish them of these that the Law was in due season given. If on the other hand they think that they have been arrested by grace, and have entirely laid aside the sinful part they were playing, then they must also plainly resolve with themselves that the Law has no concern with them, and that there is no cause why they should attend either to its prohibitions or commands. For they are now justified by grace; and the Law was not given for men in this condition, but for sinners.

The Jews had the Law given them for the sake of pointing out their iniquity, that they might openly acknowledge both the greatness of the disorder under which they suf-

fered, and their own natural powerlessness; and when at length they were healed by grace, might ascribe all to grace, and feel most unmistakably that it was through grace alone that they had recovered health and life. For it is God's will that his loving-kindness and mercy and benefits should be acknowledged to proceed wholly and manifestly from himself; that men may have no room for either pride or idle questioning; but may own that nothing is of themselves, everything from God; and so, as St. Paul bids
v. 11. them, may *joy in God* alone.

CHAPTER VII.

BUT let us now return to St. Paul. He shows to the Jews who follow Christ, and are set free by grace from the dominion of the animal and sensual, and who, as regards the state of sin, are altogether, as it were, dead, and seen no more[1] in sin:—to Jews of such a kind, I say, whose sinful character has been crucified, dead, and buried with Christ, he shows that the Law has no respect, and that it concerns them in no degree, since they have laid aside the condition by virtue of which they were under the Law; namely, the condition of the sinner, for whose sake the Law was given. On this account, so far as it regards them, the authority of the Law, and the Law itself, is made void, and may be said to have perished.

Now seeing that the Law has perished for them (inasmuch as, being breathed upon by the Holy Spirit, they have been formed again[2] to another state, with which the

---

[1] Prof. Jowett, in his note on vi. 3, well brings out the much greater significance of the ancient mode of baptism, as a visible image of the convert's thus disappearing, and being *buried with Christ*, as regards his former state.

[2] Much more would be understood by being *formed again* (as in xii. 2) in Colet's time than would strike an ordinary reader now. The relations of *Form* and *Matter*, as then accepted, have to be borne in mind.—See Hampden's *Bampton Lect.* (1833), p. 335.

Law has no concern), they have free power of surrendering themselves without danger to another law; and, as though by the death of a former husband, of bestowing themselves in marriage with another husband. The Law is dead to them, because they themselves are dead to the Law,[1] seeing that they neither appear nor are that which they were, but, on account of their being formed anew to another state, and being transferred, as it were, to another realm, are bound neither to own their ancient laws, nor to be owned of them, but to cleave chastely to the new law alone, as unto a new husband; lest, if they have forsaken him, they may seem to have broken their marriage-vow and committed adultery.

Now when St. Paul says, *When we were in the flesh, the motions[2] of sins, which were by the Law, did work in our members, to bring forth fruit unto death,* he means that, through the Law, men sinned more grievously and destructively; because that, as the Law pointed out transgressions, they sinned in a manner against knowledge. When he adds, *Now we are delivered from the law of death,*[3] he is speaking of the same Law that he spake of before; and he calls it a *law of death,* because, by pointing out and aggravating the offence, it has a greater and more agonizing power of death. And now that men have been loosed and set free from this Law of Moses—a Law that, through their incapacity, rather kills than quickens,—by being, as it were, born again from the dead, and formed anew by the Spirit, they must assuredly not bring either of these results to pass: namely, so to fall back again as to be entangled in that rudimentary Law; or fail to follow, as new and spiritual men, that form

vii. 5.

vii. 6.

---

[1] Colet perceives and explains the difficulty involved in St. Paul's comparison, that it is the Law which answers to the husband, and therefore it is the Law's death which has to be regarded.—Vaughan notices this in his Introd. to ch. vii.

[2] Vulgate, *passiones,* as in our marginal reading.

[3] The Vulgate has *a lege mortis, in qua,* etc., corresponding to "the law *of death* wherein we were held," instead of to "*that being dead* wherein we were held," as in the E. V.—Erasmus notices the difference. Our translators seem to have followed St. Chrysostom's interpretation: "As if he had said, the chain by which we were held down was deadened and broken through, so that that which held down, namely, sin, held down no more."—*Hom.* in loc.

of doctrine which is new and adapted to the Spirit. This is the doctrine of the grace and love of Christ; that they should in turn love God who loves them, and wait for God, and trust in God alone.

St. Paul next shows how powerless the Law was, and how it did not remove, but only point out, sin; and moreover how, though good in itself and in its objects, yet for evil men it was evil, according to their evil nature. For all things are received in each case according to the measure of the receiver.

Now all the evil that man has, springs up from him out of that lower part of his nature, which may be called, as I said above,[1] the animal and bestial part of man. This was committed to the inner man, and soul, to be ruled by it. But after that man loosed himself from God through ungodliness and want of faith, and sank to the corporeal, our bestial nature, now that man's state was so changed and overturned, broke forth at once in riot and madness, and seized upon the reins of government in man. His soul it placed in miserable subjection to folly and lust, and dealt with everything after the judgment of the senses. Then did there wax strong in man a republic, as it were, wholly of the people and the commonalty, administered by the decision and decrees of sense, with no interposition of the authority of understanding and reason; a republic held in blind subjection, forced in a measure to be the slave—the voluntary slave, I might almost say—of the dominant senses. This miserable and forlorn condition of man, and lamentable bondage of the soul, is here bewailed by St. Paul; and bitterly does he complain of the injustice and tyranny of the sensual body. Under that bondage, he says, vii. 15, 18. he knows not what he does in his actions; that he wills, but cannot perform, what is good; that he owns the Law to be an admonisher of righteousness, but cannot obey it. Our bestial nature does so goad on, and press, and order with such blandishments, and with such false enticements does it inveigle the soul and bind it to itself, that by what means it

---

[1] Page 16.

is to release itself, unless succoured by divine grace, it sees not.

Accordingly St. Paul, after uttering the exclamation and inquiry, *O wretched man that I am! who shall deliver me from the body of this death?*—that is, from a body which kills and hurries to everlasting destruction—thus makes answer in conclusion: The grace of God,[1] *through Jesus Christ our Lord:* the grace and love of God, that is to say, which he showed towards men, when it was his pleasure that the Word should be incarnate and die for the human race, that men might be saved from a just death. For if Jesus Christ had not died, as a sufficient satisfaction for our state, and recompense for sin, then, without further delay, all the ungodly, each for his own transgressions, would themselves have perished, and been hurried away to death and punishment. But Jesus alone suffered that to be inflicted unjustly on himself, which would justly have been inflicted upon all; that in mercy, and at the same time in a fitting kind of justice, he might reserve to himself such out of the whole number as he would have exempt from death, even that endless death into which men would of themselves have fallen, if sinners had been destroyed. By the death of Christ, therefore, which was gone through for all, men are retained in life, by the marvellous grace of God; that their sins may be blotted out by the death of Christ, even as by their own, and that in all the rest of their life they may strive after virtue, and aspire unto God.

Thus was it marvellously brought about, in merciful justice and just mercy, that men's sins were taken away out of the world, not by their own death, for endless destruction afterwards, but by the saving of their life; that, if willing, they may live in this world so as to possess eternal life with God. And that they may do this, he who, of his singular love towards them, even when they were aliens,

vii. 24.

---

[1] A difference of reading will be observed here between the Vulgate and the English version; the former having *Gratia Dei*, as translated in the text; the latter, "*I thank God*, through Jesus Christ," &c.

was willing to die for all, will give them the needful strength, and will preserve them; especially those whom he has recalled to himself and reconciled to himself and God. This
v. 9, 10. St. Paul implies by saying: *Much more, being now justified by his blood, we shall be saved*: and, a little after, *Much more; being reconciled, we shall be saved by his life.*.

To blot out sins thus thoroughly, and to purify men and reconcile them to God, the law given to the Jews was not able, although that was its end and aim, and though in many and various ways it warned men to follow after righteousness. But yet it neither gave the soul fresh strength, nor increased what it had, whereby it might have released itself from bondage, and escaped from the prison of the body. It aroused the soul to some faint light and knowledge of good, but did not also inflame it deeply with the love of goodness and of God; that, being wholly on fire, and rapt, as it were, into flame, it might leave the darksome body and attach itself to God alone. This heat, life, and strength God supplied to man through Jesus Christ; to the intent that, bursting the bonds of his sins, he might come forth free, and live in the presence of God; and regard the Law no more, which regarded sin; nor dread the sinful body, the cause of sin; but, trusting in God, hoping in God, and loving God alone, might finally be in terror of no condemnation at all, so long as he followed Christ, and fashioned himself to the best of his power after the pattern of his Master, and exhibited the form of Christ. For, as St.
viii. 1. Paul concludes from the foregoing, *there is no condemnation to them which are in Christ Jesus*, which have been withdrawn altogether from the flesh, and drawn together to the spirit; having been arrested and seized upon by grace, that they may breathe in God that giveth breath, and live in God that giveth life, and be strong in him that strengtheneth.

For such, as St. Paul goes on to say, have God for their friend, their helper and preserver. And the end of this is that, being assured they will not be condemned or accused, either by God, or by his Son Jesus (in whom they have a most loving patron and defender and liberator, aye, even at the cost of his own death, since he was willing to die for the salvation of the human race) :—

CHAPTER VIII.

BEING assured and certain of this, I say, there is, beyond question, nothing further for them to fear, depending as they do in steadfast hope on God. Nor, whilst they retain God as their helper, have they reason to think anything able to withstand and be dangerous to them; but, embracing God, or rather embraced by God, may feel confident that they are altogether shielded and safe in God. These are they, as St. Paul records, whom the Divine purpose has marked out to be called to him by his grace for justification; whom by his free inspiration he has moved, and formed anew after the likeness of his Son, and drawn from their human and customary affections, and translated to a new and divine state of life; in such wise that they should henceforth appear in no degree the men they were before, but, as being begotten again and entirely born anew, should in all their life and actions image forth God himself within them, so far as human dimness allows.

These in truth are they, as Paul writes, who are *led by the Spirit of God* to be the *sons of God*, who have within them the spirit of God and Christ; whose being, life, feelings, tastes, will, are wholly spiritual; and who (to use the Apostle's words) *walk in the spirit,* and in it do all things. These are they who, in a fervent spirit and love of God, have chased away all the wavering affections of the body; who have rendered the body a light burden, and obedient to reason; who persevere in a firm and steadfast hope and expectation of the glory of the sons of God; who suffer all things, even the most bitter, rather than either fall away from their hope, or be diverted from the love of God. For in truth there is nothing that ought to be so highly esteemed by us, as to withdraw us from God. They who, I say, are inspired with such a spirit and love towards God, and held

viii. 14.

Gal. v. 25.

by so great a hope, and endued with so great patience, virtue, and righteousness, are in truth Christ's, as St. Paul saith : that is, Christians; sons and *heirs of God and joint heirs with Christ* ; being now marked and sealed, as it were, by the Holy Spirit, that, as adopted children, they may after this life be brought into the home of their great and exalted Father, and enjoy that eternal and happy inheritance, even God himself. And that we may possess him, we must in the meanwhile, so long as we are here and abiding in this vain and shadowy life, shrouded in this poor murky body,[1] patiently endure all things, and stand fast in the highest hope. For if we have faith, the Holy Spirit himself, who begat that hope, will not suffer it to droop, nor allow us to wish for aught but what is befitting spiritual men, and pleasing to God ; seeing that *all things work together for good to* spiritual men and *them that love God.*

By this means St. Paul endeavours to persuade the church in Rome to be of a great and immovable hope, and, though harassed by adversity, to abide fixedly in God ; by whom they were called to trust and hope in him. This done, they will not be deceived by a faithful God. But if, neglecting the love and attractive influence of God (ensnared, it may be, by the allurements of the body or deterred by violence), they have fallen from God, and lived again after the flesh and fleshly appetites, which are opposed and hostile to God, and destructive to men themselves ;—if, shame to tell it, there has been this inexpressible wickedness in any man, after God has loved him so greatly, then for certain will he be deserted by divine grace, and fall headlong into a state far more miserable than before. Wherefore he must stand fast with the utmost faith in God and his Christ, and await undoubtingly what will be shown to the sons of God, and must cleave with the most burning love to God himself above all, and to Jesus Christ, as a steadfast and steadying rock.

---

[1] Colet's language here is very like that of Ficino, *Op.* (1576), ii. p. 1471, where he describes the descent of the soul into the body as a change from a state of brightness to one that is "*tenebrosum longeque dissimilem.*"

This love of his towards God and Christ, who had deserved so well of him, St. Paul avers to be such, so great and so vehement, that there could neither be, nor even be conceived of, anything in the whole universe, of any kind whatever, so mighty and effectual, as to separate him from the desire and *love of God which is in Christ Jesus*. And the Apostle makes this avowal respecting himself, that, by the example of his own most fervent love, he may confirm the Roman Church in the love of God, and establish them in the hope and expectation of what is appointed for those who love God in sincerity, so long as they are called by divine grace to such liberty in this world as to be able to love God, and trust in him, and wait for his bounty. viii. 39.

But why does St. Paul write in this place, *As many as are called by the Spirit of God, they are the sons of God;* and again, not long after, declare his own unbounded love towards God? viii. 14.

Touching the first matter we must bear in mind that the Spirit of God, who is God himself, though he is everywhere, and present to all, yet does not dwell in and enlighten all, but only those who are predestined by the divine counsel to be enlightened. Upon them, indeed (that is, upon the surface of their minds) the Spirit works pleasantly and sweetly; and by heating, as it were, and breathing upon them in a way past our understanding, first thaws and liquefies some little extent of love, and (if we may use such a term in immaterial things like these) in a measure rarefies[1] it, to the end that they may have full light and heat in their very inmost depths.

---

[1] The illustration from clouds, raised by evaporation from the surface of the waters they once formed a part of, has always been a favourite one with theologians, and the reader may find more than one specimen of it in even modern commentaries on Heb. xii. 1. Colet may have taken the idea from Mirandola's *Heptaplus (Proœm. in Lib. vii.)* : " Potest vapor conscendere in altum, sed non nisi attractus radio Solis. Lapis et corpulenta omnis substantia neque radium usquequaque admittere, neque per illum tolli in sublime potest. Hunc radium, hunc vim divinam, hunc influxum *gratiam* appellamus." Elsewhere Mirandola says that the union of the formative spirit with matter is signified by the words, "the evening

Now this infused *light* is Faith, by which the mystery of the incarnation is discerned, and believed unto salvation; whilst Love, which takes possession of the soul along with Faith, and rarefies it, so to speak, and expands it, is that whereby, so far as can be done by man, God and his Christ are received and worshipped. These two, as it seems to me, thus differ, not in reality, but in a kind of interchangeableness;[1] namely, in faith being a less united, and, as it were, a more diffused love; love, on the other hand, a more condensed and united faith. Whence it comes to pass that love in force and power far surpasses faith, and is far more effectual to raise man on high, and join him to God. And hence that saying of St. Paul to the Corinthians: *The greatest of these is Charity.* This marvellous and heavenly light, shining brightly through faith, burning fiercely through love, when it seizes on the soul of man, influences, disposes and forms it; so that there arises a new thing by the divine working, compounded of the soul itself, as the matter, and the embracing spirit, as the formative principle. Wherein the spirit excels the soul formed by it, far more than the soul excels the body which it forms. And in fact, out of soul and spirit there arises something far more truly one, than there does out of body and soul. For the soul makes less resistance to its union with the spirit, than the body does to its connexion with the soul; since the dimensions, by which the body is extended,[2] seem most adverse to unity.

Accordingly this person of the spiritual man, lovely and beautiful throughout, when begotten at length by the divine

1 Cor. xiii. 13.

---

and the morning were the first day":—"ut ex *vespere* et *mane*, id est, ex corporis nocturna, et matutini animi natura unus sit homo." *Op.* (1601) p. 22.

[1] Compare the remark of Bengel on John xvi. 27, ("because ye have loved me, and have believed," &c.): "Amor et posterior est fide et prior; nam se invicem sustentant. Imo ipsa fides imbibit amorem, et amplexum doni cælestis."

[2] Namely, in length, breadth, and depth.—See Aristot. *De Cœlo*, Lib. ii. c. 2; and compare Ficino, *Theol. Plat.* vi. 8, "Extensio namque ipsa quantitatis partes corporis disjunctas manere compellit."

spirit, consists of three natures, body, soul and spirit; so as in its threefold constitution to resemble Christ, in whom were the godhead, soul, and body. And hence those who have put on this person, from their threefold resemblance, may be termed Christians, and even, in a manner, *Christs*. To this the words of St. Paul refer: *Whom he did predestinate to be conformed to the image of his Son, that he might be the firstborn among many brethren.* [Rom. viii. 29.]

Thus is it evident in some measure, in what way men are *led by the spirit,* and in what sense they are termed by St. Paul *sons of God.*

As regards that *love,* on the other hand, from which St. Paul said that he could by no means be separated, there is this to be next said: namely, that Charity and Love are one and the same; and that the love of God within us is kindled from God's love toward us; and is begotten in us by a loving God. Hence the saying of St. John in his Epistle: *love is of God;* and a little after he adds: *Herein is love, not that we loved God, but that he first loved us.* Hence it is by God's loving us that we love him in return. [Rom. viii. 35.] [1 Joh. iv. 7.]

To what an extent this return of love and charity on our part towards God and his Christ is profitable for us, above all things else, plainly appears from the words of the Platonist Marsilius Ficinus touching the love of God. They are found in the XIVth Book of his *Platonic Theology,*[1] and are in the main to this effect:—

"Man," he says, "has two most excellent actions, regarding a most excellent object, of which the most excellent part of his soul, namely the intellect, is the instrument: and these are the *knowledge* and the *love* of God. But in this life the love of God far surpasses the knowledge of him, seeing that here no man truly knows God, nor indeed can do. But to love God is in his power; and he who by the grace of God despises and makes light of all else, does love God, in whatever degree he may know him. More-

---

[1] The passage will be found at p. 324, vol. i., of the Basle edn., 1575.—As Colet afterwards mentions, it is quoted with considerable alterations and additions.

over, in proportion as it is worse to hate God than not to know him, so is it assuredly better to love God than to know him. Add to this, that the searching out God is exceeding painful and hard, and after all brings but small profit with no small time; while on the other hand the love of God gains much fruit in a very short space, and causes us to approach God more quickly, and cleave to him more steadfastly. For while the force of knowledge consists rather in separation, that of love consists in union. Hence of necessity love is the more impetuous and efficacious, and swifter in attaining what is good, than knowledge is in detecting what is true. Furthermore it is beyond doubt more pleasing to God himself to be loved by men than to be surveyed; and to be worshipped, than to be understood. For we bestow nothing upon God by contemplating him; but by loving him we give him all our being, powers, and possessions. In searching into his nature, moreover, we appear to be seeking our own profit; but in loving him, the profit of God: whence arises the saying of the Apostle, *Charity seeketh not her own.*—And that same Apostle himself, being all on fire [1] with love, sought not his own but the things of Jesus Christ, whom he so much loved.—Well then, God bestows himself rather on those who love, than on those who search him out. And hence the saying of St. Paul: *All things work together for good to them that love God;* because to such God vouchsafes himself. And with him, through his unspeakable goodness, all things are good, even ills themselves, which are turned by him to something good. So that they who love God and possess him, must needs take in good part whatever befalls, and assign to a good end whatever is reckoned among evil things; so that, although the evil be an evil in itself, yet to those who love God, since they are good and divine, it may be able to prove a good.

1 Cor. xiii. 5.

Rom. viii. 28.

---

[1] In the Latin, *fragrans*, which I have supposed to be meant for *flagrans*, as in the *Hierarchies*, p. 133. A converse error in the *Letters on Genesis* will illustrate this, where "flagile" is found for "fragile." (Parker MS., p. 204.)

"But let me add what remains concerning love; the nature and power of which is marvellous, as may be perceived even from hence: namely, that the *love* of God cannot possibly be made a bad use of by us, though the *knowledge* of him undoubtedly may; that is, for boastfulness and pride. This was testified by St. Paul in his First Epistle to the Corinthians, when he said: *knowledge puffeth up, but charity edifieth*.[1 Cor. viii. 1.]

"Furthermore the love of God is infinitely more pleasant than the search after him with a view to knowledge; and they who love God feel far more enjoyment than they who search him out; and men become at length far better men by loving, than by inquiring into, God. And again, as it is not he who sees good, that becomes good, but he who wishes for and seeks it; so also the soul is rendered divine, not from studying, but from loving God: just as what is placed on a fire is shown to have been turned into fire, not because it is alight, but because it is hot and burning to its core. Moreover it is more honourable to man, and also, it must be allowed, more befitting the majesty divine, that God should be loved at once by feeble men, than that he should be known in some degree more minutely; seeing that, in striving to know God, we are endeavouring in a measure to narrow, and, as it were, distort him, to the meanness and straitness of our own intellect; but in loving him, we are raising ourselves to God, and enlarging ourselves to his unbounded goodness, so as now, great and lofty, to receive it according to our measure; adapting ourselves to it, not it to ourselves. Whence it is far more becoming both to God and men, that God should be loved, than that he should be searched out by us and known.[1] For weak men know but as much of God as they can contain; which is little indeed: but they love, not only as much as they know and behold, but also as much of the divine goodness as they conjecture to remain over, which they cannot know. For love is not confined within the limits of knowledge, but

---

[1] Colet expresses the same thought in his Letter to the Abbot of Winchcombe: "Unde sequitur, quod melius est ignorare Deum, quam eundem quoquo modo cognitum non amare et colere."

advances farther, in keeping with its transcendent power, and takes a wider sweep, not satisfied till it has attained that first boundless and infinite good, wherein alone it can repose. This exalted, expansive, God-embracing love, holding fast by him, and linking man closely to him, is the true worship and religion, whereby the minds of men may be

'Bound with gold chains about the feet of God.'"

Thus much have I related, after Marsilius, touching the excellency of love; using, however, my own words for the most part as I pleased, and my own manner of writing; not that I dream of being able to express it more fittingly or clearly than Marsilius (than whose language there can be nothing finer in philosophy), but because, in the use of our freedom of speech, I have taken the liberty of inserting what I would in the course of writing, and of giving such a turn to the passage as might best suit my purpose.

The drift of it all is this : that we ought by no means to wonder at St. Paul, possessed as he was with so great a love for God, asserting, with such fervour of spirit and fulness and grandeur of language, that nothing in the world could be conceived of as able to divert him from the love of God and Christ. Nor can we at all marvel that one, all on fire and burning with divine love, and who had experienced in himself the wonderful power of Charity,[1] should assign so much to love;—as he especially does in the Epistles to the Corinthians. For without it he affirms that nothing can avail: no matter how high its estimation may be as a thing good and powerful, yet nothing, I say, can avail without charity. But let me return at length to the point whence I digressed, and proceed in my exposition of the subject of this Epistle to the Romans, as I at first set out.

Having shown in the course of it, that there is no power or efficiency in the Jewish Law for restoring man, but that all his hope of salvation is placed in *faith*, that men should trust in God alone; and in *hope*, that they should look for God himself; and in *love*, that they should most ardently

---

[1] The word being used as synonymous with Christian love.

return the love of God; (and this, as set forth in the Incarnation of His Word, and in all the rest of that unutterable and most gracious dispensation touching Jesus Christ, for the recall of the human race to God; that of Christ, and in Christ, and through Christ, and for Christ, they may love God in the highest, and look for all things from him, and trust in him alone)—and moreover, having in the former chapters pointed out that, according to the purpose and voluntary predestination of God, and, as it were, by his immoveable decree, men are called by God himself to believe and trust in Him:—

CHAPTERS IX. AND X.[1]

HEREUPON the Apostle earnestly desires, yea longs intensely, that the Jews also, even though they refused to be called, may at length through divine grace be reckoned among the number of the called, and of those who trust in God. This is what, of his great love towards them, he now longs for; aye, even on condition that, if only they be saved, he himself may be made *accursed*, and an offering and victim for them, to be sacrificed for the propitiation of God.

For this is the signification of the Greek word *anathema*; since the verb *anathematize*, as Baptista Mantuanus[2] interprets it, denotes both to *execrate*, and also to *devote* (that is, *assign* and *dedicate*). Whence an *anathema*, as he also shows, is a victim over which one makes an oath; agreeably

---

[1] I have joined these two chapters together, from being unable to discover any exact point at which the commentary on chapter x. might be said to begin. In the MS. the present section is merely indicated by $ca^m\ 9^m$ in the margin; and no further mark of division occurs till the beginning of chapter xi., which is itself denoted as *ix. ca^m.*

[2] After taking some trouble, I have not succeeded in verifying this reference. It may be some excuse to plead, that no edition known to me has an index, and that Baptista's works in my copy (Antwerp edn. 1576) fill about 3,000 closely printed octavo pages.

to what St. Jerome[1] writes to Algasia, saying that he observes the word *anathema* in Holy Scripture frequently to imply *a slaying*. For the sheep that were *slain* and sacrificed for the propitiation of God towards men, were thus made victims.

Well then, St. Paul wished to be thus made a victim and oblation, that God might be rendered propitious to the Jews, with whom He was justly wroth; and that by the divine grace and mercy they might be brought into the number of the faithful. For, as St. Paul indicates, it concerned them beyond all others, to follow the call of God and Christ when summoned, seeing that with a peculiar desire (if I may so say) God had testified his good-will towards them, and given them a law, and thus long beforehand fashioned them, as it were, to receive his Christ and grace; which Christ moreover he willed should be born of their forefathers, and this grace take its rise among them. But so blind were they, and so hard of hearing when called by Christ, that they made no advance on their former privileges, handed down by Moses. Nevertheless the counsel and purpose of God were not in any wise baffled or deceived on that account; for he foresaw which way the Jews were inclined,[2] and what would at length be the issue of his grace displayed to them.

Not that his most sure and infallible providence assigned to such matters their issues: but God, seeing clearly what was to happen—everything from its own proper cause,—and what men would do of their own proper wills, both does what seems good to him to be done, and unfolds in due time his own everlasting purposes, and guides all things to

---

[1] "Quod autem *anathema* interdum occisionem sonet, multis veteris instrumenti testimnoiis probari potest."—*Op.* iii. 54 (ed. 1546).

[2] Colet in this is at one with Bishop Pearson, whose 3rd and 4th propositions are: "Deus omnes et singulos, quos prædestinavit ad vitam æternam, prævidit ab æterno ea in tempore præstituros, quæ ab iis requisivit ad obtinendam vitam æternam:" and "Deus omnes et singulos quos prædestinavit ad mortem, prævidit ab æterno ea præstituros quibus æternam mortem adjunxit."—*Minor Theol. Works*, i. p. 262.

the end which he himself wills and knows :—he who reach- Wisdom
eth from one end to another mightily, and sweetly¹ doth order viii: 1.
all things.

This unspeakable counsel, and disposal of things surpassing knowledge, we ought constantly to adore, weak men that we are; not to scrutinize; and to consider that all things have been done by God in such wise, that nothing could be either wiser, or juster, or more useful, or in every way more fitting. In this His providence, ordination, and disposal of events, all things, whencesoever they proceed, do so universally harmonize and tally together, and are so beautifully and sweetly blended by the merciful justice and just mercy of God, that, since equity and loving-kindness appear together on all sides and in every quarter of the world, there is no being in existence that can justly complain of God's dealings. On the contrary, there is reason why both that being, if such there were, and the whole universe, should rejoice in self-congratulation on the mercy and grace of God.

The Jews, then, were by no means able to frustrate the purpose and will of that great Governor. And though they did not reach the ultimate end to which the law of Moses and the teaching of the prophets strove to advance them, and to which Christ himself also at last endeavoured to draw them (I mean, to a kind of spirituality and divineness in life, wholly set free from bodily images and human affections), yet in these endeavours the purpose of God was not baffled. For it was his will to show most plainly, by so many methods, in the case of that single nation of the Jews, what might be learnt concerning the human race at large; namely, how hardly and with what difficulty men are drawn on high, out of that load of sins, under the pressure of

---

¹ The English version agrees in the text with the Vulgate *suaviter*, but has "profitably" as a marginal reading. The Septuagint word *chrēstŏs* combines these two ideas of kindness and serviceableness, as may be seen from the use of another form of it in ii. 4. It may be worth while to bear this in mind, as it will be noticed how often Dean Colet, taking his cue from the Latin *suaviter*, speaks of the *sweetness*, as well as power, with which the Divine wisdom works.

which they had not strength to lift up themselves. And if the result had been other than it was, God would then not have attained his will. Now his will was, to show openly the necessity of divine grace; that is to say, how necessary was a divine and transporting grace, that man might be set free from the state of bondage and misery in which he was. But if the Jews had not of themselves, in their own wickedness, resisted slighter efforts to draw them, the mighty power of saving grace would not have been displayed. Not that the Jews were under a necessity of resisting what would draw them, or that there was any compulsion. But God, observing all things in his wide survey, turned the evil which the Jews of their own accord were likely to do, and at length in fact did, to such an end, and of his infinite goodness diverted it to such an issue, in the way that might be most convenient and useful for the human race, that, though not the cause of evil, He yet appeared as the marvellous author of good out of evil. For, as St. Augustine finely says, *He makes a good use of our evil things, as we make a bad use of his good things.*[1]

Accordingly God turned the wicked deeds of the Jews to good ends; good, not indeed for themselves, who for their disobedience to the word will arrive at unmingled woe as the end of their wickedness; but good for the whole universe, and, as it were, for the general commonwealth; so that whilst, in keeping with God's justice, individual wrongdoers have nothing whereof to accuse God, or complain of him, yet at the same time, to a wonderful degree, in keeping with God's most bountiful grace, the system of things and the entire universe have both matter for rejoicing, and also cause to glorify God in the highest, whom even in the very midst of evils they acknowledge to be endued with so great goodness.

But we are now wandering away from St. Paul, and in disputing about the foreknowledge of God are saying more

---

[1] The passage occurs in c. lx. of Augustine's *Opus imperfectum contra Julianum* (Migne's ed. x. p. 1495): "Deus vero tam bonus est ut malis quoque utatur bene; quæ Omnipotens esse non sineret, si eis bene uti summa sua bonitate non posset."

than it seems that he would have us do. For by the weight of his authority he stops men's mouths, and, as it were, forbids us to debate of so great and so unsearchable a matter; saying, *O man, who art thou that repliest against God?* But, inasmuch as men cannot easily free themselves from wondering at the matter, lest perchance in their marvelling they should be either inwardly disturbed, or think profanely of God, I judge it right to say these few words, in order that they, whose mental vision grows dim from being strained towards so abstruse a subject, may in some degree be satisfied by this discourse of mine. ix. 20.

Now, St. Paul himself, in brief and simple language, places all in the mere will and pleasure of God; so as for those alone to come to God whom He calls; whom he has foreordained, purposed, promised, elected and predestinated. We must carefully observe, that in the Apostle's writings these words *purpose, promise, elect,* and *predestinate,* mean the same thing; and that God's *purpose* among men, his *promise; election,* and *predestination,* are one and the same; and that those whom he has promised to call, and those whom in his purpose and resolution he has called, and those whom he has elected, and those whom he has predestinated to his house and heritage, are the same.

Now, such will and purpose of God, as it pleaseth him, is not only in things eternal, for the election of men to the possession of eternal happiness, but moreover is in these earthly matters, for the attainment of some earthly and temporal happiness. This St. Paul teaches by examples borrowed from the Old Testament; in order that the Jews might clearly learn from them that in everything the end will be as God has purposed, and that his purpose cannot be baffled. For instance, it was the purpose and resolve of God, that Ishmael should be rejected, and that Isaac should be Abraham's heir. Nay further, that there might be no room for gainsaying, and that the free choice and will of God in events (namely, how it is his will to elect altogether as it pleaseth Him) might be most plainly shown,—of the twins brought forth at one birth, without any antecedent cause why either of the two should be preferred, He rejected

<small>Rom. ix. 13.
Gen. xxv. 32.</small>

Esau, and chose Jacob for Himself, to succeed to the possession and blessing of his father. What else can these things mean, but that God knows what He has promised, and of Himself performs what he has promised; and that the admission to every inheritance, whether temporal, or, most of all, spiritual and eternal, is of the promise and election of God?[1] And this sense Holy Scripture also contains in a remarkable manner, as appears in the examples brought forward by St. Paul. For in them, those who are recorded as elect, were ordained not only to their fathers' possessions on earth, but also, and far more, to the everlasting possession of God in heaven; so that, whichever of the two senses[2] you choose to follow, you may plainly see that matters are guided by the providence and direction of God, and that in human affairs it is done as He would have it. Not that this is from any violence being brought to bear; since nothing is further removed from violence than the action of God; but it is from the divine providence and will secretly and gently and, as it were, naturally accompanying the nature, will, and pleasure of man; and advancing along with it so marvellously, that both whatever you will and do is known by God, and also whatever He has known and determined, that must needs be done.

Now, he determined and decreed with himself—not to wander from St. Paul—what men were to be his sons, and who should attain eternal happiness; so that the Jews had neither the power nor the right to claim for themselves authority and position with God, in the way that they did,

---

[1] It will be observed how careful Dean Colet is throughout, to apply this reasoning about predestination to the purpose for which St. Paul originally introduced it, namely, to lessen the pride and self-confidence of the Jew. The author of the Comments on *Romans* in Jerome's works has some wise remarks on this passage in the same spirit, and adds : "Non enim Apostolus tollit quod in propria voluntate habemus, qui superius dicit, *Ignoras quia bonitas Dei te ad pœnitentiam adducit* . . . *Si quis autem mundaverit se ab his, erit vas in honorem sanctificatum*," &c.

[2] Namely, of being fore-ordained to *temporal*, or *spiritual* privileges and blessings.

as of hereditary right, in drawing their descent from Abraham. For even Abraham and Israel themselves could not demand anything as of their own right; but, if they sought to be counted among the sons of God, they must look for that from the divine election. In this the purpose of God cannot be baffled. For what he has determined and promised in the future, depends not on the wills of men, but on his own power and choice. This is what St. Paul teaches the Jews, when he says that not all the seed of Abraham are children of Abraham, nor all Israelites, who are born of Israel. But they who are so, are the promised and chosen by God's free will; even as Isaac and Jacob were, whilst Ishmael and Esau were disowned and rejected. And this we may perceive even in regard to their temporal affairs. But still, in this proceeding, and the election to earthly possessions, Holy Scripture, in accordance with its design, has portrayed this deeper purpose of God, and the method of coming to a heavenly inheritance; the partakers of which it calls children of Abraham and Israelites. These are they who have attained to the faith of Abraham, that was so acceptable to God, and to the vision of Israel. These again are they whom God himself has decreed to be faithful and believing, that is, *seeing*. These in sooth are the true children of Abraham; and, because elected to the faith of Abraham, children of God, and truly Israelites, because through faith they see God. These, lastly, are they whom God has promised and purposed and predestined to be children of Abraham, that is, representers of the faith of Abraham; and Israelites, that is, *seers of God*.[1] These are

Ix. 6, 7.

---

[1] Erasmus, in his *Annotationes* (in loc.) calls attention to this interpretation of the name Israel, which he says had hitherto been ill understood. The reason given for the change of the name Jacob to Israel, as it stands in the Vulgate of Gen. xxxii. 28, is "quoniam si contra Deum fortis fuisti, quanto magis contra homines prævalebis," which, it will be observed, varies somewhat from the English version. Jerome (*Quæst. Hebr. in Gen.*) admits that in his time the commonly received interpretation was *vir videns Deum*; and Erasmus regrets that he did not adopt this meaning in the present instance, instead of countenancing the other meaning, "*Prince* of God," which has been commonly accepted among ourselves.

called children of the promise and election of God; being verily born, nay rather re-born, of the promised seed, even Jesus Christ, of whom the Isaac of promise was a type.

<small>Rom. ix. 7.
Gen. xxi. 12.</small>
Hence St. Paul bethinks him of the passage in Genesis, *But in Isaac shall thy seed be called;* in the Isaac, that is to say, who was promised and fore-chosen. And he proceeds to explain that not all *the children of the flesh* are born of Abraham; nor indeed because any has been born of Abraham, is he on that account a child of God: but they that are *the children of the promise* (to wit, the promised and elect) *are counted for the seed*, that is, the heavenly offspring, which will be propagated from Christ, the spiritual Isaac. Thus he teaches that all things are done for men by the promise and free election of God; they themselves contributing nothing towards that election, lest the counsel and purpose of God should seem to depend on the will and deeds of man. This is the application of the passage quoted by the apostle concerning the twins brought forth almost at the same instant; touching whom it was said, even before they
<small>Rom. ix. 11, 13.</small>
were born, *Not of works, but of him that calleth, Jacob have I loved but Esau have I hated;* and *the elder shall serve the younger; neither having done any good or evil; that the purpose of God according to election might stand.* For he purposes and promises what he will; and by election performs what he himself has promised; that men may own God's benefit to be untouched by others, and see himself wholly in it; to the end that, if they glory at all, they may glory in God as the sole author of their glorying.

This is the apostle Paul's opinion concerning the manner of attaining the heavenly inheritance; an opinion most true and religious and worthy of the divine majesty; namely that, whatever there is which affects the blessedness of mankind, it rests wholly on the purpose and will and grace of God.

Now, how true and just this is, and how fitting both to

God and men, man indeed, in his blindness, may not be able to perceive. Yet assuredly he ought not, in so great and exalted a subject, to abuse the little power of intellect that he possesses, either by scrutinising it too eagerly, or forming any rash decisions, or despising what he cannot see, or finally despairing of himself, in an abject fear and terror of the power and will of God. For whoever does this, beyond question makes an unworthy and mournful misuse of his intellect; a faculty given him in order that he may subject it to God, with trust in him; to the end that he may be raised through grace out of blindness into light, and out of folly into wisdom; that is, from distrust and questionings, to faith, and to the discovery of the reality and truth.

Wherefore let every one consider, who is pondering in a purblind way on the divine and arbitrary election of men to heavenly life,—let such consider, I say, in the first place, how great is the sublimity and loftiness of the divine majesty, and how it surpasses by the vastest possible interval not only weak men but the most exalted angels; so that not even the highest spirits of all know all the things that are of God, *who dwelleth,* as St. Paul elsewhere says, *in the light which no man can approach unto.* Let him consider in the next place his own low and base condition; how far distant from God his own mind is, both of itself and from its being depressed into this heavy and gloomy body, whereby the soul is so hoodwinked as not only to be unable to look upwards at things heavenly (much less at things divine themselves), but even to behold without error all that is present and set before the eyes. As he considers this with himself, and calmly recollects it, let him marvel in no wise that there should be declared and handed down by most divine men, to whom God has revealed it, things concerning God and the mind of God at which he is lost in amazement; things that, in his weakness, he at first rather shrinks from, than accepts, and feels to have been truly spoken. Nay, rather let him marvel that in so humble and low a condition, and in a body, moreover, so over-

1 Tim. vi. 16.

shadowing[1] and sordid, he can raise his eyes to matters of such loftiness and purity and brightness. For assuredly it would be a greater marvel that those things could be contemplated by weak men than that they could not.

I do not mean to say that what our most good and kindly God purposed in His own mind, and decreed, and accomplished, for the salvation of men was so accomplished, nor was it the will of God that it should be so accomplished, and the benefit so bestowed on men, as that it could in no wise be *known* by men themselves. But yet in truth these matters were so set forth, and appear in the eyes of men to be such and so marvellous (as is but reasonable, seeing that they proceeded from God), that men may be obviously reminded, in the first place, that things of this sort, far transcending as they do the human reason, cannot be scrutinized by them; and secondly, that, if they wish to scrutinize them, they must be changed from the state in which they are to one wholly different, namely, the divine state, and must suffer themselves to be drawn towards the things which they seek to know, not do anything themselves that those things may be narrowed down to them.

For, if man endeavours to draw them to himself, and examine them by the natural powers of his own mind, it cannot fail but that they will certainly degenerate at once, so to speak, from their truth and sweetness, in keeping with the fickleness and incapacity of the human mind, and prove for him in a measure delusive and insipid; much in the same way as to sick people wholesome things become unwholesome, and to the feverish sweets appear bitter,[2] and also as the sun's rays look red when streaming through red glass, and a sweet-scented liquid, if placed in a foul vessel, becomes noisome. *For everything ultimately becomes*

---

[1] See note above, p. 26. The reader will call to mind the expression in the *Intimations of Immortality*:—
"Shades of the prison-house begin to close
About the growing boy."

[2] Compare Baptista Mantuanus, *De Patientia*, i. 4: "Nam propter bilis admixtionem palato infirmo mel amarescit, et oculis ægris odiosa est lux, quæ jucunda est sanis."

similar to its receptacle.[1] Whence the prophet Isaiah denounces those who, through their own baseness, unsettle and defile all things, saying, *Woe unto them that call evil* Is. v. 20. *good, and good evil; that put bitter for sweet, and sweet for bitter.* That is to say, those are to be denounced, and heartily detested, who wish to measure and define all things by the nature and powers of their own mind; especially divine things, which exceed all the limits of the human mind. For if these are to be rightly understood by feeble men, and as their lofty nature deserves, then beyond question men must be elevated to them, not they depressed to men. Ungodliness and pride, I repeat, must yield to humility and grace. For through ungodliness and profane haughtiness we draw what is divine down to ourselves; but through humility on our part, and the divine grace, we are drawn to what is divine, and are enlarged so as to receive it; a more fitting result than that those things should be confined and straitened so as to be received by us. Accordingly man must submit himself to God and the divine inspiration, if he would contemplate to any extent the wisdom of the divine counsels. And just as primal matter,[2] in order to be formed, is naked, that there may be nothing in it to counteract the formation; so it is needful that man should strip off all his own powers, and patiently subject himself in every way to God, if he would be enlightened by inspiration to understand things divine, lest, if he do anything of himself, he hinder the divine working and reforming of himself.

---

[1] The words in the Latin are underlined; but I am in ignorance whether the sentence is a quotation, or only meant to express a general principle.

[2] See note above, p. 20. Colet's own language, in his Exposition of 1 *Corinthians*, will best illustrate this: "Homo quasi materia rudis est, spiritalis formæ expers, idoneus tamen ut formetur a spiritu; qui ipse homo suapte natura privatur deitate. Causa autem transmutans hunc carnalem hominem in spiritum, et efficiens, spiritus ipse Dei est."—*Cambr. Univ. MS.* Gg. iv. 26, leaf 142.

The mention of *causa transmutans* is a passing corroboration of what Bishop Hampden wrote about the "doctrine of Transmutation" passing from Aristotle into the tenets of the Schools.

This was wisely taught by St. Paul when he wrote to the Corinthians: *If any man among you seemeth to be wise in this world, let him become a fool, that he may be wise.* That is, let him acknowledge his own foolishness, and be conscious that he has no wisdom, nor of himself can have, and let him lay aside altogether every conceit of knowledge, and all trust in himself and in his own strength (which is no strength at all but rather weakness), and in entire subjection to God let him trust in God alone, and from God look for the reformation of himself, and the power and faculty of discerning and judging all things aright.

<small>1 Cor. iii. 18.</small>

He that shall have done this humbly and as a suppliant, with dutiful and constant prayer as well, that he may be raised from darkness into light, will assuredly feel that he has not pleaded with God in vain, nor sought ineffectually for the light of knowledge; but by the divine ray, and by grace, he will be drawn from what is low to what is lofty, and from wavering reason to certain, undoubting and steadfast faith. This faith is a kind of light infused into the soul of man from the divine sun, by which the heavenly verities are known to be revealed without uncertainty or doubt; and it as far excels the light of reason, as certainty does uncertainty, or as the solar light does colours.[1] And, more, just as in certainty there is no uncertainty, nor colouring in light, so likewise in the splendour of faith no shadowy reasoning ought to appear; for if this be introduced, faith is shaken. And when from this low, erring, and unquiet reason, never finding a spot wherein to rest, you are brought back to the straight road of faith and the truth of Christ, beware of ever straying from it again, and reasoning, and seeming to yourself wise, and supposing that by the strength of reason you can attain aught of truth; since this would be like seeking light in darkness, and wishing to be wise in the very midst of folly. For in truth all the force of human intellect is purblind and sightless as regards the light of God and divine things: of which St. Paul bore witness, when he said that *the wisdom of this world is foolishness with God.*

<small>1 Cor. iii. 19.</small>

---

[1] See the *Hierarchies,* p. xli. n. 2.

And what is this but to say, that he who thinks himself wise, cannot see? Hence the saying of the Apostle that I cited but now; *If any man seemeth to be wise, let him become a fool, that he may be wise.* For the acknowledgment and confession of ignorance is in God's sight the beginning of wisdom. Nor is there in fact anything that so dispels the divine grace, as a high opinion of ourselves, and a conceit of there being some wisdom in us. Let him who is of this temper and mind plainly settle it with himself that, as long as he remains in this opinion, he cannot be a partaker of the divine grace.

<small>1 Cor. iii. 18.</small>

The result then is this. Does any wish to see how true, and good, and just, and worthy of God, and suitable for men, and in short how fitting and well-adjusted to the whole universe is all the dispensation which God made regarding His Son, the incarnate Word, in a manner and with a grace that are unutterable? Would he see the end to be men's revocation to Himself, and restitution to their primeval state; nay to something even higher than the state of Adam in Paradise; a drawing to far greater height of those, whom that inscrutable mind has marked out (even *before the foundation of the world*, as St. Paul writes to the Ephesians) to be so drawn and united with Himself? Does any wish and long to see this, I repeat, and to see moreover how marvellously just and merciful at the same time is God, in the choice of those men who are fore-ordained to complete the number of the angels; so that, whether He choose or reject, there is joy on the part of many, with complaint from none? Would any, I repeat once more, see and mark this? Then he must wholly strip and lay bare himself, laying aside all the thoughts of his mind that he was wont to entertain, and by which he deemed that he had learnt something; and, in subjection to God, and sighing for God, he must acknowledge first and foremost his own folly and worthlessness; he must own his errors, lament his sins, implore for grace, and offer himself in patience, purity and simplicity to God; in order that he may be touched and moved and affected by the simple and pure divine ray and grace, and be formed again into a new man, spiritual, that

<small>Eph. i. 4.</small>

is, and divine; that in due course he may have, not the blind intellect and gross will of a grovelling soul, but a new will and new intellect, such as follow the form [1] of the spirit; to the end that, through this new form, power, will and action, he himself may appear an entirely new man.

Now the *intellect* of the spirit is faith in God; and its *will* is charity and the love of God. These are begotten in the soul of man by the beneficent ray of God; who in His own being has both light and heat in a wonderful degree; and who, when He finds a soul washed and scoured and bright, takes possession of it, and fills it at once with sweetest warmth and light. This *warmth*, and clear flame, so to speak, kindled in the soul, is *charity*. The *illumination*, and infused light, by which the soul may have light in its inmost recess, and see what is abroad with perfect truth, is *faith*. These are the new powers, both true and efficacious, that spring from the new and spiritual form of man; endowed with which, man is the author and worker of actions and works wholly new; of such a kind namely, as that in all of them his faith in God and love of God may shine forth, as a cause does in its effects; so that, whatever he has either done or said or thought within himself, may wholly proceed from a heart so faithful and loving, as to show that nothing else has any weight with him, but faith and the love of God. When a man has attained to this excellence and perfection, both through his own humility and above all through the divine grace of God, then will he immediately, as if emerging into light, see distinctly by the eye of faith both himself, and God, and the divine grace and mysteries, and in fine Jesus Christ and the election of men

---

[1] This term has been before explained. The following passage from Ficino's Commentary on the *Romans*, will not only serve to illustrate it, but also to show how the *forms* of Aristotle had become blended with the *ideas* of Plato: "Plato Plotinusque esse res veras dumtaxat ideas existimant. *Formas* autem naturales rerum verarum, id est, *idearum, imagines* esse, ex influxibus invisibilium idearum, in ipsa mundi materia, quasi speculo, resultantes ad sensum."—*MS. Harl.* No. 4695, leaf 30. In the collected works of Ficino (1576), this and other treatises are very inaccurately printed.

unto salvation. He will see these things, I say, with reverence and devotion; and will cease from endless reasonings about a matter that far transcends all reason; but rather, raised on high, and stationed on the lofty watch-tower of faith, and with the love of God brightly blazing,[1] will most gladly and delightfully rest in it, waiting with full resolve for the fruit of his faith and love, and of his faithful and loving works and actions. And this firm hope and expectation our good and faithful God will not frustrate, since it is by His own love to us first, that He has awakened it in man.

But I am now wandering far away from my subject, St. Paul; not being able to restrain myself from breaking out on the slightest occasion into lengthy discourse, as often as I have any field for speaking of the predestination of God, and the judgment of men concerning it. And because this judgment is apt with many to waver and be unsteady, I therefore, out of the goodwill and affection I bear to men, am delivering a longer address, not being so much afraid of weariness on my readers' part,[2] as desirous of confirming the weak and wavering.

But now let us return to St. Paul, who forbids man to dispute about the counsel of God; saying, *O man, who art thou that repliest against God?*—that is, Canst thou make any reply, for thine own defence, if God will be the plaintiff, and (as he may) bring a heavy charge against thee? As though to say, Thou canst make no reply; but, acknowledging thine own wickedness and iniquity, must needs stand mute and speechless, even as a potter's vessels before the potter. For these, had they understanding, would not ask the maker why, out of the same lump, vessels were fashioned for many and various purposes and uses; nor would those designed for baser offices complain of that allotment of themselves. So neither is it the part of man, the handiwork[3] of God, to complain, or to inquire what the

ix. 20.

---

[1] Latin *fragranti*. See note above, p. 30.
[2] It will be observed here that Colet speaks of *readers*, not *hearers*
[3] It is difficult to express the exact force of *figmentum* by a single

reason is, why some are chosen for glory, others are left behind. For that would be to argue with God; than which there can be nothing more wicked and detestable. And if any one were to search never so carefully, why some are saved, and others will be condemned; he would find no other reason than this, namely, that grace is the cause of salvation, man's guilt the cause of condemnation. He would find men saved by the goodness and grace of God, though most unworthy of salvation; and others, most worthy of death, justly and by right of their sin condemned. *What if God* (as St. Paul adds) *had been willing to show his wrath, and to make his power known?* Let the sentence be read interrogatively,[1] and then it is an unfinished and suspended one, arising from the impetuosity of his language. And there may be understood after it: *Then assuredly long before this God would have destroyed men altogether.* Therefore does St. Paul, showing the clemency and grace of God, subjoin the word *endured.* Understand *But;* and read: *But he endured* and suffered *the vessels of wrath fitted to destruction* (that is, those deserving condemnation) to continue in the world, *that he might make known the riches of his glory*

ix. 22.

---

word in English. In our version it is rendered "the thing formed;" but in this we lose the relationship to *figulus,* "the potter."

In the Commentary on the *Romans* that passes under Jerome's name, a very remarkable interpretation is given to the argument from the potter's handiwork. Instead of the phrase being understood to express the vast distance between God and man, and thus teach humility and acquiescence (as in Is. xlv. 9), it is taken as implying man's free-will, as though the force of it were, "The vessel of potter's clay cannot answer its maker; but thy very question is an expostulation with him, and shows thee to have an independent will:" "Hic autem in eo in quo contradicit, queritur de Dei voluntate, ostendit liberi esse arbitrii, qui audet de Dei judicio retractare." (Frankf. ed. ix. p. 230.)

[1] Erasmus (*Annotationes* in loc.) states that some copies of the Vulgate in his time had *Quid si,* &c., and this reading appears in an edition of 1516. Erasmus suggests more than one way of completing the sentence, but not this one proposed by Colet. Dr. Peile translates: "*But* is it any impeachment of his unsullied righteousness, *if God with final purpose to let His wrath be seen, and to make known what* when He will *He can do,* hath borne with, *in much long-suffering, vessels of wrath, when now ripe for destruction?*"

on the vessels of mercy;[1] that is, that he might manifest his grace on those on whom he would have mercy, and on those whom *he had afore prepared unto glory.*

For when, out of a lost and abandoned world, wholly condemned by its own crimes, God chose for himself those whom he would set free from just condemnation, he so manifestly declared his grace, that, except by grace, none can now truly say that he is saved. This saving grace he bestowed, as it pleased him, in common to all nations, both of the Jews and of others; because God is not an accepter of any man's person or quality; but draws out of every nation, and makes acceptable to himself, whom, and in what way, he will. This St. Paul establishes by the testimonies of the prophets Hosea and Isaiah; of whom the latter foretold that there would be summoned to God a certain *remnant* of Israel; to wit, the apostles and disciples of Christ, and the rest of the church among the Jews: the former, Hosea, that there would be such also out of other places and peoples. For, as Isaiah foretold, God was purposing one day to set before all mankind a form of doctrine; not such as was that of the Jews, long, intricate, and imperfect; but a short, simple and perfect one; such as men might learn with the utmost ease, and express in almost a single word. This doctrine, at the time when St. Paul wrote to the Romans, was set forth by God, through his Son, and exhibited to the world. It is the doctrine of Faith; that men should believe and trust in God, and in his messenger Jesus Christ, and confess their faith by words. This doctrine Isaiah calls a *brief and summary word;*[2] seeing

Is. x. 22.

Hos. ii. 23.

Is. x. 23.

---

[1] In the Latin, *iræ*, by an error for *misericordiæ*.

[2] This expression will not be found in the English version of Isaiah x. 23, but may be compared with Wycliffe's translation: "Forsothe a word makynge an ende, and abreggynge in equyte, for the Lord schal make a word breggid on al the erthe." Colet's application of the passage is due to the influence of the word *verbum* on his mind, which appears in the Vulgate of Rom. ix. 28 as an equivalent for the Greek *logon*, *i. e.*, the summary *reckoning* that God would take with his people; which is what Isaiah is really speaking of. See the note on Colet's *Hierarchies* (1869), p. 9. Baptista Mantuanus uses the expression in the same way as Colet: "At Christi verbum

that in it are contained *in brief* all doctrine, wisdom, virtue, and the reward of virtue, happiness. For he who has believed in Christ, and in accordance with that faith has practised what Christ delivered, will undoubtedly be saved. And this doctrine of faith, this reconciliation of mankind, this life and salvation, was at length offered to all alike by a merciful God : even as angels sang to the shepherds, *Glory to God in the highest, and on earth peace, good will toward men.* For there is peace and reconciliation to those who believe[1] in Jesus Christ, the messenger of truth, and pointer-out of the way of salvation. This is the very gospel; *the power of God unto salvation,* as St. Paul in another place calls it, *to every one that believeth; to the Jew first and also to the Greek.* And this gospel, even this good news, and short doctrine of faith, was set before the eyes of men, and was, in a manner, in the mouth of all, that they might believe and see the messenger of faith, Jesus Christ, and make confession of him. For he was so preached throughout the whole world, and the voices of the apostles so went (as David foretold they would) into all the ends of the earth, that they who believed the preaching of the apostles, may most justly be accounted to have believed Christ himself, and God. For they could not believe in Christ, unless they heard of him; nor hear, unless there had been some to preach; nor could there have been preachers, unless they had been sent. Wherefore such as believed them that were sent, even the Apostles, believed Christ himself.

An inference of this kind is drawn by St. Paul, in order to prove that faith must of necessity be placed in the

Luke ii. 14.

Rom. i. 16.

Rom. x. 8.

Ps. xix. 4; Rom. x. 18.

Rom. x. 14.

---

abbreviatum, quod unius horæ spacio disci potest nobis, ostendit quod philosophi frustra laborantes toto vitæ spacio quæsierunt."—*De Patient.* iii. 1.

[1] It will be remembered that in the Vulgate the sense is, "Peace on earth *to men of good will*"—*hominibus bonæ voluntatis*—instead of " good will to men." Faber's preference for the latter translation of the Greek is made the subject of some entertaining remarks in the *Epistolæ Obscurorum Virorum* (ed. 1557, leaf I. 7), where Magister Lupoldus is made to exclaim, on hearing it, " Sancta Maria, ego nescio magis quam Bibliam habebimus."

Apostles and ambassadors of Christ. For when by their efforts and pains there was published abroad the will and instruction of Christ, that is, the law and system of faith; namely, that men should everywhere trust in God alone, and believe themselves to be saved through Christ; there was no room for any one to say that he had never heard aught concerning Christ and saving faith. For by means of the Apostles, all had discourses and preaching on the subject within their reach—so close at hand, indeed, that nothing essential to their salvation appears to have been wanting, except the good will of the hearers themselves. Hence St. Paul cites the words of Moses, the Hebrew Lawgiver, addressed once on a time to the Hebrews themselves (as is recorded in Deuteronomy), after their laws had been enacted, and written and delivered to them, and repeatedly published. In these words he admonishes them that, so long as they had their laws and complete rule of life at hand, they were not to seek from any other source for a rule of life, or virtue, or religion; nor to inquire who would bring them, out of heaven, or some more distant region, a law by which they might live rightly and religiously, as though they had not any of the sort; but own the law that was plainly set before their eyes and often impressed upon their hearing, and obey it. Failing which, so long as they had at hand a light whereby the right way of living was shown, they could have no excuse for their fault. The words of Moses are these: *For this commandment which I command thee this day, it is not hidden from thee, neither is it far off. It is not in heaven, that thou shouldest say, Who shall go up for us to heaven, and bring it unto us, that we may hear it and do it? Neither is it beyond the sea, that thou shouldest say, Who shall go over the sea for us, and bring it unto us, that we may hear it and do it? But the word is very nigh unto thee, in thy mouth and in thy heart, that thou mayest do it.* By which words it is manifest that he warned the Hebrews, that, so long as there was a law given to them, and at hand, there could be no excuse for going astray. Deut. xxx. 11-14.

Now, what Moses said touching that law, namely, that it was open and by their side, so as not possibly to be overlooked, the very same may now be aptly said touching the law of Christ, the light and reason of faith, seeing that it has been proclaimed and published by the Apostles in the sight of all men. Nay more, since Christ is the end of the Mosaic law, and since all that Moses wrote points to Christ, he appears, while speaking of his own law, to have prophesied also of the law of Christ, and of faith; and in pronouncing the above words concerning his own law, a law which had reference to the coming law of Christ, he appears to pronounce them at the same time prophetically concerning the Christian law itself, and faith; which he foresaw would be not less present to all mankind, than his own was to the Jews. On this account St. Paul, in quoting those words of Moses, explains them of Christ and his law. For when Christ was now come, and through his Apostles had made [known][1] to the whole world both himself and his doctrine, and the law of faith, then might it justly be said, as

x. 8.   St. Paul says in the language of Moses, *The word is nigh thee* (nigh to every one, that is), *even in thy mouth and in thy heart; that is, the word of faith which we preach.* This *word* requires belief, as the law of the Jews required observance; in order that, just as those who kept the law of Moses lived in safety under it, without bodily death or punishment, so they who believe the Gospel of Christ, and trust in God, and confess the faith they have in Christ as their Lord, may, if they persevere, that is, in this faith, have everlasting life both in soul and body, and obtain eternal happiness.

But when the gospel of God was preached, they did not all show faith in it. And among those who failed to do so were the Jews first and foremost. This is proved by the

x. 19.   question thus put by St. Paul: *But I say, Did not Israel know?* That is, Were the Israelites of the number of those who did not *know*—in other words, did not *believe* the gospel? For observe in this passage, that to *believe*, and *obey*, and *know* the gospel, have with St. Paul the same meaning. Accordingly, after asking the question, Were the Jews of

---

[1] Some such word as *notam* appears wanting before *fecerit* in the Latin, unless the word has been *patefecerit*.

the number of those who heard, but knew not Christ, nor believed in him—as if implying that they certainly were such in the highest degree—he then proves it also by the testimonies of the prophets Moses and Isaiah; who by their prophetic utterances plainly testified how slow to believe in God the Jewish nation would ever be; and how other nations would be far more inclined to receive the faith and the truth. Hence it is that St. Paul grieved so bitterly over their lot, and wished himself to be made a sacrifice, so that they were reconciled to God, and drawn again to the light and perception of the truth. For he implies that, in their grossness and ignorance of mind, they had rejected the offered truth, and in kicking against the *stone of stumbling* had hurt themselves; not suffering Christ, the *rock of offence* (that is, the rock that was a bar to them when sliding into the abyss) to be an obstacle to their sins; but in thus spurning, and, as it were, striking at the stone with their feet, that it might be removed out of the way, lest it should hinder their headlong fall to death,[1] they stumbled so heavily upon it, and inflicted such a wound upon themselves, that it was needful for that mischief long afterwards to remain in them, as a mighty argument of their folly and guilt.

ix. 3.

---

[1] Colet appears to have taken from Origen this explanation of the "stone of stumbling." In the quotation made by St. Paul from Isaiah, the language of two passages is blended together, namely xxviii. 16 and viii. 14. In the application of that language to Christ, it became a question how he could be called a "stumbling-block," or "rock of offence," since we naturally regard that as a cause of injury, not a safeguard. And so Chrysostom understood it: "Stumbling comes of not taking heed" (he writes), "of gaping after other things." And as the Jews fell against it from having their eyes fixed on the Law, he says it is so called "from the character and end of those that believe not." But Origen, whom Colet follows, regarded it as a barrier placed across a dangerous way, not to trip men up, but to keep them from falling. Christ by his preaching, he says, "began to bar their ways of destruction, and thus became for them a *stone of stumbling and rock of offence*, from suffering them not to enter the *broad way* that leadeth unto death."—*Comment. in Ep. ad Rom., Lib. vii.* (ed. 1837, Pars ii. p. 190).

CHAPTER XI.

NEVERTHELESS, as appears afterwards in the continuation of his discourse, St. Paul, moved by prophecy and taught by the divine Spirit, foretells that the time will one day be when the Jews, through divine grace, shall regain the favour of God, and repent, and acknowledge Christ, and accept and reverence all the saving mystery of God touching Christ, and in fine, trust in God as they ought. This, after his manner, St. Paul establishes by the testimony of the prophet Isaiah; in whose prophecies it is written, that through Christ their stain shall be washed away, and their sin blotted out. Now Christ from his very first coming did cleanse, and by his Spirit still continues to cleanse, those whom he will, till his coming again. For, as Jesus himself saith in the Evangelist St. John, *the wind*[1] *bloweth where it listeth.* Accordingly St. Paul saw and foretold that the Jews would be cleansed by the Spirit of God; but when this will be, and which of them will be called, and how many, is known (as Origen says[2]) to God alone. For they will not all be called, but a more abundant multitude of them than of other nations in proportion, for filling up the number of the elect.

The mention of this call of theirs is at length most wisely added by St. Paul, that he may bring to the Jews the hope of grace, may provoke them to lay hold on grace, and keep the gentiles from priding themselves on their desertion, or boasting of their own abundance of grace, since the Jews also, if God will, may so greatly abound in it. Nay, more, he even shows that the gentiles themselves also may most easily fall away from grace, unless they take heed, and walk circumspectly and humbly, and own

---

[1] See note above, p. 11.
[2] "Quis autem sit iste omnis Israel, qui salvus fiet, vel quæ erit ista plenitudo etiam Gentium, Deus solus novit, et Unigenitus suus, et si qui forte amici ejus sunt," &c.—*Comment.*, ut supra, *Lib. viii.*, p. 269.

Marginal references: Is. i. 18. John iii. 8.

that by grace they stand, not of themselves, but are upheld by the author of grace. He measures all things in his mercy, and weighs them in his faithfulness; and, just as He graciously takes hold of and draws to himself those who submit, and begin to believe and trust in God, so likewise does He at once forsake those who boast too proudly, and turn to themselves, and cease to trust in God; yea and leaves them devoid of all grace. This the chief of the apostles, St. Peter, testifies in his Epistle, saying, *God resisteth the proud, and giveth grace to the humble.* [1 Pet. v. 5.]

Thus does St. Paul, with singular wisdom and skill, temper his language in this Epistle, and balance it, as it were, in such equipoise, as to make Jews and gentiles on a level together; that each party may acknowledge that it has no reason for preferring itself to the other. And it is to this end chiefly that the Apostle's discourse tends, varied and diffuse as it is. For in it he shows, first of all, that Jews and gentiles had been on a level in wickedness; on a level also in weakness, and equally powerless to rise again. In the next place, after declaring that by God's grace alone any raising up[1] of mankind is possible, he shows that both the Jews and the other nations are on an equality respecting it, that all moreover have sinned unto condemnation, that all need grace for salvation, that the reconciliation of men with God depends on humility and faith; that those are humble and faithful whom God has subjected to himself and made faithful; that, as regards those whom He wills to recall to himself out of the whole lost race of men, to serve and believe in Him, those who are not yet called *may* be called, whilst those who are called, may still be rejected; that, in the wonderful dispensation of events, the Jews were suffered to wander away from God, that so by a just occasion grace might be offered to the gentiles; that the gentiles had believed, in order that by their example the Jews might have an incentive to faith; that at length, to fulfil the promises made to their fathers, God will draw to himself as many as shall be deemed sufficient, although they

---

[1] Reading *relevationem* for *revelationem*.

.have been enemies to the Gospel; that in the bestowal of His grace, as is most fitting, He works in the way that pleases him best; that He engrafts whom He will as branches on the tree of faith (whose root is Christ, planted by him in Judea to grow there), and whom He will, He breaks off; in fine, that he chooses out of the whole world and multitude of men, whom, and when, and how He will; and that He will accomplish all that he has fore-known and predestinated touching the salvation of men and the number of the faithful, in the way that shall seem best to him, and at the time that shall be most fitting.

After pointing out these things, and making what is divine in the work of man's salvation to rest in the power of God, as undoubtedly it must be made to rest, and after he has said much concerning the unutterable and amazing counsel of God; last of all, in admiration of so great and so unsearchable a matter as this dispensation, St. Paul exclaims to himself in these words : *O the depth of the riches both of the wisdom and knowledge of God! how unsearchable are his judgments, and his ways past finding out! For who hath known the mind of the Lord? or who hath been his counsellor? Or who hath first given to him, and it shall be recompensed him again?* As if he said, None giveth counsel to God; nor is there anything before him. *For of him,* the true first principle, who is in all; *and through him* alone, without helper; *and in him,* than whom nothing is more capacious, who contains all things; all things have their source and being and preservation.

xi. 33-36.

Thus have I brought down to the present point the exposition I undertook to write on this portion alone of the Epistle to the Romans, which ends with the above passage of the admirable St. Paul. And truly my exposition has grown to far greater length than I at first intended. But the mingled brevity and condensed richness of St. Paul demanded of me a fuller explanation. Yet I think that no one can explain all. For so great is the treasure, and so abundant the store, of wisdom and divineness hidden in the Apostle's language, that, whatever any one may have quarried and brought forth from the mine, there will still ever be an inexhaustible remainder, to be brought to light by some wiser man.[1]

As for the contribution, whatever it be, that I myself have made towards this subject, although I have not written so much for others as for myself, yet if it chance that these comments of mine, be they what they may, shall fall at any time into the hands of others, I pray them to take in good part whatever they may read in them, and ascribe to God alone whatever they shall find well said. But if there be aught to offend those that are of better judgment, I will not object to its being disproved, refuted and thrown upon my hands again. For I acknowledge my own weakness; I acknowledge also that all things are of grace; so that we both may and must adopt that saying of the Apostle: *We are not sufficient of ourselves, but all our sufficiency is of God.* 2 Cor. iii. 5.

THE END.

HERE FOLLOWS THE REST OF THE EXPOSITION ON THE REMAINDER OF THIS EPISTLE OF ST. PAUL TO THE ROMANS, WRITTEN BY JOHN COLET.

THOUGH I determined with myself that I would not continue my exposition on this Epistle written by St. Paul to the Romans, beyond what was lately delivered by me, and brought down to the passage in which the Apostle concludes his appeal (whereby he endeavoured to turn the whole Roman Church to God, and persuade them to attribute nothing to themselves, but ascribe all to God, and

---

[1] Colet at times seems scarcely able to find words to express his admiration of St. Paul. In his letter to the Abbot of Winchcombe he says, "Ut pelagus quoddam infinitum sapientiæ et pietatis mihi unus videtur Paulus esse." And in the MS. *Exposition of 1 Cor.*, he speaks of his "adamantina mens," and calls him "unus omnium divinissimus et consideratissimus." He afterwards learnt to feel, as Erasmus tells us, how the light even of St. Paul himself grew pale in presence of the Master.

trust in God alone, and look for all from God) in these
xi. 36. words: *For of him, and through him, and to him, are all things; to whom be glory for ever. Amen:*—yet the truth is, being often and pressingly asked by certain friends, themselves also attached hearers of my interpretation of St. Paul (to whom, as in friendship bound, I communicated what I had written on the former part of the Epistle), I was at length induced to promise that I would go on with what I had before begun, and apply to the rest of the Epistle what still remains of my exposition.

This I will now do, following the track of St. Paul as I previously did. And though I may prove at times to wander away from my set task, as the method of a clearer exposition shall demand, yet I will recall myself, and return to the path, in such a way as in the end to be considered to have made no deviation from St. Paul's route.

In this way accordingly let me begin in order what remains.

CHAPTER XII.

THE Apostle has been writing all that he could to the Romans,—to those, that is, who professed amendment of life and the worship of God and Christ. And the end of it all was, to take away arrogance and pride, the root of all dissension among men; and persuade them that they must trust in God alone, from whom proceeds to mankind everything that is counted good.

Accordingly he now goes on to beseech and adjure them all, to draw together and collect themselves; that is, to withdraw themselves wholly from the defilements of this world, and rein-in the body to be obedient to the soul and reason, and submit themselves, as matter fit and cleansed, to the divine reformation; that every one, being seized by divine grace, and inspired by the divine Spirit, may become wholly new and divine; and that there may be reared, and stand forth visibly on earth, formed of all thus renewed, a new and heavenly City of God.¹ Thus at length, as we ask in the Lord's Prayer, God would reign on earth, as in heaven, and exercise dominion among men themselves; so as for nothing to be either desired or done by any, that should not seem done according to the will of God himself.

This is what St. Paul here enjoins; namely, that the Romans should be transformed to a new sense and judgment of things; that they should prove and make manifest by their deeds what the will of God is, and what is good, and perfect, and well-pleasing to God instead of to themselves; that they should henceforth show that they have now not their own will, but the will of God in them, and that God reigns in them, who is goodness and perfectness itself; making them do all things well and perfectly, and causing the whole society of the church to be in a good and perfect state. This in truth will be done passing well, if men, now turned away from God, return to him, and if all things belonging to man have, so far as they can, an upward aim and direction; the body towards reason, the reason towards God; that the former, by obeying the soul and reason, may become in a measure *rational*; and the reason and soul of man, by being subject and surrendered to God, may itself become divine; through the presence, that is, of the divine Spirit, from whom it receives a new enlightenment, and one of far higher excellency than its own.

So long as he retains this enlightenment, man, as though now fashioned in a new form more distinctly after the image of God, appears to be not so much man as God. And he does retain it (or rather, is retained by it; since it is the part of the higher to embrace and retain) so long as his own soul keeps his body in check, and upbears it in subservience to itself. But if the soul has neglected this, and suffered the body to run to waste in lusts, then will it be itself also neglected and forsaken at once by the sustaining Spirit, and the whole man will fall downwards, in wretched

xii. 2.

---

¹ It is but natural to think that Colet had in his mind the "gloriosissimam Civitatem Dei" of Augustine.

plight, prone and headlong to earth and destruction. For in what direction one part of man is borne, whether body or soul, thither is the whole man instantly drawn; so that he must needs tend wholly either upwards or downwards. If he tend in that upward direction, humbly and with trust in God, he will be laid hold of by the Spirit and drawn still higher, and his soul will be sustained by the Divine Spirit in a divine state beyond itself; his body being the constant servant of the soul. But if in a downward course the soul follows the lead of the body, and of the blind and wanton senses,—few words will tell the tale. The hapless soul, forsaken by its preserving Spirit, will sink along with the body to everlasting destruction.

Rom. xii. 1. On which account St. Paul beseeches the Romans by the mercies of God, to render their bodies obedient to reason, that they themselves may then be easily made spiritual and divine. For when the body is transformed by the soul, and made, so to speak, *soul-like* (that is, so far as its grossness allows, like to the nature of the soul), then at once the soul itself, if it trust in God, and love God, is transformed by the divine grace and Spirit, and becomes spiritual and like to the nature of God; and the whole man is again brought upwards, in fair guise, to a divine state; the soul leaning towards God, the body towards the soul; and there exists upon earth a being that is plainly a god; since *he that is joined unto the Lord,* as it is in the Epistle to the Colossians,[1] *is one spirit.* Hence David said that it was *good for him to draw near to God,* and with reason; since there is nothing else that works, or can work, the good of men. For God alone is good; and whatsoever is good is so through his goodness.

1 Cor. vi. 17.
Ps. lxxiii. 28.

In St. Paul's exhortation to them in this passage, to *present their bodies a living sacrifice,* he is covertly reproving the sacrifices of all those who slew and offered cattle; especially the Jews, who (as Aristeas[2] writes) were accus-

---

[1] In error for Corinthians.

[2] In his *Ancient History of the Septuagint* (Donne's translation, 1685, p. 51), where an account is given of the water-supply of the Temple, which was required to be very copious, by reason that "in their Festival Daies many thousands of victims are offered."

tomed to make oblations of victims on festival days by slaughtering thousands of sheep, and to glut the whole temple with blood; thinking that by this act they gave great pleasure to God. Whence Isaiah, speaking in the name of the Lord, exclaims: *To what purpose is the multitude of your sacrifices unto me? I am full of the burnt offering of rams, and the fat of fed beasts; and I delight not in the blood of bullocks, or of lambs, or of he goats. Incense is an abomination unto me; your hands are full of blood. Who hath required this at your hand?* Wherefore the prophet adds: *Wash you, make you clean; put away the evil of your doings from before mine eyes.* For this is the sacrifice that is pleasing to God, a victim fat and without blemish; namely, a man cleansed from evil. To this the sacrifices of the Jews point, as signs and tokens; and that slaughtering of beasts is a sign that the beastlike appetites in the body ought to be destroyed; that the body, cleansed and holy, may live in obedience to reason, and may please God. For in truth God is not gratified by dead, but by living offerings; nor is it anything in cattle that he requires, but in men themselves; in whom he would have all brutal appetites slaughtered, as it were, and consumed by the fire of the divine Spirit; that the body, cleansed from all vices, holy and without spot, may live to the soul and to God.

On this account St. Paul besought the Romans, to present their bodies a holy sacrifice, living, obedient to reason. By which he meant, that each should recall and draw in his own body to obey the soul and reason; in order that the soul, now unfettered, might have power to withdraw itself from this world, and deliver itself in subjection to God; that, being transformed by him, and strengthened with divine energy, it might both be more firmly concentrated, and restrain more resolutely the intemperate and truant body. And this power, whereby each soul becomes more vigorous, when placed in subjection to God, is a spiritual life, consisting of spiritual light and heat. For, as the body lives by light and heat,[1] and grows through

---

[1] "Vita quidem tanquam lumen in naturali calore consistit."—Ficino, *De Vita produc.* ii. 2. There is much to the same purpose

the combination of light and heat infused into it by the soul, which is called the life of the body, whereby it has all power of sense, appetite and action; so, in well nigh the same manner, the soul itself also has life, growth and strength, by means of a certain life, consisting of spiritual light and heat, streaming down upon it from the Soul of all souls, even God. By whose ray a man is then *at one*, when, with a soul marvellously united, illumined and warmed, he has both light and heat and firm consolidation; when every sense is true, and every action good. For from unity comes compactness and power; from light, truth and uprightness; from heat, goodness and honest action. From its union with God, by the uniting ray of grace, the soul is born again and has a new existence :—for nothing can have existence, save unity. From its illumination, it trusts and believes in God; and in its faith has the clearest vision, in its vision the clearest faith. Lastly, from its heat, it loves and longs for God, and for all divine things for the sake of God.

Thus the *will* of him who is born anew to God by the divine Spirit, is love of God and of things divine; the *understanding* is the vision of God and of things divine through faith; the *being* is unity and establishment in that state, to which he has been drawn and carried by that wonderful and mighty principle, which we may call either the divine spirit, or ray, or force, or influence, or grace. This establishment and being, as it seems to me, is *hope*, whereby we exist and stand. For it is by hope that we both live, and have our being and standing; as, on the other hand, by hopelessness we are cast adrift, run to waste, and fall. And as the latter finds no place wherein to stand,

---

in Scotus Erigena's treatise *De divisione Naturæ*, where he says that *calor* and *color* are both the same word, and that *forma* is derived from an old word mentioned by Festus, signifying *hot*. " Et *forma* vocatur a *formo*, hoc est calido . . . antiqui siquidem formum dicebant calidum." Hence he goes on to describe the decay and dissolution of the body, if there be a deficiency of this vital heat, which is equivalent to a withdrawal of the sustaining *form* : " Ac sine mora totum corporis ædificium solutum collapsumque rigescit, frigore vim caloris superante."—Joannis Scoti, *Op.* (Migne's edn.) pp. 495-8.

so hope has whereon to plant itself and rest; so that the establishment of the soul in God appears to be hope, its light and clearness, faith; its heat and power, love. We may conclude therefore, that by hope we have existence; by faith, knowledge; and by love, goodness; and that in these three consist the life and growth of the soul, whereby it lives, and has being, knowledge, and love of God; whereby it stands, and preserves and sustains itself; whereby also it reins-in the body and binds it in obedience to itself; whereby, in a word, the whole man is good, beautiful, and happy.

This life and happiness the soul has not from itself, but from another source on high, even *down from the Father of* *lights*, from whom, as St. James writes, *is every perfect gift;* who framed the world and the race of men; who in righteousness suffered the sins of the many; who in compassion recalled the few; who bound some (namely, the Hebrews) by a law; who also warned them ofttimes by his prophets; who lastly, in a boundless mercy and loving-kindness, chose to have pity on the whole human race, at fitting time, and in a wonderful way and method. For he—the mighty and loving Father—willed that his own Son, co-eternal and co-equal with himself, and of substance and essence entirely the same, should become man, that through him men might be recalled to God, and rendered gods. This Son of God and man, himself God and man (which in Greek is called *Theanthropos* [1]) is Jesus Christ, the mediator between God and man, uniting in himself each extreme in a wonderful manner, so as for those extremes to be fitly and graciously connected together by this unutterable mean. The Word was made flesh, and God was made the Son of man, that flesh might have access to the Word, and man become the son of God. God put on our human nature, that man might put on the divine. God humbled himself that man might be exalted. In Christ there was a uniting of

Jam. i. 17.

---

[1] Colet uses this word also in the Exposition of 1 *Corinth*. In both cases it is spelt in English letters, though a few words in Greek letters are found in that treatise.

humanity and divinity, that men might be united with God.

O marvellous and wonder-working mean between the extremes, to be worshipped and adored with all reverence! *Neither is there any other name under heaven* (as St. John[1] truly wrote) *than this hallowed name of Jesus, whereby men must be saved.* He, as he most truly testifies of himself, is *the way* and *the door;* and, as St. Paul writes, is *the power of God unto salvation to every one that believeth; to the Jew first, and also to the Greek.* He, in his inestimable counsel and dispensation, came and appeared among men upon earth in the flesh, for this chief, nay only, reason, that he might turn men from their proud trust in themselves to a humble faith in God; that they who relied too presumptuously on their own individual strength, a mere thing of nought, might humbly turn to God, and trust in him alone; might ascribe nothing to themselves, but all to God; might look for nothing from themselves, but everything from God; in a word, might love and long for God alone, and not in anywise for themselves.

For this was the end, this the purpose of Christ's embodiment and incarnation, that the world, which before Christ's coming trusted and believed in itself, should trust and believe in God. Such trust in self was the cause from which every kind of evil and misery sprang. For in truth, when the world, in its self-regard and self-reliance, magnified itself, there grew up one after another, to the whole world's destruction, blindness, dishonesty, lust, perverseness, arrogance, ambition, covetousness, envy, hatred, war, robbery, murder, luxury, gluttony, fornication, neglect of God, disregard of men, violation of law everywhere, both human and divine, and whatever ills there are besides; so that with justice this relf-reliance of mankind, which in truth is hateful pride, may be called the root of their common ruin. Hence it is that Holy Scripture bears witness,

---

[1] So in the original. The error was probably caused by Colet's having in his mind the passages of St. John (xiv. 6, and x. 9), alluded to just after.

Acts iv. 12.

Rom. i. 16.

by so many testimonies, against pride; though for the present I will be content with that single text of the Preacher, which says that *pride is hateful before God and man;* and a little after calls pride *the beginning of sin.* This is because they wrongly trust in man, who is but *earth and ashes;* whereas men are born to look upwards, and expect all things from God; to depend on him; to him alone entrust themselves; on him rely, and in him repose. And until this be done, there can be no end of evils. Ecclus. x. 7, 13.
Ib. 9

For this world is so wholly placed in the power of the wicked one,[1] that its countless wickedness cannot be overcome save by infinite good; nor will men be ever devoid of evils, unless they be rescued from the throng of ills by some power far above them; and unless by pure Goodness they are made good themselves, that in the good they may conquer the evil. For it is goodness alone that conquers evil: and men endowed with goodness are alone able to repel and triumph over evil. This goodness, shed forth by a good God upon the evil, and benefiting those who were evil, is the power that renders the soul strong and victorious over evils, and that unites, stays, establishes, illumines, enlightens, kindles and enflames it. And what else is this than the grace of God, and the love of God, and the gift of God; aye even (as St. Augustine[2] will have it) the Holy Spirit of God himself? 1 Jo. v. 19

For he in his oneness unites the parted, in his firmness stays the wandering, in his brightness illumines the obscure, collects the scattered, reconciles the divided, adjusts the dismembered, arranges in beautiful order what was in shapeless disorder. In a word, he brings it to pass by his saving power, wherever and in whomsoever he dwells, that

---

[1] Latin, *in maligno positus est;* which, as *malignus* precedes in ver. 18, would not be correctly rendered by "lieth in wickedness," as in our version.—See Beza's note.

[2] Colet seems to be referring to the last Book of the *Confessions,* in *cc.* vii.-ix. of which the operation of the Holy Spirit is reflected upon. "*Amor illuc attollit nos, et spiritus tuus bonus exaltat humilitatem nostri de portis mortis. . . . Dono tuo accendimur et sursum ferimur.*"

beauty and goodness shall everywhere appear in a marvellous degree.

Now the loving Jesus came, that he might bring upon earth and set before men this very spirit and grace and gift of God; the spirit, namely, that first reconciles men to God, and then to one another. And this the angels testified; who when Christ was born sang to the shepherds, *On earth peace, good will toward men:*—peace, that is, and reconciliation, both towards God and towards one another; if, taught by Christ, they are willing to trust in God. This trust in God is humility; as on the other hand trust in one's own self is pride. For as, by trusting in yourself, you break loose; so, by trusting in God, you subject yourself to God. And this humility is beyond doubt man's greatest exaltation. For what is there more exalted than to be subject to the Highest, and in this subjection to come near to the Highest? On the other hand also, what is a lower, more abject and prostrate thing, than by turning towards oneself to become averted, withdrawn and remote from God? Wherefore there is nothing so low and sunken as pride, nothing so raised and elevated as humility; since the latter tends upwards to God, the former downwards to man. The one is a departure of man from himself, and an approach to God; the other is an approach to man, or rather to something lower than man, and a departure far away from God.

Luke ii. 14.

This pride, as I have often said, is nothing else than man's overweening trust in his own powers; and is what brought down, first the angels, and afterwards men. *I will ascend, I will be like the Most High:* so spake Lucifer in his pride. Adam also, the first man, sought to taste the forbidden fruit, that he might become like God; and this pride was a departing far from God, and laying himself low. Whereas they who, in no reliance on themselves, but in subjection to God, put their trust in him, are drawn on high through their trust. And the reason is that they mistrusted themselves, and trusted in God; and owning their natural weakness, and distrusting their own strength, they recognized the greatness and power of God, and set their love

Is. xiv. 14.

and admiration upon it; confiding themselves to it, and placing in it alone their hope. And this hope, as St. Paul avers, *maketh not ashamed :*—does not beguile men, that is, nor deceive them. The reason is, that God loves men who hope, and causes them to love him in return; diffusing his love through men's hearts by the Holy Spirit which he gives them.

Rom. v. 5.

But, to keep my discourse clear of ambiguities, let me define the terms I employ. In laying down three things, by which the soul exists in its new and divine life, namely, Hope, Faith, and Charity, I placed Hope under the head of *union* and *being;* Faith under that of *illumination* and *wisdom;* Charity under that of *heat* and *love*. Moreover, in speaking but now of reliance on God, which I called humility and subjection, I used the words *trust, trusting*,[1] and others of the same derivation.

Now lest any one should infer from this, that the *Faith* above mentioned, which consists in light, is humility, and the first principle whence man's salvation springs, I wish my readers to take note, that by *trust* I occasionally mean *hope,* and employ the two words *hope* and *trust* promiscuously, as the custom of the Latin language permits; since those who hope are said to trust, and those who trust, to hope. Nor is this at variance with the usage of Scripture, and with St. Paul's manner of speaking. For he writes to the Corinthians: *Seeing then that we have such hope, we use great plainness of speech:*[2] and to the Hebrews, *If we hold*

2 Cor. iii. 12.

---

[1] I have chosen the word *trust*, rather than *confide, confidence,* &c., as an equivalent for *fidere* and its derivatives; but in fact no English terms will quite suit Colet's reasoning here, since it turns on the verbal affinities of the Latin. In speaking of the three stages of ascent to God—Hope, Faith, and Charity or Love—he has been applying to the first, or lowest, of these three gradations, the terms *fidere, confidere,* and the like. But as the word for Faith, namely, *fides,* is of the same family as these, the hearer might become confused between the terms proper to the first stage of *Hope*, and the second of *Faith.* Hence the passing caution he inserts. For the classification under these three heads, see the *Hierarchies,* p. 192.

[2] In the Vulgate, "magnam *fiduciam*," the same word as is rendered *confidence* in the next quotation. See the previous note.

Heb. iii. 6. *fast the confidence and the rejoicing of the hope firm unto the end.*

This hope is the beginning of man's journey towards God, a collecting of the soul,[1] and a uniting and drawing of it to God, that it may be illumined and inflamed. For if it be divided and scattered through the body, it can neither retain light nor preserve heat. And so the first requisite is, that the soul be brought together from distrust, which is manifold, to hope, which is one; that being made one it may be illumined, and being illumined may glow with heat:—be brought together, I say, to one,. by the drawing of the Holy Spirit, that it may hope in one God, and in hope believe, and believing, love; that so love may spring from faith, as faith from hope.

No doubt these three things, faith, hope and charity, are infused into the soul at the same moment by the one good and beautiful Spirit of God. But still, if there is nothing to forbid precedence being imagined in things instantaneous, and our arranging a first, second and third; then certainly reason demands that faith should precede charity, and hope faith. For hope consists in union, faith in light, charity in heat. And if the order of things requires that everything should be in a state of unity before it is in that of light, and should have light before heat, then of course it would be necessary for Hope to hold the first place, being as it is a

---

[1] There is extant, in private ownership, a very interesting manuscript collection of apophthegms, entitled *Truths worthy to bee known, often to bee thought on. Collected and written by John Collet in the eightieth year of his age.* This John Collet, son of Thomas Collet (of the same stock as the Dean), was born in 1633, and wrote a most beautiful hand, as is shown by his MS. volume of "Historical Anecdotes," Sloane Coll. No. 3890.

In the above-mentioned collection are many passages remarkably similar in tone to these *Dionysian* passages of the Dean. Thus, for example, at p. 23: "One of the principall means to obtain divine love is for a man to re-collect all the powers of his soul with himself, and to call them off from the different objects upon which they shall bee set, that hee may lift them up to God. . . . (Otherwise) we shall never attain to true Introversion, nor to unity and simplification of the spirit, which is the immediate disposition to the presence of God in our souls."

kind of unity and steadfastness of mind; Faith the second, being an illumination of the mind and recognition of God; Charity, the third and last, as it is a love of God when known, and a longing for him.

These three, if three they be in any distinguishable manner, I consider to have the above order. But if in truth the three are but one thing (as may perhaps not unreasonably be supposed, seeing that the divine ray is one and wholly indivisible),[1] and if there is no essential difference, but only some divided appearance in the image presented,[2] then every medium, by its own proper density, deceptively parts and decomposes the ray in itself, though being in fact one and single.

However it be, supposing a plurality to be agreed upon, and the three to be distinct, I think they must follow in the order just mentioned; the first being hope and trust in God; the second faith, and the seeing what is revealed; the third charity, and the loving what is believed. But although a precedence among these three virtues be here imagined, yet they are so linked together, and connected by so close a bond, that it is not possible either for hope to exist, unless full of light and heat; or for faith, unless in a state of hope and love; or, lastly, for charity, unless united with the highest hope and brightness.

Such a one and beautiful goodness, and good and beautiful oneness, and one and good beautifulness,[3] is the very

---

[1] "The purgative, illuminative, and unitive life, are not three ways, so different as one thing differs from an other thing, but as modes from the essence of the thing modified, since they are all three rooted in charity. For true Charity purifies the unclean, illuminates the blind, and unites the separated. Purgation, illumination, and union, cannot bee wanting in him that loves God, seeing that the love of God does not admit of corruption, darkness, or separation."—P. 10 of John Collet's MS., quoted above.

[2] The word *phantasma* is here used in its strict sense of "an image presented to the mind," as in the *Phædo*, § 81 D., and *Republic*, *lib.* ix. § 584. Later on, if I understand him aright, Colet twice employs it as synonymous with *phantasia*, "the power which the mind has of making such presentment."—See note below, p. 76.

[3] Colet is fond of this way of expressing himself, when he means to signify that any three things, A, B, and C, are so closely asso-

life of the soul, rendering it strong, beautiful and active for good. Its unity is sure hope; its beauty, shining faith; its goodness, burning charity. There has risen upon the earth the *sun of righteousness,* the one beautiful and good Christ; *in whom are hid all the treasures of wisdom and knowledge;* in whom *dwelleth all the fulness of the Godhead bodily.* He, in his power, and brightness, and grateful heat, has marvellously drawn men's minds together to hope, illumined them by faith, kindled them by love. This Sun, shining upon the minds of men (of those, I mean, who cease to trust in themselves, and who, when so drawn together, readily begin to trust in God, that is, to hope), at once unites them in strength, elevates them to the light, kindles them into flame; to the end that they may have the strongest establishment, as hoping in God; may have the clearest vision of all that is possible, as believing what is revealed; and may burn with the most fervent desire, as loving God and the mysteries of God.

Mal. iv. 2.
Col. ii. 3.
Ib. 9.

This Christ, *the brightness of his* Father's *glory,* the light of the world, the life of men, the head of the church, the soul of human society, in a marvellous manner, as was fitting, was brought forth among men of a Virgin, that he might reconcile men both to God and to one another, and might establish a city upon earth whereof he himself should be the Lord; and might fashion out of men a body, as it were, of which he should be the head; that from it, as from a fountain, there might be diffused life (that is to say, unity, light, and spiritual heat) through the members in seemly order; that every one might be a partaker, so far as his capacity admits, and so far as is sufficient for him. He would have all unite in one fellowship, as members of one body; and each occupy his own place therein, and act according to his own measure; not essaying more than his strength allows, nor failing in any way to do what his strength permits; but set down all to Christ, and contri-

Heb. i. 3.

---

ciated, that the properties of A and B are in C; of A and C in B, and so on. Compare the "loving Wisdoms" and "wise Loves" of the *Hierarchies,* p. 20.

bute, so far as he can, the grace bestowed on him to the common good; ever mindful that he is a member of the body of Christ, and called to live not to himself alone, but to the body; aye even to die, if need be, for the safety of the body.

For all the parts of this holy society, which Christ would collect together, must imitate a whole and sound body and its members. For although they be many, varied and diverse, both in form, power and office, yet still, through the harmonizing effect of the natural life, that flows from the body's head to all the joints and members, all the parts have such coherence and sympathy, and do so assiduously render mutual help to one another, according to their means, by giving and receiving aid, that in the whole body there is presented, not a plurality of parts, but a united whole composed of the several parts; with no private interest among them, no care for individual advantage, but everywhere, and on the part of all, through the silent teaching of instinct, a singular desire for fellowship and unity and the welfare of the whole body. In such a body every member seems to own that it is then in best health when the whole body is healthiest, and to feel that what it contributes to the common share of the body it contributes to its own self; and that it cannot seek life and strength for itself by any better method (in fact by no other method), than by doing all it can for the growth and strength of the whole body; seeing that on the health and strength of the whole body its own healthy state depends; and that, except in the health of the whole, it can in no way be healthy itself.

This pattern of nature, the best subject to show what is right,[1] must be closely copied by that Christian body, as I have just said, which consists of Christ, as head, and faithful Christians, as members. It was the purpose of Christ, himself the author of nature, to express nature herself

---

[1] "Naturæ ratio, quæ est lex divina et humana," etc. Cic. *De Off.* iii. 5. The whole chapter affords a striking parallel to the passage Colet is here enlarging upon, or to the fuller development of it in 1 *Cor.* xii. 12-26.

among men, and to bring back to the order and beauty of nature what had diverged from order, and to reform the human race, all deformed as it was, and disfigured and abominable through diseases and transgressions. This could not be done without some mighty living force, which, being in all its fulness in one, might be poured out from that one upon the many; which might go forth, and recall, restore, win back and re-establish for mankind their pristine state; arranging men in some right order among themselves, and reforming all things to a better condition; so that there should be no longer evil and iniquity among men, but goodness and equity in all. Thus would there be order and agreement on the part of all, fellow aspirations, common desires, mutual good-will, courtesy and beneficence, compassion and support in changes of fortune, common joy and sorrow, loss and gain; in a word, all things common, and nothing whatever private, whether in blessings or misfortunes; but congratulation and rejoicing together in prosperity; in adversity, sympathy and condolence; so that, by this mutual and intimate agreement and concord, there would seem to be formed, out of what was many and various, something that was one and the same, so to speak, throughout.

This is, in every body, the business of the head, from which life emanates, namely, to conciliate in unity and fellowship the members to which the life flows forth and is diffused. And this is done by the force of that undivided life so diffused. For with uniting power it everywhere tends to what is one and single; and unity and simplicity are the surest proofs that it exhibits of its presence, since these are naturally followed by soundness in the whole body, and vigorous strength, and healthy complexion. This life in the body is a combination of light and heat,[1] poured forth, as we know, from that inmost and highest soul, which is the truer and purer heat and light; truer and purer, as being spiritual, recognized not by sense, but by the intelli-

---

[1] Literally, "light warmth and warm light." The same expression has occurred before, p. 62.

gence which is akin to it. Of this older and purer life, the light and heat felt in the body (which I call the *life* of the body) are a later and grosser image, reproducing it roughly and coarsely, as in a poor and unfitting substance. And this life is conveyed into the body from the soul, by certain well-adapted means, that unite the two extremes together; consisting of the higher and more refined elements of the body, and the lower and, so to speak, more concrete ones of the soul. These are called by physicians *vital spirits*,[1] and are particles of lucid nature blended together from the clearer part of the body, and from the lower and obscurer part (as it may be called) of the soul. These spirits, coming midway between the exalted soul and the humble body, cause both the body to resemble the soul, and the soul to recognize the body. In the soul itself heat and light are intelligence and will; in these middle spirits sense and desire; in the body again, they are sensible light and warmth.

Thus do these two principles, light and heat, emanate and proceed together in order from the highest to the lowest; and as they pass downwards and become deteriorated, they acquire different names. But wherever they are conveyed, their effort is to preserve themselves as far as they can, and to confine and keep together in unity the scattered substance that they have penetrated. It is the constant care of each higher gradation to sustain in union the next lower to which it is neighbour. There is also an anxious attention on the part of each towards the one higher than itself, that by that higher one it may itself be sustained in unity and life. For nothing in the whole universe can live

---

[1] Compare Mirandola's *Heptaplus*, iv. 1: "Verum inter terrenum corpus et coelestem animi substantiam opus fuit medio vinculo, quod tam distantes naturas invicem copularet. Huic muneri delegatum tenue illud et spiritale corpusculum, quod et medici et philosophi spiritum vocant." What is said as to the "lucid nature" of these spirits may be illustrated from Lord Bacon's *Natural Hist. Cent.* vii. "the spirits of animate bodies are all in some degree (more or less) kindled and inflamed; and have a fine commixture of flame and an aerial substance."

apart and wholly separate by itself, save only that one First Cause, which has need of nothing, and alone is self-sufficient. But whatever else is in the world, being incomplete and insufficient, must needs live with others, for existence and well-being. Wherefore there is nothing more agreeable to nature, or pleasing to God, than that beings, singly deficient, should seek sufficiency in the bonds of society; wherein, by mutual helps, every one that needs has succour brought him. For there is nothing that can truly say, *I have no need;* nothing but what may be, and ought to be, helped by others; and this, not merely inferiors by superiors, but perchance even yet more, superiors by inferiors. Because the machinery of the universe has been so adjusted, that no one thing can dispense with another; and in such a way, through the wisdom and love of God, is it formed and joined together, that nothing can be so pleasing to God as a wise society of all things, mutually loving and beloved. This was religiously observed first of all in the great body (the *animal,* as Plato[1] calls it) of the world; and all living creatures in succession, following the example, strenuously observe it also; not only each one in its own organization, but, far more remarkably, in the mutual seeking for classification and society, through the secret instinct of nature, on the part of those that are of the same species. But of all beings endowed with reason in this visible world, the race of man alone deviates from this course, through some weakness or other, and perverseness; no doubt from a deficiency of the *life* that wins and binds together, that is, wisdom and love.[2]

margin: 1 Cor. xii. 21.

Therefore it was that Jesus Christ, *the power of God and*

margin: 1 Cor. i. 24.

---

[1] *Timæus,* § 30, D. "For the Deity intending to make this world like the fairest and most perfect of intelligible beings, framed one visible *animal* comprehending within all other animals of a kindred nature . . . . For these reasons, and out of these elements, which are in number four, the *body* of the world was created in the harmony of proportion, and therefore having the spirit of friendship."—*Prof. Jowett's Transl.* ii. p. 525.

[2] Corresponding to the "light and heat" that together formed the life of the body. Shortly after, he slightly alters the terms to "wisdom and *goodness* (or *kindness*)"—*bonitas.*

the wisdom of God, came down to bring back the human race to a wise and good way, order and society, by infusing into men wisdom and power; that they might have in common the heat and light that tend to life; and, being associated together by the strait bond of love, might be collected and drawn as one to God from whom they came forth. For as the diffused life of the body is brought back to the soul, as to a fountain-head, so too all the life of men, whereby they hold and unite themselves together (I mean, wisdom and goodness), must be referred to God from whom it came. For God is the soul of men, no otherwise than is the soul of each body; and every society has life and health in God, as the body has in the soul. It was his will also to be in man, and become incarnate, and be, as it were, in the place of a head, that he might diffuse life over all. And, as though to form for himself a purer, that is, a more *single*, portion of mankind, he chose some whom he breathed upon with his spirit, and made them, as it were, *vital spirits* between himself and the rest of mankind, to carry light and life to the whole world and body of men. Hence the expression in the Gospel: *Ye are the light of the world*, and *the salt of the earth*. For the Apostles, whose *sound went into all the earth*, were *media*,[1] bright and warm with life, resembling *vital spirits*, filling men with light and heat. The speech of those Apostles was the Gospel; a speech and language full of light and heat, as proceeding from men themselves on fire; and it dispelled the shades of ignorance, and mastered the chillness of sins and wickedness, and caused those on whom it seized to be all aglow with wisdom and the love of God. The very fire itself, the very soul of men

Mat. v. 13, 14.
Rom. x. 18.

---

[1] The thought may be illustrated from a passage of the *Heptaplus* before quoted. After the Spirit of God had brooded upon the face of the waters, the first creation was that of Light. Hence Mirandola makes *light* a connecting link between the *soul* and *body*; as the Apostles, the "lights of the world," are represented as being between God and man. It may be remarked, in passing, how fond Colet is of arranging things in triplets: a result, probably, of his study of Dionysius. In the accounts left us of his works, he is said to have so arranged the sayings of Christ.

in Christ their head, even his divinity, enlightened and inflamed the Apostles. These in succession, as angels and ministering spirits between the head and the body, illumined and quickened by the heat of devotion the body, that is, the remaining host of men; such part of them, I mean, as could give entrance to the vital rays, and be influenced by them. These were they whom divine providence made fit. And of those so called and attracted by the rays of life there is formed one body; whose head is Christ, whose soul is his divinity, whose members are men living by the divine inspiration and grace.

And among these, according to the varied bestowal of the spirit, there are various states and conditions of life. For some in this body are like the vital spirits within, that go between as nimble and active couriers, to quicken the members, wherever and whatever they be. Whilst yet among these spirits there is a long gradation; some of them possessing greater light, others less; but still the office of all in general is, to purify, illumine and warm; to quicken and support. Some effect this in the body with regard to the faculty of imagination [1] and the *common sense;* others

---

[1] As *phantasma* a little later on is contrasted with *ratio*, "reason," it seems clear that in both these passages the word is used, not in its strict sense as above (see p. 69, *n.*), but as equivalent to *phantasia*. In the third book of the *De Anima*, which Colet seems here to have in view, Aristotle distinguishes *phantasia* from *sense* and *judgment*, and compares its office to that of the monumental imagemaker, who is able to reproduce the likeness of some departed one. Hence it will answer most nearly to our "imagination," in the strict sense of the term.

Communis sensus is also defined by Aristotle in the same treatise (*Op.* 1607, i. p. 1410) to be the faculty by which the *common* properties of bodies become sensible to us; these common properties corresponding to the *primary qualities* of Locke, namely, shape, motion, number, &c. And he makes the seat of this faculty to be the "common *sensorium*, which is in the heart of each animal."—See Lewes' *Aristotle* (1864), p. 239. But writers of Colet's age appear to use the term as more nearly equivalent to *phantasia*. Thus Ficino calls it an "imaginaria quædam virtus" (*Op.* ii. p. 1450). Mirandola compares it to a central ocean, the five senses being as rivers that run into it, or as Mediterranean seas connected with it (*Op.* 1601, p. 22). In the following passage of Codrus Urceus (*Sermones*,

with regard to the sight; others to the hearing; others to the sense of smell; others to the taste; others to the setting free of the tongue; others to readiness of hand; others to swiftness of foot. In this way, by the presence of the soul, and the infusion of spiritual light, there are formed various members in the body, according to the measure of the spirit, and they are marked out for different offices.

So, in the same manner, by the presence of God waxing strong in men and in Christ their head, there is a spiritual and divine irradiation of mankind from God, their soul; streaming first on men of singleness—the Apostles; then on others in order; on every one, that is to say, according to his capacity, and as the soul has rendered him suitable. For it passes on from the more single to the more manifold, and deteriorates in its progress, in proportion as it sinks on grosser matter. The first creation and appointment was that of spirits; and these are themselves varied and diverse at the outset, according to the variety of their substance. For whilst the soul that takes up its abode in them, and animates and enlightens them, is altogether one and the same; yet, just as the corporeal part differs in grossness and refinement, so also is there a different and varied participation of the light-giving soul and life;[1] and thus the vital spirits are from the first differently constituted. And this no doubt was done in the body by the exalted providence of the soul; that, as there are various and different members in the body, so also there might be various active and enlightening spirits; that every part of the body might have something adapted to it. In like manner the divinity in Christ the head (that highest soul, namely, of the human society, that has its vigorous existence in the head), first imparted itself to the more single and unalloyed portion of

---

1502, leaf L.) the reader will find a good parallel to the expression in the text: "Ut, exempli causa, vini aut mellis saporem, sive aquæ frigus aut ignis calorem, aut purpuræ aut atramenti colores, prius gustu aut tactu aut visu percepi; deinde *communi sensu* percepta speculatus sum."

[1] "Non est alius Deus, sed diversi sunt oculi." — Erasmus, *Enarr. in Ps.* lxxxiii.

the human race, and formed, as it were, *vital* spirits; who themselves also differ from one another in their participation of the divine light and life, according as they were perceived to be differing in singleness and multiplicity when the light first seized upon them. For what the qualities of fineness and coarseness are in bodies, in relation to the light diffused from the soul for the body's life, such in fact are those of singleness and multiplicity in souls, in relation to the rays of divinity. And more, just as each one is single or manifold, one or divided, so is he *deified* in greater or less degree[1];—animated, that is, and reformed by the divine spirit, that he may be a spiritual vitality, or a vital spirit. In this class of men, who have great illumination, like spirits, are the Apostles, whom Christ called the lights of the world. And St. John in the Revelation plainly calls them *spirits* of God, *angels*, and *stars*.

Rev. iii. 1.

Now these Apostles are themselves illumined in varying degree, as may be the more suitable to the places whither they are sent; and they also variously illumine the lower and grosser body (that is, the rest of the church, and the world), and cause various lights, or *colours*[2] rather, to exist in the gross material; that every one may both appear, and be, good and beautiful, in proportion as he is a partaker of enlightening and warming grace. This is St. Paul's meaning when he says: *To every one according to the proportion of faith.* A further result would be, that some would have within them a kind of clearness of light, whereby to discern easily, in inferior matters, what was white and what was black; that is, what was good and what bad; others

Rom. xii. 6.

---

[1] "Singulares ergo et simplices, id est, secreti a multitudine ac turba nascentium rerum ac morientium, amatores æternitatis et unitatis esse debemus, si uni Deo et Domino nostro cupimus inhærere."—August. *Enarr. in Ps.* iv.

[2] Colet has elsewhere defined *colour* as that which "consists of darkness and light."—See the *Hierarchies*, p. 5 *n.*, and xli. *n.* 2. Ficino, in his additional notes on the *Timæus*, defines it as "participatio quædam luminis varia, pro natura cujusque, in superficie corporis emicans, accommodata visui." (*Op.* 1576, ii. p. 1807). The Pythagoreans identified it with the superficies. See Aristot. *De Sensu et Sensili*, c. iii. (*Op.* 1607, i. p. 1433).

also would be as the ears of the Christian body, to judge what was discordant, and what harmonious, to faith; some would perceive, as by the organ of smell, what exhalation from men's actions has a sweet odour and perfume for the senses of God, and what, moreover, from out of them, has an ill and noisome odour; some would mark immediately, when any doctrine was set before them, what had a good and pleasant savour, and what a bitter; some lastly would easily feel what was warm to the touch among men, in the warmth of God, and what was cold. The *common sense*[1] and *imagination* does all this; and in a higher and more excellent degree than *imagination, reason*[2] does it; that is to say, spiritual reason; whilst the *mind* of the Christian Church, even the inner divinity itself, does it in a way the highest and surest of all. For this can none escape; this is none other than God that *trieth the hearts and reins*. And the more humbly men advance to him, the more are they drawn together for their special duties; and out of this onward flow and diminution there arises order among men, and a graduating of the abilities and members of the body of Christ. To so notable a degree is this done, that, along with want of honour, there springs up a greater necessity and usefulness; that compensation may be made, and an equalization of the members; to the end that in proportion as each excels in comeliness, it may be excelled by others in necessity. Ps. vii. 10.

This was most wisely noted and taught by St. Paul, in his first Epistle to the Corinthians, in the words: *Much more those members of the body, which seem to be more feeble, are necessary*. And he adds, *Ye are the body of Christ, and members in particular*,[3] thus acknowledging the ramification 1 Cor. xii. 22.

Ib. v. 27.

---

[1] See note above, p. 76.
[2] Compare the fine passage of Ficino (*Theol. Platon.* ix. 3): "Offert igitur phantasia nobis lumen adeo clarum, ut nullum aliud videri possit fulgentius . . . . Sed ratio interim e summa mentis specula despiciens phantasiæ ludos, ita proclamat: Cave, animula, cave inanes istius sophistæ præstigias," etc.
[3] The Vulgate *membra de membro*, "members depending one on another," seems to have arisen from the similarity of the Greek

of members, and their diminution and variety, with compensation accompanying; so that, if we take all into account, and weigh in an even balance, the result is equalization and unity, arising from an equipoise of excellence.

1 Cor. xii. 24.

Hence in the same passage St. Paul says: *God hath tempered the body together, having given more abundant honour to that part which lacked; that there should be no schism in the body, but that the members should have the same care one for another.* Wherein it must be heedfully noted, that God fashions for himself a body, namely the Church, such, and of such men, as he wills; men whom he has not only inspired and reformed in a measure befitting his body, but has also rendered fit for reformation, and capable of receiving the divine form and life. So that not only is the reformation of each individual, and the fact of his having a place in God's Church, to be assigned to God, but also the very ability of each, and capacity of receiving form. For, if we follow the teaching of St. Paul, which we must follow before everything, no one can be able and fit to be brought to unity and illumined by faith, except in such degree as the bountiful grace of God has enabled him. He it is who knows whom he will choose, and chooses whom he knows, and adapts them when known to his own fashioning and forming. For *the Spirit,* as St. John the Evangelist testifies, *bloweth where it listeth:* and St. Paul says to the Corinthians, *Now hath God set the members every one of them in the body, as it hath pleased him.* For he fashions men when fit, and fits those that are to be fashioned. It is by him that the matter is formed and arranged. From God comes undoubtedly the whole quickening and salvation of man; so that man has in himself nothing whatever whereof to glory, but has cause to own that all things are from God, and that to God alone, who *is the King of glory,* all the glory must be ascribed.

John iii. 8.

1 Cor. xii. 18.

Ps. xxiv. 10.

But now at length let us return to our St. Paul, who

---

words *melē* and *merē;* the real sense of the clause being "severally members thereof."—See the Amended Version by Five Clergymen, Lond. 1858.

would have the Church imitate the structure of the body, in its order, adjustment, connection, mutual offices and tempering of forces; since it is from moderation, order and love, that all things are established in beauty. Whereas immoderateness and extravagance, disturbance of order, and dissension, weaken and disfigure all things. But force, when occupied in keeping order and unity among things allied, consists chiefly in maintaining moderation and temperance; that none should aim above his height, nor transgress the appointed bounds, but be sensible of his own powers, and confine himself within their limits. This is what every member in the human body does, so long as it continues sound. Nor is unsoundness and disease anything else than a member's deviation from the life and form bestowed upon it by the soul, and a bursting the bonds, as it were, of the confining form,[1] and a self-caused detachment of the member. Hence there arise, and become manifest in the body, weakness and deformity and disease; the beginning of dissolution. For the death of the whole body is nothing else than a declining and becoming detached from the sustaining form. It is from form; and from being well strung together, that the body's strength and health proceed; whilst on the other hand from relapsing into itself (into its own multiplicity, that is), spring weakness and sickness, the prelude to death. Accordingly, just as the whole body has health and strength, so long as it is firmly held together by the whole animating form, so does every member in like manner retain its vigour, so long as it is confined within the limits of its own special form. But

---

[1] A little later on he speaks of this as the "animating" and "sustaining" form. Some traces of the old theories are visible in Lord Bacon; as when he makes one radical difference between animate and inanimate bodies to be, that the former "are all figurate and determinate, which inanimate bodies are not; for look how far the spirit is able to spread and continue itself, so far goeth the shape or figure, and then is determined."—*Nat. Hist., Cent.* vii. This being "figurate and determinate" was due to the union of living *form* with matter, the departure of which brought on "deformity" and death. Virg. *Aen.* vi. 724 *sqq.* and Lucr. ii. 949 *sqq.* were often quoted in illustration of this principle.

if it break the bounds, it sickens, and through weakness suffers from immoderate feverishness and heat. Confined within its form, it has a gentle and agreeable warmth, from the tender fostering of the vital spirit; but when it has left that, and fallen back upon itself, then has it a gross and distempered heat, and burns immoderately; and this unregulated fire and inflammation in a member is disease. The soundness of the body consists therefore in an obedience to the form and life assigned to it, in observing moderation, and in a voluntary remaining within bounds.

So too in like manner is it in the Christian Church, in which the souls of men live by a spiritual life diffused by God; everyone, I mean, according to the measure of life given and received. This life, as has been often said by me already, is a loving faith and belief in God. And it is distributed to men by God in a certain ratio and wise proportion; to the end that they, believing in God, may live in him; and that all may be faithful with a faith varying in degrees of greatness; for the construction of one faithful Church, with Christ for its head, the abode of Truth and Divineness itself, whence has flowed forth all faith and life into the souls of men.

Now if the whole Church and all its parts have life from God and Christ through loving faith; and if this faith be as it were the life of the body, that is, the Church; then assuredly it must needs be, that the Church will live and be in health so long a time as it is held together in one faith by its soul, that, is by God. And this will be, so long as men obey and cleave to the measure of their faith, and allow themselves to be kept within the bounds of it. For faith is a gentle, agreeable and clear intelligence[1] of things, cherishing and strengthening the soul, and supporting it in sound health. But if anyone shall abandon faith, and relapse into himself, into the heat and madness of his own disposition; if, loosed as it were from the bonds of faith, he feebly run to waste beyond the limits of belief, and endeavour, in his weakness, either to think or do anything, the issue must

---

[1] Faith corresponding to *intellectus*, as love to *appetitus*.

needs be, first, that his soul is out of health, through loss of the life of faith; and secondly, that he does whatever he attempts, feebly and ineffectually. This lapse from faith in each one's case, into his own weakness and private opinion,[1] is clearly a madness and folly of the soul, feverish now, and almost raging, in distempered mood, and roaming in darkness; since it is forsaken by pleasant and calm faith, which is the sweet life of the soul, its light and steadfastness, calming the soul, and keeping it collected, and suffering it not to fall away from unity and trust in God.

Well then, the cause of every disease, nay rather every disease itself and discord in the Church, is the distempered state of reason, and its aberration from living faith, and wanton transgression of bounds, and departure from *the measure of faith*. For this faith, as the Apostle says, is xii. 3. dealt by measure and proportion, to the end that, out of many and various faithful ones, there may be formed one body in fair and harmonious symmetry; order and measure being everywhere sacredly and religiously observed.

On this account he warns the Roman Church, that no one should *think of himself more highly than he ought to think, but* Ib. *to think soberly;* that is, should not exceed the measure of faith; but that everyone should curb his reason with the bridle of faith, and keep himself within its bounds; the which if he overstep, in self-reliance and untempered reason, he then does *think more highly than he ought to think*, and, deeming himself to be wise, is plainly a fool. Such wisdom without faith is in truth lack of wisdom, and a debasement from true wisdom to what is lower and worse. For as a member, if forsaken by the vital spirits, and by soft and gentle warmth, has a more consuming inward fever and burning, since this burning is itself neither more nor less than defect of warmth; so in the body of Christ, the Church, he who has withdrawn from faith, and in self-reliance

---

[1] The reader should be careful not to detach these words from the context, any more than what Colet says about "heretics" a little after. They can only be estimated aright if we remember that his subject now is the unity of Christ's body.

endeavours to use his reason, and be wise of himself, has assuredly fallen from the better wisdom, and in his own wisdom is not so much wise as inordinately unwise, seeing that he has relapsed into himself, into what is worse, grosser and more obscure. In this state of mind there is nothing but unbounded error and wanton strife, the end whereof is dire weariness and confusion. This is the goal that all heretics have reached, and for no other cause than that they trusted too presumptuously to themselves, and their own weakness, and would attempt more by powerless reason than by strong and prevailing faith. It is the chastening of our reason, accordingly, and observance of the measure of faith, that preserve the society and unity of the Church; when each individual has neither any feelings nor desires, except as they spring from faith and the love of God, nor essays more than he believes pleasing to God when done, nor in short omits any means whereby he thinks he can please God and men. For we are not only bound to take heed that we go not beyond the limits of faith, but also to show care and diligence in constant well-doing, so far as our faith allows; that our life may not grow slothful through idleness, nor ourselves be thought to have received from God a gift and ability that we turn to no account. For as in the body no member is unemployed and without an office, so in the Church there ought to be no one but is doing something, and contributing some benefit to the community. Furthermore, just as in the human body all the members assist one another with a rare sympathy, by mutually rendering and receiving services; and tend, succour, and support one another; so likewise ought there to be in the Church, and among all faithful people, such a mutual love and interest, as for each to believe that his own powers, whatsoever they be, were given him for no other cause, than that he should be always exerting them for the assistance of others, the profit of the society, and the pre-

xii. 5. servation of unity and peace. For *we, being many,* as St. Paul says, *are one body in Christ, and everyone members* and *ministers one of another :* that is, we have all been quickened by faith for the formation of one body, that everyone should help and sustain another in health, according to the ability of faith; that through the aids thus alternately rendered, mutual love may be able to appear among men themselves; an image, I mean, of that exceeding love which was and is betwixt Christ and his Church; that they may love one another, *even as Christ loved the Church.* Eph. v. 25.

From the presence of God, and the outpouring of his grace, and the varied bestowal of faith and love, there grow up among men various members, so to speak;—various powers (that is), faculties, offices, actions, and services. These are briefly and cursorily recounted by St. Paul; rather to give a specimen and sample of them, than to enumerate all exactly and in their true order. Thus [he mentions] *prophecy* according to faith, and the foretelling future events; *ministry,* which the Greeks call *diaconate; teaching,* and *exhortation,* and *giving,* and *ruling,* and [*mercy,* which the Greeks] call *alms ;*—faculties that are conspicuous in men according to the measure and proportion of grace and faith bestowed. He then adds, what ought to be in the whole Church,—true *love* of God, *abhorrence of evil, cleaving to the good,* mutual and *brotherly affection* among the faithful, *preferring one another in honour,* earnestness and *diligence, fervency*[1] of life, observance of the time, *rejoicing in hope, patience* in adversity, *perseverance in prayer,* liberality, hospitality. He adds, after these, continual blessing, even towards evil speakers and evil doers ; common joy, common grief; community of mind and of every desire; lowliness, condescension, courtesy, love, fellow-feeling, agreement, unity; such as springs from a mutual adaptation and conformity of different parts. But as for haughtiness, pride, disdain, self-conceit, contempt of others, avenging of wrongs ;—he shows them to be abominable in men, and resolutely forbids them, as a nursery of mischief and destruction. For St. Paul would have all vengeance and retaliation to be left to God alone; who has said by his prophet: *Vengeance is mine, and I will repay.* Among the mem-

Rom. xii. 6, *sqq.*

Rom. xii. 19; Deut. xxxii. 35.

---

[1] Colet uses *calorem vitæ* as an equivalent to the Vulgate *spiritu ferventes.*

bers of Christ's body, even the Church, he feels that there ought to be faith in God, and reason subject to faith; humility, toleration, constancy in good at all times and without cessation, a doing good even to those who do us evil and provoke us wrongfully; that every member, so far as it can, may imitate Christ its head, who was perfect lowliness, goodness, patience, kindness; who did good to the evil, that by his goodness he might make them good instead of evil; herein imitating his Father in heaven, who *maketh his sun to rise on the evil and on the good.*

Matt. v. 45.

For there is nothing that conquers evil, but good; and if you aim at returning evil for evil, and endeavour to crush evil by evil, then you yourself descend to evil, and foolishly shift to a weaker position, and render yourself more powerless to confound the evil. Nay you even increase the evil, when you make yourself on a level with evil men, seeing that you wish to encounter evil ones while evil yourself. For you cannot render evil for evil, without having done evil in so rendering. In fact, he who begins, and he who returns, evil, are both engaged in evil; and therefore are alike evil. On which account, the good must on all occasions be on their guard not to return evil for evil; lest, by this descent to evil, they cease to be good. But we must constantly persevere in goodness and in reliance upon God; that, as nature demands, we may conquer opposites by opposites, and evil by good; acting with goodness and patience on our part, that evil men may become good.

This must be allowed to be the only means and way of conquering evil. And they who imagine that evil can be dissipated by evil, are certainly fools and madmen; as matter of fact and experience shows. For human laws, and infliction of punishment, and undertaking of wars, and all the other ways in which men labour to do away with evil, aim in vain at that object, and in no respects attain their purpose. Since it is plainly evident, that, whatever efforts men may have made, in reliance on their own powers, the world is none the less on that account full of evils; and that these are growing up day by day, and multiplying with all the more vigour (though foolish men see it not), the more men are attempting to uproot them by their own efforts.

Let this be a settled and established maxim, that evil cannot be removed except by means of good. For as it is light that scatters darkness, and heat that banishes cold, so undoubtedly in like manner is it virtue and goodness only, that overcomes evil and exterminates vice. And moreover, just as the sun, were he to overshadow himself, in order to drive away the darkness, would be less efficient, and would by no means accomplish his end; so beyond doubt will those, who depart from good, and as it were obscure themselves, and return like for like in the case of evils, never obtain what they are striving for. For whatever seeks to conquer, must needs make itself as unlike as possible to that which it seeks to conquer; since victory is gained in every instance, not by what is like, but by what is unlike. Hence we ought to aim as much as possible at goodness, in order to conquer evil; and at peace and forbearance, to overcome war and unjust actions. For it is not by war that war is conquered,[1] but by peace, and forbearance, and reliance on God. And in truth by this virtue we see that the apostles overcame the whole world, and by suffering were the greatest doers, and by being vanquished were the greatest victors; and, in short, by their death, more than by aught else, left life upon the earth. Sooth to say, the Christian warrior's prowess is his patience, his action is suffering, and his victory, a sure trust in God; a

---

[1] How much more significant this becomes, when we recall the events of the year, during the course of which these words were uttered. In June, 1497, there was fought the battle of Blackheath. In September of the same year Perkin Warbeck landed in Cornwall, and was joined by "many thousands who had lost relations and friends in the fierce fight at Blackheath, and who were anxious for revenge." In the winter, and, it is possible, whilst these Lectures were being delivered, the prisoners taken after the engagement at Taunton were being tried by Commissioners, of whom Robert Sherborne, then Dean of St. Paul's, was one.—See the *Pictorial Hist. of England*, bk. vi. ch. i.; and Bacon's *Henry the Seventh* (*Works*, ed. 1730, iii. p. 471).

confidence that he is either justly suffering, or patiently enduring, the evil. Which thing he does, not in evil, but in his all-powerful goodness and mercy; since by his bountiful grace he would make good those that are evil. Him, even God the Father, every good man is bound to imitate, and to endeavour by ceaseless goodness to overcome the badness of others; and (as Jesus Christ, who is perfect goodness, teaches) we ought to *love our enemies, and do good to them that hate us, and pray for them that persecute us, that we may be the children of our Father which is in heaven; for he sendeth rain on the just and on the unjust.*

Agreeable to this is what the Apostle, the expounder of the gospel, and possessor of the *mind of Christ*, here writes and enjoins, saying: *Be not wise in your own conceits,* nor haughty and self-relying; *recompense not evil for evil;* a thing which does not conquer, but increases, the evil. But be ye good, and practise goodness constantly both before God and before men; that through your manifest goodness wicked men may at length submit, and desire to become like you. Be not angry with the angry, nor repel force by force; but be at peace with all men; and bring it to pass, as much as in you lieth, that others harm you not: that is, offend no one, but be careful at all times, however men may rage against you, not to be yourselves provoked, nor strive against them in self-defence. But keep patience unbroken, and maintain peace undisturbed, at least in yourselves, and *give place unto wrath.* Suffer God to avenge your wrongs, you who know not wherefore and to what end he suffers evils. Interfere not, by your pride and reliance on your own strength, with the great and excellent providence of God; for this is to *mind high things,* and to be *wise in your own conceits.* But be lowly-minded, and rely on God alone: persevere in goodness, and suffer evils. For if these cannot be conquered by your goodness, then believe that God for some better end suffers for a time, and, as it were, endures the evil. Wherefore leave the removal of it, in strong faith, to God; and do ye, in the meanwhile, not cease to do good unto all, that ye may conquer them by goodness. Feed your enemies; and if an adversary thirst,

Marginal references: Matt. v. 44. — 1 Cor. ii. 16. xii. 16.

give him drink; and whatever service you can confer, render it cheerfully and willingly to all. For assuredly by this alone will you conquer evil, and win over even the ill-disposed to yourselves as friends. By your love and kindness you will warm those that are in the chill of malice and wickedness; and by your tenderness you will soften the hard and unbending. For just as men grow sweet by goodness and gentleness, so on the other hand do they grow bitter and harsh by unkindness and ill-treatment. But soft, sweet, powerful goodness and kindness at length fuses all things, and by its beneficent heat causes the hard to soften, and the bitter to grow sweet; so that the rugged become smooth, the savage tame, the proud humble, the evil good; in a word, the human become divine. This is what St. Paul means by *heaping coals of fire upon his* xii. 20. *head;* heating a man, namely, and fusing his dross-like badness, and soothing his implacable mood: which you will either do by goodness and sweetness, or you will never do; seeing that it is only by its opposite that anything is overcome. But if evil provoke you to return evil, then are you being conquered by the evil, and beginning to be yourself evil. Whereas if, on the contrary, your goodness, clemency, kindness and beneficence attracts those that are evil, and draws them gently to a better state, then have you vanquished the evil by your goodness.

This kind of contending with evil men was alone used by those first soldiers in the Church, who fought under the banner of Christ, and conquered gloriously. And St. Paul, in his wisdom, perceiving the force and power of goodness to be such, sent this golden maxim to the Romans; namely, *Be not overcome of evil, but overcome evil with good.* This is to the same effect as he said just above: *Recompense not evil for evil;* since this is being conquered by evil, and drawn into it: but persevere in what is good, both in secret before God, and openly, yea boldly, before men. For in dealing with them everyone must hold so fast to patience, as to feel bound to die rather than suffer it to be overthrown in his own case; and testify to virtue by death, sooner than increase vice in any measure by his life. This was what the martyrs did; concerning whom it is said, *How precious in the sight of the Lord is the death of his saints.* Whose martyrdom was nothing else than patience, and a bearing witness to virtue.

Ps. cxvi. 15.

But now let us proceed to what remains, and to the sequel of this Epistle ; in which, as I write, I discover such fruit and profit, and in the contemplation of each part am possessed with such great pleasure, that I cannot pass lightly on, though so disposed, at least in so fruitful and pleasant a land. This however I will not omit; namely, that when I expounded to my hearers the words of St. Paul about the various parts of the Church,[1] I said that those were called Prophets by the Apostle, who, drawn towards the one and exalted, surveyed the true causes of things, and the right rule of life, in eternity itself: those Teachers, who afterwards delivered that rule to the people in their addresses ; and that the Ministers were those between the two, who received from the Prophets what they were to convey to the Teachers.

This was the order I thought St. Paul wished to convey, because it is in striking agreement with reason, and because it contains also a resemblance of that Heavenly Hierarchy,[2] where the first orders burn and cleave to God in ceaseless contemplation ; the last have regard to the lower matters here on earth, and are engaged in constant administration and guardianship ; whilst midway between them speed to and fro the ministering spirits, who receive from the higher what in turn they convey to the lower. This order St. Paul would have to be imitated in the Christian church : that there should be some to depend on God without ceasing, by whose connection with God all the rest of the Church might be sustained ; some again to receive attentively the divine and vital aliment thus derived from the first ones, and deliver it to those who were to distribute

---

[1] In the Exposition of 1 *Cor.* xii.—It has been said, in the *Introduction*, that there are reasons for thinking this Epistle (1 *Corinthians*) to have been lectured on before the *Romans.*

[2] See *Dean Colet on the Hierarchies* (1869), p. 31, and *passim.*

it diligently and unceasingly to the people. These third ones in order are the Teachers, who give to the multitude the means of being stable and strong in God, and of thinking and acting in concert, and mutually helping one another in love, and living in harmony and perfect holiness, and growing up to unity in God; that so they may appear to spring up, and be nourished and supported by one God to unity; and have their *roots* (namely, those first ones in the Church) planted in God himself, and from them derive the divine nourishment of wisdom and goodness, and digest it for the strengthening and banding together of the whole body, so compactly and firmly, that the very *gates of hell shall not prevail against it.* For this is what the divine mind and purpose of St. Paul is aiming at.

But now at length let me return to my task.

CHAPTER XIII.

AFTER this there follows in the Epistle a most prudent admonition to all the faithful then in Rome; opportunely given, as must be confessed ; to the effect that they should act circumspectly, and be careful on all occasions not to come into collision with the Emperor and authorities of Rome, in those matters especially which concerned the manners and usages of the Roman state, and the laws passed about the exaction of tributes and customs. These, so long as necessity compelled, they both might and must obey, provided their religion were not violated. For if they would not obey them, but were to refuse payment of the tribute exacted, and set at naught the Roman magistrates, and the authority of the State and Empire under which they were living, then they would at once provoke the others to wrath and cruelty, and cause themselves to be in some cases put to death, in others banished from the State. Wherefore it is St. Paul's wish, while the Church is as yet in its infancy, and especially in the case of those at Rome, under such wide control of heathens, that all things should be done discreetly, soberly, and patiently about money matters, or whatever else the world is covetous of; that they should make no opposition, but pay readily the tributes and customs exacted from them; that they should also *fear*, and, as the manner is, *honour* those Roman magistrates. For, as St. Paul implies, God allows and suffers such magistrates, and the power of the unbelieving, for a time. But on what account, and for what end, he alone knows. He disposes all things in this world, and ordains them as he will. Were they to resist, they would be resisting the will of God. Wherefore the Apostle covertly advises them that all things, whatever they be, must be borne; and teaches that they must ever encounter evil with good; and that the evil, if possible, must be conquered by the good. Failing this, they must still not depart at all from the good, nor render evil for evil, which is a decline from good to evil; but persevere resolutely in goodness and endurance of evil; that capricious evil may at length be overcome by unswerving good, and what is in truth the weaker thing by its stronger opposite.

There were at Rome, we must remark, sons of God, and brethren, and Christians, beset on all hands by evil men; enemies of virtue, and of the true religion which those servants of Christ professed. With these enemies and opponents they were to engage, with no other arms than the contrary qualities. For it is not cold that conquers cold, nor darkness darkness, nor in a word like that conquers like; nay rather this does but increase it; but it is heat that conquers cold, and light darkness, and in fact opposites their opposites. Thus, in like manner, it must needs be good alone that conquers evil; and pride, unbelief, false worship, hatred, unjust deeds, war, murder, and all other crimes, must be overcome by their opposites; namely, humility, faith in God, true worship of God, love, forbearance, peace, and the not refusing to die in holding fast to what is good. These arms of light, I repeat, if they advance resolutely, conquer and overcome and scatter far abroad what is opposed to them, and at length illumine all things by their radiance. With these arms, Christ, and his Apostles, whom he called *lights of the world*, both finished their fight and won the victory.

ROMANS XIII.

In this way alone has been introduced whatever light there is in the world. In this way alone also is preserved and increased by men, every portion, whether of light or goodness, that has been introduced. And the wider the departure made from it, the more are smoke and darkness and evil and misery stirred up in the life of men. He that sees not this, but fancies that force must be repelled by force, and war by war, and evil by evil, in his unhappy blindness sees no light. And how great the error is in which he is involved, may be clearly recognised from this, namely, the fact that he will never, by any efforts, attain what he is endeavouring and longing to accomplish; nor in this way, 'tis most certain, will he ever perceive an end of evils; but rather evils after evils springing up so thickly, that the more he toils in extricating himself by that method, the more will he involve himself in evils. And the cause that as yet in this world, which wholly *lieth in wickedness*[1] we are surrounded and almost overwhelmed by so many evils, is none other than this, namely, that in our folly and blindness we do not seek to conquer opposites by opposites, but wish rather to increase one evil by another; not perceiving, when we recompense evil by evil, that we are increasing the evil, not dispelling it. Now the Apostle Paul, taught by Christ, saw the marvellous truth of the evangelic precept, that evil must not be rendered for evil. And had this precept been religiously and constantly observed, we should now have had an end of our evils. Therefore he has both explained it more at large on various occasions in his other letters, and in this Epistle to the Romans expatiates on it more fully; to the intent that at Rome, where evils swarmed on every side, those that worshipped the name of Christ might in no way render evil

1 Joh. v. 19.

---

[1] See note above, p. 65. To what is there said may be added, in confirmation, a passage from Ficino (*Argum. in Lib.* iii. *Enn. Sec.*): "Ideoque angeli a fato solvunt animas; demones autem eas fato devinciunt. In dæmonibus positum est propinquum corporei mundi hujus imperium. Unde fit ut, si ad angelos comparatio fiat, mundus hic jure dicatur *positus in maligno.*" (*Plotini Op.* Ed. Creuzer, i. p. 230.)

for evil, but suffer evil, that by steadfast goodness and inoffensiveness they might at length, with God's help, lay low the troublesome and aggressive evil; and, giving no offence to any, walk gently, courteously, religiously, and harmlessly in the State. He would have them deal with everyone without despising any, but respect everyone, and render to everyone his due, readily and cheerfully; that by such goodness and sincerity of life they might win the kind favour and good will even of the bad, and procure for themselves rest amid the restless and unprincipled citizens of that State; so far as to be able to serve God and Christ without disturbance and molestation.

This Epistle to the Romans was written during the reign of Claudius,[1] at the close of his reign, about the twentieth year of St. Paul's ministry. At which time also, as I gather from the histories and from the letters of St. Paul himself, both Epistles to the Corinthians were written, as well as that to the Galatians: but this one to the Romans after them, not long before St. Paul's last journey to Jerusalem. For he was imprisoned by Festus, the Governor of Judea, four or five[2] years after the despatch of these letters, and sent by him to Rome. This was the twenty-fifth year after

---

[1] This is somewhat earlier than the date now usually given for the *Romans*. Pearson, in his *Annales Paulini* (*Minor Theol. Works*, 1844, i. p. 386), places it at the end of the third year of Nero's reign, or at the end of A. D. 57. Lightfoot (*Bib. Dict.*) differs but little from this, assigning the Epistle to A.D. 58. The best authorities agree with Colet in making the *Romans* to have been written after 1 and 2 *Corinthians* and *Galatians*.

[2] If Colet interposes four or five years between the date of the *Romans* and the second year of Nero, he makes the Epistle to have been written two years at least before the end of Claudius's reign. This, as said above, is now judged too early. The chief date to be fixed, as a pivot, is the accession of Festus; and this is now assigned to A. D. 60.—See Mr. Davies' Art. in the *Dict. of the Bible*. This agrees with Bishop Pearson, who makes the year A.D. 60 to correspond to the sixth and part of the seventh of Nero. Hence Colet, in placing Paul's trial by Festus in the *second* of Nero's reign, is four years too early. The source of this discrepancy appears to be, his making St. Paul's "commission" to be in the year of the Crucifixion, instead of four years after.

ROMANS XIII. 95

the death of Christ, and after St. Paul's commission, and the second year of the reign of Nero. After this date he survived for twelve years, and taught in Italy, and served under the banner of Christ till his death,—thirty-seven years from his first conversion. He perished in the first persecution of the Christians that continued under Nero, on the same day as St. Peter, in the fourteenth year of Nero's reign.[1]

I mention this, that St. Paul's great thoughtfulness and prudence may be remarked. For being aware that Claudius Cæsar had succeeded to the throne; a man of changeable disposition,[2] and bad principles, and sudden purposes; a man too who, as Suetonius writes in his Life, *banished the Jews from Rome, as they were in constant insurrection at the instigation of CHRESTUS*[3] (on account of which insurrection I suppose St. Paul to have written this Epistle, and that what Suetonius meant to convey was, that the Jews had been banished by Claudius on account of their disputes about Christ);—St. Paul understanding, I say, that the Roman Emperor, as Suetonius also relates,[4] was levying

---

[1] This is the date generally agreed upon, so far as the year of Nero's reign is concerned; but if thirty-seven years be allowed from St. Paul's conversion (even though we place that as early as Colet does), the martyrdom of the Apostle will be brought down to A. D. 70 or 71. Bishop Pearson fixes it in A. D. 68.

Dean Colet probably took his chronology, in the first instance, from the *Chronicon* attributed to Ivo, which he quotes by name later on. We there find the appointment of Festus placed in the second year of Nero, and the statement that the two Apostles suffered on the same day.

[2] "Moreover, in the examination, trial, and deciding of controversies, he was wonderous variable: one while circumspect, wary, and of great insight: otherwhiles as rash and inconsiderate: now and then also foolish, vaine, and like to one without all reason."—Sueton. *Claudius*, xv. Holland's *Transl.*

[3] "Judæos impulsore CHRESTO assidue tumultuantes Roma expulit."—*Ib.* c. xxv.

[4] The words which follow are quoted from Suetonius' Life of C. Cæsar Caligula, c. xl.: "Vectigalia nova atque inaudita, primum per publicanos, deinde, quia lucrum exuberabat, per centuriones tribunosque prætorianos exercuit: nullo rerum aut hominum genere

some *new and unheard of taxes,* originated by Caligula, *letting no description of persons or things escape without some amount of tribute being imposed upon them ;* lest the brethren at Rome should chance to become weary of their vexations, and break forth into some contumely and defiance of the Roman magistrates, and refuse to obey their decrees;—St. Paul, I repeat, writing to those who professed the service of Christ, to teach them something as to the behaviour they were to show towards the Romans, and unbelieving rulers, whose subjects they could not but be, if they lived at Rome, nor avoid submitting to all their decrees, but must needs give them somewhat, which was theirs, that they might keep on the other hand what was their own, and *render,* Matt. xxii. as the Saviour commands, *unto Cæsar the things that are Cæsar's, and unto God the things that are God's ;*—that most wise Apostle Paul, I repeat again, perceiving that this must be done, exhorts and commands them so to do, and on no account to contend with the Roman powers, or give them any cause for being incensed and angry ; but to maintain sincere charity among themselves, without variance, and to be kind both towards one another and towards all else ; that they might stand firmly together in kindness, and by kindness, so far as possible, ever prevail over their adversaries, and draw them to goodness, and likeness to themselves, whilst they themselves were on no account to be drawn to evil.

Rom. xii. 17. *sqq.* This is the point of that expression of St. Paul : *Recompense to no man evil for evil. Provide things honest not only in the sight of God,*[1] among your own selves, *but also in the sight of men ;*—those outsiders and heathen, with whom you live : *Avenge not yourselves* from the wrongs of the unbe-

---

omisso, cui non tributi aliquid imponeret."—I do not find where Claudius is stated to have continued these.

[1] This addition to the words of the English version is due to the Vulgate, which inserts after *providentes bona,* " non tantum coram Deo, sed etiam," *etc.* Erasmus observes that the words are not in the Greek, nor required. Dionysius Carthusianus explains them in much the same sense as Colet : " Videlicet, in secreto, vel quantum ad cordis intentionem."—*Enarr. in Rom.* (1533), f. 30.

lievers, *but give place unto their* [1] *wrath;* and be at peace with all men, and *as much as lieth in you, live peaceably with all men* on all occasions; and cause all others also, to the utmost of your power, to live peaceably with you. Let there be no retaliation and revenge for wrongs among you; *for it is written, Vengeance is mine; I will repay, saith the Lord.* But succour the bad, and cherish your enemies, and, after the manner of the good God, be ye good, and doing good, to all alike. This is the only way of conquering evil, and making men good instead of bad. Hence the Apostle commands: *Overcome evil with good.* And then he adds the precepts referring to the power and authority of the Romans; which he says must not be resisted, seeing that all things are as Divine providence ordains them, and remain such time as the will of God allows. Wherefore every one *must needs be subject to the higher powers,* as St. Paul teaches; the powers of the heathen, that is, in whose hands all power in secular matters then lay. For such was the disposal of the affairs and governments of the world by God: and men must endure this, lest they should seem to bear God's providence and disposal of things impatiently. xiii. 1.

He then relates the duty of a sovereign and governor of the nation, and covertly teaches what sort of men the rulers of states ought to be; with a sagacious foresight, in my opinion, of the possibility of its one day coming to pass, that this letter of his should make its way into Roman hands. Accordingly, he speaks in such a way of the Roman magistrates, as at once to instruct them, and win their favour for the Christians; since he was admonishing Christians not to oppose the Roman rulers, but obey them, as being ordained by God, and executing here on earth a ministry of God, namely, to punish the bad, but support and defend the good and innocent. In this way, without xiii. 3.

---

[1] In the original Greek there is here the definite article, "*the* wrath;" which raises the question "*whose* wrath? that of God, or of the adversary? The amended version by Five Clergymen (Lond. 1858), has "give place unto the wrath [of God]"; but Peile, Vaughan and Jowett agree in the interpretation given by Colet.

difficulty, on seeing men of the Christian religion taught by their own masters to be constantly good and harmless, and offend no one; and on hearing at the same time that it was the duty of magistrates not to injure such;—in this way, I repeat, and by these words of St. Paul, should they have ever chanced to read his Epistle, it follows readily that they must needs have been strongly induced to deal mercifully with the inoffensive Christians, and allow them to remain in the state without injury. This would follow, I mean, on their hearing that rulers were not to be objects of terror to the good, but to the bad; and that they were *the ministers of God*, and bare the sword to inflict punishment on wicked men and evil-doers, not on good men, and well-doers, and endurers of evil. For this moreover is the only way, as I have said over and over again, of overcoming evil and obtaining rest; namely, inoffensiveness and patience. Therefore he admonishes the Christians at Rome to obey the inevitable, and bear all things; not only because the wrath of unbelievers is thus best avoided, but also, and chiefly, because patience is itself true fortitude, and a virtue well-pleasing to God. Whatever was demanded of them in the way of tribute, let them promptly pay, and conduct themselves respectfully towards the revenue officers and collectors themselves; and, so far as was possible and lawful, satisfy them with all deference and courtesy; that by such gentleness and civility on their part, expressed both in look and gesture and actions, stern, harsh unbelievers might be constrained at length to soften down in some measure, and grow gentle. Wherefore St. Paul enjoins that there should be rendered to them *tribute*, and *fear* and *honour*, after the manner and custom of the state. The doing of this self-same thing is wisely recommended to the Churches of Asia by St. Peter, the chief of the Apostles, who thus writes to them in his Epistle: *Submit yourselves to every ordinance of man for the Lord's sake: whether it be to the King, as supreme; or unto governors, as unto them that are sent by him for the punishment of evil-doers, and for the praise of them that do well. For so is the will of God, that with well-doing ye may put to silence the igno-*

rance of foolish men : as free, and not using your liberty for a cloke of maliciousness, but as the servants of God. Honour all men. Love the brotherhood. Fear God. Honour the King.

See how harmoniously one and the same Spirit spake in each Apostle, and bade those first Christians to endure as best they could, without any subversion of their faith, the kings and rulers of their time, and their laws and statutes. We are bound therefore to conduct ourselves gently, lowly and submissively towards those who are outside the City of God, and are enemies of our religion; that we may propitiate them, and render them gentle towards us (for like invites like); and by kind acts and words and friendly looks, to call forth kindness and goodwill towards ourselves on the part of all men whatsoever. *Being reviled, we bless*—thus writes St. Paul to the Corinthians; *being persecuted, we suffer it: being defamed, we entreat.* Thus did the good Apostle endeavour to draw forth goodness by goodness, and by the goodness in himself to conquer the evil of others. And we are all bound to imitate him, as he did Christ; and before all things to maintain in ourselves—every one in himself, and all in the society and church of Christ,—that which we seek from others, namely, mutual love and charity; a thing which cannot be great and accumulated enough. For the earnings of love[1] have no end; since in a thing infinite, such as love is, what end can be discovered? Wherefore St. Paul bids us love without end. *Owe no man anything,* he says, *but to love one another.* For in this we must needs be ever debtors, seeing that we cannot discharge in its full extent our mutual debt of love. For in loving one another we strive to reproduce the divine love, which is endless; and by virtue of love to approach the divine unity,

1 Cor. iv. 12.

Rom. xiii. 8.

---

[1] It will be seen that I have taken *merementum amoris* as equivalent to *id quod amor meretur*. But I feel uncertain in what sense Colet used the word. In the Medieval Lexicon of Maigne d'Arnis, *merrementum* and *merramentum* are found in the sense of "timber for building," the earlier *materia;* and so I have explained it in another passage of Colet (*Sacraments*, p. 39); but this meaning does not seem available in the present instance.

which is perfect unity and simplicity. Hence the expression of Virgil:—

Love has no bounds, in pleasure or in pain.[1]

Therefore let each be inflamed by his own love towards another, and continue endlessly loving, and love without end; for there is nothing more excellent and powerful than love. It is the author of what is good, the banisher of evil, the fulfilling of the law, the bond and consolidation of human society. For where holy love bears sway, there no wrong, nor unfairness nor transgression can have place. *Love,* saith St. Paul, *worketh no ill; and love is the fulfilling of the law.* St. Paul would have the Christian society, called the Church, be so wholly and fervently inflamed with love in itself, that the clear, unallayed heat of love might have full force in it; a heat so strong and powerful, as to warm, purify, refine, draw into its flames, yea, seize on, and keep inflamed, like flashing and flaming fire, all who are near it,—the men standing coldly outside the church; that the fire may daily increase itself more and more with this blazing fuel,[2] even the number of those that believe and love; and may spread itself at length through the whole world; seizing upon all things, purging away their dross, drying them, and rendering them hot and fiery; that so on earth and among men there may reign only the fire and heat of love; all the cold and watery matter[3] of vices having

---

[1] *Eclog.* ii. 68, Dryden's Translation.—Colet's quotation may be a defence for what has been called the amatory motto of the Prioress, in Chaucer's beautiful description:—

"And thereon heng a broche of gold ful shene,
On whiche was first ywriten a crouned A,
And after, *Amor vincit omnia.*"

[2] Compare with this the kindred passage in the *Hierarchies,* p. 62.

[3] Water, from its unstable nature, was regarded allegorically as an inferior element to earth. If by *earth* (for example) was meant the Jews, then by *water* would be meant the Gentiles. Christ, drawing his converts from the former, was a shepherd; the Apostles, drawing theirs from the latter, were fishermen. In his Convocation Sermon, Colet used the same figure of speech as in the text, speaking

ROMANS XIII.

been utterly consumed. This is the fire which Christ said that he was come to send upon the earth. This is the wonderful fire, which St. Paul in his Epistle to the Hebrews calls *a consuming fire :*—a consumer, that is, of vices. This fire moreover is that whereof Isaiah says that it doth *purely purge away the dross.* And now what else is this fire, so powerful, so glorious, but God himself, who is Love; who is *in us,* as St. John saith, and *we in him;* who doeth in us these things that are *marvellous in our eyes.* So long as we keep within ourselves this God and Holy Spirit; or rather, so long as we are kept by him (and we *are* kept, such time as we will not break loose in arrogance and pride)— so long shall we be both healthy and strong; so as to have an invincible constancy in ourselves, united by the power of the Divine Spirit and love, and to overcome others, that are weakened by mutual hatred.

After this St. Paul admonishes the Romans to *know the time* in which they now are; a time of light and of the day, a time for arising and journeying, a time for watching and labouring, a time for virtue and good acts, a time for life and rejoicing ; a time, lastly, for procuring salvation and happiness. For the Sun of faith and righteousness, Jesus Christ, has arisen and shone upon the earth ; and now it is day with men, clear and bright. Now, by the powerful rays of Christ, the clouds of evil works have been dispelled, the shades of darkling thoughts have been put to flight. The minds, that is to say, of all the faithful, have been enlightened, so that they can now perceive what they ought to think and do ; and whither, and to what end, they are to direct the whole course of their life ; and can catch a distant prospect, as it were (so keen is the eye of faith), of that City set on a high mountain, and that country to which they are journeying, even the heavenly Jerusalem. And they that hasten thither, while it is day, and shall have drawn near before night has overspread the scene, and ere yet the

---

of those who were "*enervati aquis* hujus mundi." In the Greek *Catena Patrum,* will be found a very noble application of the thought, in the comment on *Rev.* xv. 2.

[margin: Luke xii. 49. Heb. xii. 29. Is. i. 25. 1 John iv. 13. Ps. cxviii. 23. Rom. xiii. 11.]

gates have been shut to, will be admitted within full readily, and have free gift of the citizenship; and, living according to the rights and laws of the citizens there, will have full fruition of the rewards and happiness of that everlasting city. Let us therefore *know the time*, as St. Paul bids us, and *awake out of sleep*, and mark how near our salvation is at hand, and how much more speedily our Saviour came than we believed. *Let us therefore cast off* all *the works of darkness*, of night, and of the devil; works without the light of virtue, and murky vices; *and let us put on the armour* and accoutrements *of light;* even faith in God and love of God and Christ. With this armour let us oppose the darkness; in these accoutrements let us work in Christ, our light and day, and do the works of light. In the light of Christ, who is our sun and day, let us see our road, and distinguish the strait and narrow way towards the City, from the broad and well-trodden road that leads to destruction. For strait is the way that leads towards heaven; and none discerns the narrow gate by which he enters, unless the eyes of his understanding be shone upon by Christ, his sun, and illumined by the light received from him. This light is loving faith; and he that is lit by it, under Christ, can assuredly not err from the path, strait though it be and eluding the common gaze, in his journey back to his father's home, to which, like an exile, he is being recalled. For the word of God, as David says, will be *a lamp unto his feet, and a light unto his paths.* So long as he retains this light, and keeps unextinguished the lamp kindled by God (for, as David also sang, Thou dost *light my candle,* O Lord; that is, O Lord, my God, thou dost enlighten my darkness):—so long, I say, as he keeps that spiritual light, and holds fast the kindled lamp, so to speak, of his understanding, so long in truth can he not wander from the way, nor be ignorant whither he is going. For that enlightening Spirit not only shows the way by his clear illumination, but also gently draws after him, as one may say, the traveller along the road, and leads him by a straight course to the fulness of the spirit and of light; the which when the wayfarer has reached, he will be wholly absorbed in the light that sates not, and be in bliss.

Thus by the light received we journey towards the light; and by faithful love towards true goodness; and through a part towards the whole; and this part, as St. Paul teaches the Corinthians, will be done away, when we shall be in the whole and fulness itself. *For we know in part,* he says, *and we prophesy in part. But when that which is perfect is come, then that which is in part shall be done away.* Here we are children, then we shall be men; here we know *through a glass darkly; but then face to face:* here, in a word, *we know in part; but then shall we know even as also we are known.* For then this measure of the spirit and light that we now have, will be advanced to the full and perfect light. Wherefore St. Paul admonished the Thessalonians, to *quench not the spirit,* that is, the spiritual light, by which they that are here journeying to their native country may see where to place their steps. And if this be extinguished by our wickedness, then in misery and darkness we shall know not whither we go. On which account St. Paul here bids us put on the armour of light, and *walk honestly in the day* and in Christ, and also advance towards the very day and sun, which is Christ, and leave behind us, more and more every day, darkness and the deeds of darkness, with the works of night;—such as are drunken riotings, wanton chamberings, envious strife, and whatever the caprice and forwardness of the flesh lusteth after—and journey on in the course we have begun, even in all our life, with holiness, sobriety, temperance and cleanness, beneath the light of day, the rays of our sun which is Christ; and lightly and cheerfully ascend the hill—that *holy hill* of the Lord, I mean, in which none dwelleth, but *he that walketh uprightly and worketh righteousness.*

1 Cor. xiii. 9.

1 Thess. v. 19.

Rom. xiii. 13.

Ps. xv. 1.

CHAPTER XIV.

THERE now follows in St. Paul a wise admonition and precept, that in the Christian society count should be taken of those that are weak in the faith. For faith, as we have before laid down, is a spiritual light bestowed on the minds of men; on those, that is, who are chosen to believe in God. The partaking of it is in various degrees, and (as St. Paul elsewhere says) *according as God hath dealt to every man the measure of faith*, that he may not think *more highly than he ought to think, but think soberly*. For some have the light, which we call faith, in such moderate degree, that their mind is still blind to very many things, and discerns not all clearly, nor readily allows and approves of anything but what by frequent use and custom has been, as it were, impressed upon their eyes. Whereas that which is unusual, and not seen before, their dull and blunted vision discerns not openly, nor grasps boldly, but shrinks from in the blindness of distrust, and shuns, being as yet powerless and weak to apprehend what each thing is, and what has not before come into use. And so, according to his little measure, such a one makes a distinction of matters and seasons, and separates and discriminates many things that pertain to life and conduct. Neither does he easily own anything to be agreeable and useful for himself, unless after taking count of old-established custom; feeling confident that what is approved of by use will not do him harm, but shrinking from other things as hitherto untried. Nor can he be induced to believe (so slender is his faith) that he can meddle with such things without peril.

Some however have the light of faith in such abundance, that they look down as from a height on what is beneath them, and have clear discernment and judgment about all things. These shrink not from anything through blindness, nor stagger and totter at anything through infirmity; but with strong and penetrating vision discriminate all things, and are confident that they can assay and adventure all, especially in those matters which are not essential; such as the meat and drink about which St. Paul is now mainly speaking. Because in the Roman church, consisting as it did partly of Jews, partly of Gentiles, there was considerable discussion as to what was lawful for each to taste. The Jews, in pursuance of their old law, delivered to them by Moses, held it an established custom to abstain from many kinds of meats; for instance, among animals, Lev. xi. 3. whatever did not both divide the hoof and chew the cud; among fishes, whatever had not both fins and scales; among birds, all the more predatory and rapacious kinds; and lastly, every creeping thing that creepeth upon the earth, or lives in holes in the earth itself. From these Moses enjoined the Jews on all occasions to abstain.

Now although it is to a higher truth that these enactments point, and though they are only signs and reminders of the things pertaining to the soul, (as Moses himself also most plainly declares, when he adds to those enactments the words : *Ye shall*[1] *not defile your souls, nor touch ought of* Lev. xi. *them, lest ye be unclean. For I am the Lord your God: ye* 43, *sqq. shall be holy, as I am holy. Defile not your souls with any manner of creeping thing that creepeth upon the earth. For I am the Lord that brought you up out of the land of Egypt, to be your God; ye shall therefore be holy, for I am holy :*—so that it is to the sanctification of the soul that those figures, and external acts, and bodily abstinence, according to the design of Moses, refer)—yet, inasmuch as the Jewish race was a stiff-necked one and dull of sight,[2] he would train them carefully in those outward and visible signs; in order that they might either be often admonished to keep their souls pure, or else be led with more ease at length, as men trained in those examples, to the true sanctification of the soul, by that Master of truth, whose coming Moses foresaw. But when this Master of truth—himself also the very Truth —was come, and when he taught the true method of purifying the heart, multitudes of the Jews, who followed this teaching, and refused not to be cleansed in heart, yet could not on a sudden be drawn away from their custom and practice in regard of tasting food, which through long-con-

---

[1] It will be observed that the English Version differs considerably from the Vulgate in this passage.
[2] Colet speaks in much stronger language than this, in the remarkable *Letters on Genesis:* "ut ruditatis homunculorum, et paulo ante in luto et latere versatorum, videatur meminisse;" and again, "utque videar eciam animadvertere te non *lutulentum hebreum* sed politissimum philosophum esse."—Parker MS. ccclv. p. 205.

tinued use had become so deeply fixed in their minds. For their mind, contracted by a kind of narrow usage, was unable to take a wider survey, and discern the truth in each case. Hence arose distrust, which is a sort of ignorance arising from littleness of faith.

Now assuredly everything that is done with good faith in God, is not to be despised. Nor are they to be looked down upon who timidly refrain from things in which is no danger, provided they do so in good faith, believing that they please God by their deed; but we should rather have compassion upon their infirmity, and tend them gently and brotherly in our society, with thoughtful considerateness, that they may be able at length to make their way to a better and stronger state. It follows that they who are stronger in faith, and think that they can do all things, should be very careful to take count of the others' infirmity, and not so abuse their own power, as to seem forgetful of brotherly love, and of what others can bear. For that which is lawful in itself and in the abstract, is not lawful for all, and at every time and place. Whereas what is done agreeably to faith and love and brotherly affection, can be unlawful at no place or time. It is not so much what we have the power to do, that has to be regarded, as what is conducive to society, to union and peace; in order that the charity which *seeketh not her own* may appear in us. These also, if at times they see others venturing on more than they dare themselves, and taking more kinds of food than they think they themselves can, ought not to measure the deeds of others by this narrowness and infirmity of theirs, nor pass sentence on others according to their own feelings, nor condemn in another what they think deserving condemnation in themselves. For this is just as if a sickly person were unwilling that a stronger man should eat what he himself, through his weakness, doubts whether he could digest. There is nothing that ought to be less practised among men, than one person's measuring another by the standard of his own power; nothing more to be avoided, than thinking all opinions deserving condemnation which are unlike our own; especially in these matters, in which, although one opinion may be better than another, yet neither is bad in itself, provided it be supported with humility towards God, and in good faith. Of such a kind are matters of food and drink, which neither advance nor retard us, whether we abstain from them or use them. This also St. Paul testifies, in what he writes to the Corinthians: *For neither, if we eat, are we the better; neither, if we eat not, are we the worse.* For it is not *meat* (that is, an observance and discrimination of repasts) that *commendeth us to God.* But the manner, intention, and end, have undoubtedly great power either way. And what this end and intention is, and in what manner each one is acting (in what may be done without danger as things indifferent) is not for us to judge, but for God alone; for we are his servants, and do all in good faith as serving him. And whether this be rightly done or not, is plainly for the Lord of the servants to examine and decide; since whatever they are, they are his servants. Whether you have done well or ill, whether you live or die, it appertains to the Lord alone both to approve and to disapprove. For before his judgment-seat we shall all stand, to render every man an account of his own life: whereas servants, as amongst themselves, will neither accuse nor condemn one another. But seeing that they who are servants to God are at the same time his sons (for we have God both for our Lord and Father, and on that account are ourselves all brethren together) therefore this brotherhood in God demands that we should love one another as much as possible; should pity, cherish, and aid one another; and by condescending, and often accommodating ourselves to our brother, seek his salvation more than our own glory.

1 Cor. viii. 8.

And since in this we are often compelled to do what does not seem best to us, we should persuade ourselves that what is done out of charity and love for our neighbour is always best; and that what is most pleasing to God is not what most pleases us, but what tends to the common welfare and peace of the Church, and bears on its face the evidence, not of love of self, but of love of others. For Christ also, as St. Paul says, *pleased not himself.* Accordingly, let every

Rom. xv. 3, 2.

one of us please his neighbour for his good, to edification;—
edification, that is, of the Church; and not please himself,
to destruction. For this would be pride and self-esteem;
a thing hateful to God, and mischievous to the Church.

xiv. 22. Hence St. Paul says, *Happy is he that judgeth*[1] *not himself
in that which he alloweth,* nor sets himself up in his own
opinion of himself. For though it may chance to be a just
opinion to form, yet unless you mark carefully how that
which you have power to do is suitable and useful for the
society, what you fancy just will be plainly unfair. Therefore do not always put into execution what you yourself
approve of, though on the other hand never hesitate to do
what love, and the imitation of Christ, and charity towards
a neighbour, demand. Offend not his weakness by your
strength, nor overbear his hesitation by your boldness.
Do not do what is guarded against in sick chambers, that
is, eat what may raise a qualm and disgust in the weakly
one, though you in your robust health may be able to do so;
nor be ever acting as in your own opinion you think you
can; but, forgetting not charity, look at the same time to
what another's opinion may be able to receive and bear, and
what can be done agreeably to the common feeling and
health of the whole body (that is, the Church), and to union,
concord and peace. And ever remember that, since you
are a member of the body ecclesiastical, it is your duty not
to break loose into some opinion of your own, but to accord
with the other members; that the health, soundness and
vigour of the whole body may be preserved.

But on this point let us briefly run over St. Paul's own

---

[1] I have been obliged to render thus literally the Vulgate *judicat*,
to be in accordance with Colet's argument. The meaning of the
word is much disputed. Chrysostom's explanation is somewhat
singular: "And if all accuse thee, and thou condemn not thyself,
and thy conscience lay no charge against thee, thou art happy."
The gloss of Dionys. Carthus. is *damnabilem facit semetipsum, alium
scandalizando*. Peile and Vaughan both agree with the English
Version in understanding self-condemnation to be meant, arising
from inward doubts and misgivings. The amended Version of Five
Clergymen retains Colet's word:—"Blessed is he that *judgeth* not
himself."

ROMANS XIV.

words. He says, *Him that is weak in the faith*—not believing, that is, that he can safely do all things—*receive ye into your society, and bear with his infirmity, and deal kindly and considerately with him, that he may be advanced to greater faith and resolution ; not to doubtful disputations,*[1] not by discussing and debating with him (for who that is strong has any desire or duty to wrestle with the weak ?) ; since he cannot bear the strength of your reasons. Nay, any reasoning of that kind is only a sort of contest and strife of words; and this ought not to be in the Church. But that weaker one in the faith, whoever he be, should be dutifully, gently and lovingly cherished, and, with robuster strength at his side kindly and courteously and suitably leading him, he should be upborne ; just as in the body, should a member have become enfeebled, an adjoining member, that has more vitality and vigour, through nature's bounty, lends zealous and cheerful help, to raise it to equal vigour with itself. Even so let the faith and charity, whereby we ourselves live, so shine and burn in us, that by our shining love our weaker neighbours may be quickened to fresh life, and rendered stronger. And if this cannot be done, then let such be removed, kind-heartedly and without offence. For it is the duty of every Christian to cherish the good, so far as he can ; and by his own goodness either prudently to increase another's good, or patiently to maintain it. And in this endeavour, whether to increase or maintain the good of others, our own goodness shines most brightly forth. Now faithful love is, as it were, a bright heat and spirit, whereby men, the members of the Lord's body, are quickened variously and in varied measure, that they may combine for the building together of the one body, having the same aim, and bound together by mutual faithful love. In which body if any one, through deficiency of faith, seems to droop and waver beneath a too heavy

---

[1] The Vulgate reads *non in disceptationibus cogitationum*, which, as Erasmus points out, should rather have been *ad dijudicationes disceptationum*. The amended Version before referred to gives the sense correctly : "yet not for the deciding of doubts."

load, we must lighten his load for him, and according to the measure of our own faith treat him compassionately; provided only that he is striving with all his might, and thinks sincerely that he is pleasing God.

xiv. 2. *For one believeth that he may eat all things.*

St. Paul is speaking of meats, in regard to which some acted too scrupulously, not from bad intention, but from weakness. Some in truth there were, of such great faith, and with such confidence in God in his various creatures, that by the light of faith they saw there was nothing for them to shrink from in the different kinds of food, since all the things of God are good and clean. They could see too that the tradition of Moses was not concerned about meats, as its highest object, but that all his enactments about eating or avoiding meats were symbolical, as it were, for the dull Jewish people, of the things that came into their minds and thoughts, and that went abroad through the mouth, after being in their thoughts. For, as that disperser of the shades of the Mosaic twilight, Jesus Christ, saith: *Not that which goeth into the mouth defileth a man; but that which cometh out of the mouth.* And so *one believeth* (that is, sees by the light of faith) that all things which are set before him are to be eaten without making a difference. But another is not of such great faith and enlightenment as to see that all things are to be eaten: and he is one whom grovelling habit in abstaining from meats has blinded; whose clouded mind is not clear as yet with faith sufficiently strong. Therefore let such a one in his weakness *eat herbs,*[1] that is, what he can assimilate and digest; and let him do what he thinks is within his power, and advance just so far in what he ventures as his own faith extends. But let him not go

Matt. xv. 11.

---

[1] It will be observed that in the Vulgate the verb is in the imperative, *manducet,* "let him eat." Origen also read the clause imperatively; and this gave him occasion to observe that, as the Mosaic Law gave no commandment about eating herbs, St. Paul must have an inner meaning in the text, analogous to his comparison between *milk* and *strong meat* elsewhere. Colet, though he often refers to Origen, keeps clear of these fancies. Dr. Vaughan understands the expression *eateth herbs* still more literally than Colet; giving as the reason for such a practice, that thus only could the risk of pollution from idols be wholly avoided.

beyond, lest he overstep the bounds of the light which he has, and fall into darkness; which is sin. For *whatsoever is* xiv. 23. *not of faith is sin,* just as what is not in the light is in darkness.

Now as to the metaphor used by St. Paul, drawn from a sick and infirm body, to which herbs, or whatever else of that description is easy of digestion, are offered: (by *herbs* being meant every vegetable whose leaves and stalk we use for food, and which when boiled is not rejected even by a weakly stomach)—as to this, I say, we must notice that, corresponding to the office in the body of the stomach or ventricle, in which the food is received and digested, is that of the mind in man's spiritual nature. And just as in the former receptacle digestion is carried on by light heat,[1] so what comes into the mind is retained, and converted into good nutriment for the soul by the digesting powers, so to speak, of faithful love. For this is the soul's vigour; and the more it is wanting, the less bold and efficient is the soul in any attempt. On which account, just as they who overload their stomach suffer from surfeit, so they who attempt anything beyond their faith bring on a kind of indigestion of the soul, whence may spring disease and destruction to it. Such an attempt is sin, and a load that is burdensome by reason of distrust; for this latter is a kind of dull, feeble chillness of the stomach, arising from deficiency of faith and love. Let no one therefore attempt more than he believes he can do without danger; lest, if he act in distrust, he should sin through that very distrust.

Let not him that eateth despise, proudly and haughtily, xiv. 3. *him that eateth not; and let not him which eateth not,* and is weaker, *judge him that eateth* and is stronger in faith, nor condemn him in his own judgment, thinking that he is acting ill, because he sees him do what he himself dares not to do. For this is a mark of the strength to which God has brought him, and in which He can also sustain him. In this

---

[1] *Lucido calore,* that is, by the combination of light and heat which Colet has before spoken of as constituting animal life. The reader may compare what is said by Lord Bacon: "It is true that concoction is in great part the work of heat, but not the work of heat alone," &c.—*Nat. Hist. Cent.* ix., § 838.

way the Apostle covertly intimates to the weak, that it is a token of strength not to put a difference between meats; that they may follow the example.

xiv. 4. *For God hath received* that stronger one; has brought him, that is, to this strength. *Who art thou that judgest another man's servant?*—one bolder than thou in eating meats, whom it is his master's business to judge. For *to his own master he standeth or falleth;* abideth, that is, in his strength, or falleth from it. *Yea, he shall be holden up.* He shall stand,[1] saith St. Paul; that is, he shall persevere in that great faith, so as to believe that there is nothing unclean in meats; and this, not by his own strength, but by sustaining grace. *For God is able to make him stand.*

It is characteristic of St. Paul ever to hope for the best. Nor is this strange; since with great love, such as was in St. Paul, there is ever joined great hope, and an expectation in every case of better things. At the same time he here tacitly approves of that faith, by which a man believes that nothing is common, since he implies that to believe thus is to *stand*, and that such believers will stand, and that this standing is from God; in order that weaker ones may acknowledge that their own conduct proceeds from infirmity. For there are degrees of faith; and one believes that he may eat at all times and of everything. This is the mean-

xiv. 5 ing of St. Paul's expression: *Another esteemeth every day alike.* Placed on a high watch-tower, such a one sees all things. And, a little after, *He that regardeth the day, regardeth it unto the Lord.* For to *esteem every day*, and *regard the day*, is to see all things in the light of faith, and to believe, and to have a knowledge of both times and circumstances. Just as, on the other hand, he who makes a distinction and *esteemeth one day above another*, and from the narrowness of his faith cannot discern every time, is in some measure ignorant of times and circumstances; on which account there are some that he distrusts. Whilst another, in the largeness of his faith, surveys all. In this way every one is *fully persuaded in his own mind* and judgment.

---

[1] The Vulgate having *stabit;* which is not a full equivalent to the Greek, " he shall be established," or " be made to stand."

Consider here, whether that expression, *One man esteemeth one day above another*[1] may not refer to the Jews, who thought that, from the time of the giving of the Law by Moses, observances must be kept up in regard to meats, such as did not exist before. For it was said to Noah after the flood, *Every moving thing that liveth shall be meat for you*: whilst Moses, as it is recorded in Leviticus, says, *This is the law of the beasts, and of the fowl, and of every living creature that moveth in the waters, and every creature that creepeth upon the earth; to make a difference between the unclean and the clean, and between the beast that may be eaten and the beast that may not be eaten.* Gen. ix. 3.
Lev. xi. 46.

Remembering this, the Jews sought to distinguish the time of the law from the time before the law; and, by observing the Mosaic distinction in meats, to *esteem one day above another; one day* being the time subsequent to the giving of the law, and *another* being the time before it;[2] and to separate their own *time* from the *time* of the Gentiles, who at every period of time were indifferent with respect to meats. They would have their own *time* and *day* begin with the Law of Moses; at which point they were taken away from the rest of the world, as from men unclean, and by the precepts of their laws were debarred from the

---

[1] The Latin of the Vulgate should here be noticed: *alius judicat diem inter diem: alius autem judicat omnem diem.* The meaning of the original Greek is disputed. Augustine renders it *alternos dies*, but follows this with what Erasmus justly calls an extraordinary interpretation; namely, that by "one man—another" are meant, not two individuals, or classes of men, but *mankind* and *God*. Jerome renders it *diem plus quam diem;* which is the sense Dr. Vaughan supports, comparing i. 25, where the preposition is rightly translated *more than*,—literally *beyond*. Prof. Jowett, however, maintains that the expression can only mean *alternate days*. He would have the reference be to eating flesh *every other day*, instead of every day.

[2] Whence did Colet get this notion? Not from Origen, who has a mystical interpretation of the words, but not this one. He makes the inner meaning to be, that the one who takes note of alternate days, is he who has such moderate ability as to gather *some* only of the manifold senses of Scripture; while he who takes note of every day, is the one of such capacity, as not to let a single jot or tittle escape him. (*Comment. in loc.*)

customs and common habits of mankind; that so they alone, as it were, out of all, through certain rules of abstinence and peculiar ceremonies, might be holy and clean. Those accordingly who *esteemed one day* and time of special abstinence *above another* day and time of eating in common, were the weaker Jews. It is to them that the words refer: *Another esteemeth every day alike.* And hence this passage of St. Paul may not unreasonably, as I think, be thus explained:—*One man*, a Jew but weak as yet, being confined within the narrowness of the Mosaic law, *esteemeth* and distinguisheth *one day*, that is, the time of his own abstaining, *above another*, that is, the time of the Gentiles, and of eating promiscuously. But *another esteemeth* and regardeth *every day* and time as a time for eating in common. This latter is one of the Gentiles; or some Jew, who has burst the barriers of the Mosaic law in the greatness of his faith, and gone forth into the light, so as to gain a wider view of all things. Thus *every man* is *fully persuaded in his own mind,* in esteeming meats and seasons.

And seeing that in these things there is not much of consequence, and that in either case what is honestly done on the part of the doer, and with a view to please the Lord, *may* be done; therefore men ought not to contend about those trifles; but the strong should rather bend and conform to the weak, and to the weak become weak, that harmony may be preserved. For *he that regardeth the day* and *eateth, eateth to the Lord; and he that eateth not,* and *regardeth not the day,*—that is, who has no appreciation and true understanding of the time (I mean, of the fact that at every period of time, and of all kinds of meats, so far as the meats themselves are concerned, it is lawful even for the Jews under the law to partake; seeing that the meats are not essentially unclean, although by certain properties they may typify this or that uncleanness)—he that so eateth not, *to the Lord he eateth not*: each of them moreover *giving thanks* in sincerity, and hoping that he pleases God.

Wherefore, since the acts and wishes and thoughts of servants, aye even their very life and death, and whatever they are, belong to their lord; let not a servant take upon himself to judge a fellow-servant. But let them, each in his measure, with mutual help, serve him who is their Lord, their examiner and judge. Now our Lord is Christ, who has redeemed us by his death, and has risen again to have dominion over all; both over the living, with mercy unto salvation; and over the dead, with judgment unto condemnation. Far be judgment and condemnation, therefore, from those who are fellow-servants and brethren together: that they may beware of judging, not only others, but even their own selves. For St. Paul says to the Corinthians: *Yea, I judge not mine own self. But he that judgeth me is the Lord. Therefore judge nothing before the time*—and in this day of man—*until the Lord come, who both will bring to light the hidden things of darkness, and will make manifest the counsels of the hearts; and then shall every man have praise from God.* But meanwhile, so long as we are living here in the Church, each brother must take heed to deal brotherly and kindly with his brother, whoever he may be; to have compassion on his weakness, cherish and comfort him; shunning whatever makes the weaker one to stumble, and not thinking of what he himself can do, but what his brother can bear; he must seek no display of his own strength, but show charity towards his brother; making himself weak along with him, even as God became weak for us, who *made himself of no reputation, and took upon him the form of a servant,* and suffered, as it were, along with us, that by his loving conformity he might reform us to be gods. He sought our gain, rather than self-display; leaving us an example how every one should behave towards his brother; how dutifully, how kindly, how conformably; that one should reform another, not with arrogancy and harshness, not with stumbling and offence, but humbly, gently, quietly, and in an acceptable way; and while zealous for his salvation, lead him considerately, at the same time, to soundness of mind.

1 Cor. iv. 3-5.

Phil. ii. 7.

It was thus that Christ, our brother, acted; and his whole life, deeds, and words, are nothing else than a pattern, modelled and placed before men for their imitation, if they would follow whither he has ascended. For, like a good teacher, he portrayed in himself the true manner of living; that men, gazing upon his life, might plainly read the way in which those must live in this world, who after this life would live for evermore. Now the Jews were offended at Christ, not because he did anything to offend them, being as he was most loving to them, but because they in their maliciousness, which takes all things in ill part, chose to be offended with what was good. Hence he is called a *stumbling stone and rock of offence* to them, because they, in their evil and bitter nature, could not bear his goodness and sweetness: whilst to the Gentiles he is a rock of *foolishness*; because they, in their foolish worldly wisdom, the enemy of the divine wisdom, judged the true wisdom of God to be foolishness. For as all things are evil to the evil, so to the foolish all things are foolish. To the good and wise, on the other hand, to whom it is given to know the mysteries of God, that Rock, even Christ, was no rock of offence, but one that gave marvellous delight by its goodness. No foolishness, again, was it to such like, but the very wisdom of God.

Rom. ix. 33.
1 Cor. i. 23.

So far then as in us lies, let us be a cause of stumbling and offence to none, but avoid offence as we would a precipice. Let us ever do, not what is allowable for ourselves, but what is expedient for others; not what we ourselves are able to do, but what may on every occasion benefit the society and body of the Lord, whereof we are members, so long as we will agree with other members.

And since there was a dispute in the Church at Rome about meats, St. Paul interposes his own decision with authority, and delivers as his sentence this weighty and noticeable one; namely, that in meats there is nothing essentially *common*, that is, unclean.—For whatever had been commonly in use among all other people than themselves, the Jews called unclean, esteeming nothing clean but what was in a special manner peculiar to themselves. Whatever had been in use among the Gentiles they considered unclean, and called it *common*.—But the power of faith, as we know, is marvellous, so as to make everything done contrary to faith to be a mischief and a sin. As every one believes, so will it happen to him. And as is the faith in our soul, so the things that come into our mind turn to good or ill for us.

Accordingly St. Paul, while asserting, as one who knew and was *persuaded by the Lord*, that there was *nothing common*, through Christ,[1] yet added : *But to him that esteemeth anything to be unclean, to him it is unclean.* For him who mistrusts its being good, the thing is evil ; just as what he cannot digest is indigestible for him. He who wishes to do a thing, about the goodness of which he is distrustful, appears to have a wish for sinning, and to be doing of his own accord what he himself thinks bad. And if he force himself, then is he heavily loaded and distressed by the troublesome nature and weight of the matter. That which we do distrustfully cannot by any means be good for us, since it will lie heavy on us as an undigested mass. *If therefore*, he adds, *thy brother be grieved with thy meat,—* be disturbed, and offended, that is, when he sees thee taking a wider range in meats than he himself can—*thou walkest not charitably,* nor according to love, who takest no count of thy brother : thou hast no pity on thy brother, but makest profane boast of thy boldness, albeit in a matter of itself good ; to the offending, and scandalizing and injuring of thy weak brother. *Destroy not with thy meat*—with thy boldness in eating, and conceit of thine own power—that poor creature *for whom Christ died ;* sinner though he was, and unworthy of Christ. *Let not then our good,* namely, spiritual quickening, unity and brotherly peace, be blasphemed ; be slandered, that is, and *evil spoken of.* *Behold,* says David, *how good and how pleasant it is for brethren to dwell together in unity.* Let not our good, I say, be evil spoken of, for the sake of eatables, and such like earthly matters, lest we give occasion to the revilers to blaspheme about our meats. *For the kingdom of God is not meat and*

Rom. xiv. 14.

Rom. xiv. 15.

Ps.cxxxiii. 1.

---

[1] Where the English version has "of itself," the Vulgate has *per ipsum*, the sense of which is ambiguous. Most interpreters understand the original expression in the same way as the E. V., but Ambrose rendered it in the same way as Colet :—" *beneficio Christi nihil commune esse.*"

drink: that is, the kingdom of God is not attained by an observance of meats; it is a matter which has no concern with it. In these things let discretion, not angry passions, be employed. For men are advanced towards heaven, and gain the kingdom of God, neither by their manner of eating and drinking, nor by their choiceness in repasts, nor by distinction in meats, nor, in a word, by anything that is earthly; but only by *righteousness, and peace, and joy in the Holy Ghost*.

Now what St. Paul says in this passage about meat and drink, that they neither are, nor constitute, the kingdom of God, may also be said with the greatest truth about money, possessions, tithes, oblations, and whatever else is of an earthly nature;—I mean, that they are not the kingdom of God, nor do they constitute it. Hence the deplorable folly of those, who imagine that Christian men, yea, even churchmen, ought to strive about these matters, as if the Church of Christ consisted of them; little knowing by what the Church has been begun, or increased, or preserved; little knowing also by what the Christian Church is shaken, disturbed and overthrown. If you cast your eyes around, and survey the whole field with care, pondering well each single object, you will find nothing that has befallen the Church to have done more mischief, than possessions, and titles of *meum* and *tuum*, and power of claiming property. Hence have sprung avarice and greed of money; a disease that has now grown to such strength in the Christian Church, and is spread so widely throughout the whole Body of Christ, absorbing and infecting the chief members even beyond the rest, that, unless Christ have mercy on his own Body, and aid it in its peril, it assuredly cannot be far off from being doomed to destruction. But He knows his own time and opportunity; and all things are suffered for an end well seen by divine Providence.

I write not thus from an unwillingness that the Church should have possessions, or priests tithes and offerings; but in order that they should on no account contend about such matters. For the Church is not tithes and oblations; as men, for the most part of narrow and grovelling minds, are wont in their conversation rashly to assert. But, as St. Paul says, the Church and *kingdom of God* (the coming of which upon the earth, sooner or later, we are taught by the Lord's Prayer to ask) *is righteousness, and peace, and joy in the Holy Ghost.* Wherefore priests and pastors of the Lord's flock ought rather to importune men to make tithes and offerings to God of *these* things above all others. For what has God to do with honey, cheese, corn, money and sheep? Not that oblations of these are to be omitted. But they are not to be exacted by priests before everything else, as is often contentiously done.[1] If you seek first those former things, these latter will follow of their own accord; and the more readily and plentifully, the less desirous of them you may seem. *Seek ye first the kingdom of God,* our Saviour bids us, which is *righteousness, peace, and joy in the Holy Ghost; and all these things shall be added unto you.* It was the search for this upon earth by Christ and his apostles, that established and extended the Church. Then at length there were gradually added to their zeal and diligence in preserving righteousness and peace, manifold possessions, not sought for by the leaders of the Church, but voluntarily offered and given by men, on account of the approved merit of ecclesiastics. And in maintaining these the same method only must be used that served for procuring them. Wherefore there ought on no account to be any insisting upon tithes, or contention, in a churchman, such as may betoken a mind bent upon earthly things, and

Rom. xiv. 17.

Matt. vi. 33.

---

[1] This grievance came to a head in 1522, when a hundred *gravamina* were presented by the Emperor and his party to the Pope's representative, of which the sixty-first was, " Quomodo novæ per violentiam instituantur decimarum præstationes."—See the *Fasciculus rerum expetendarum, etc.* (1535), f. 184. Erasmus, in his *Praise of Folly,* exposes the same abuse :—" The inferior clergy, deeming it unmannerly not to conform to their patrons and diocesans, devoutly tug and fight for their tythes with syllogisms and arguments, as fiercely as with swords, sticks, stones, or anything that came next to hand" (Bishop Burnet's *Transl.* 8th Ed. p. 132). And Colet himself, with a boldness that excites our astonishment, had denounced it in his Sermon before the Convocation.—See Hook's *Lives of the Archbishops* (1868), vi. 294.

may cause offence to the Church, and blasphemy against Christ. But rather, as St. Paul teaches the Corinthians, we are bound to endure every fraud and wrong. For he says in that Epistle: *Now therefore there is utterly a fault among you, because ye go to law one with another. Why do ye not rather take wrong? Why do ye not rather suffer yourselves to be defrauded?*

_{1 Cor. vi. 7.}

That ruler of the Church is foolish and mad, ignorant of Holy Writ, ignorant of Christ, ignorant of his own duty, who will contend with his parishioners about tithes and offerings; a shepherd contending with his sheep, a father with his sons, a minister of God with them that are sons of God and brothers to himself. Sooner than be at strife with those who are in such close relationship, a relationship that surpasses all human kindred, you should utterly cast away and despise whatever there is on earth. And think not to seek for an excuse in your misdoings, and to say that you are not seeking your own gain, but what belongs to God, and the Church's portion.—How God's? How the Church's?—Our God takes no pleasure in those paltry gifts of thine, nor does the Church of God consist in such things as the world holds in esteem, but shines most brightly in despising them. It is virtue, faith, charity, righteousness, that make an offering acceptable in the sight of God. And if you continue to seek these first and foremost among your people, the other things will follow, even though you seek them not, and more bountifully than you ask.[1] As our Saviour said to the scribes and Pharisees of old : *Woe unto you, scribes and Pharisees, hypocrites! for ye pay tithe of mint and anise and cummin, and have omitted the weightier matters of the law, judgment, mercy and faith :* so may it be said to these forward and meddlesome priests, who in

_{Matt. xxiii. 23.}

---

[1] "In viris Christianis mundus sequitur fugientes. Unde tot facultates et opes in ecclesia, nisi ex fuga?"—Coleti *Ep.* Erasmo. As written to Erasmus, the above words were half in jest. But Erasmus was of the same mind. "Ubi coaluerint," he writes, speaking of nations not yet converted, "et in nobis mores vere Christianos compererint, *ultro plus offerent,* quam ab eis ulla vis queat extorquere."—*Ichthyophagia* (*Colloq.* 1727, p. 285).

words confess Christ, but in deeds deny him, who cause the name of Christ to be evil spoken of among the Gentiles, who under the cloak of religion seek their own gain and not the gain of Christ: Woe unto you, petty priests, hypocrites! who insist on the tithing of corn and sheep and money, but insist not on the weightier matters of the law, the righteousness and mercy and faith that are left behind: for these ought the people first to do, without therefore leaving the others undone. And they will doubtless not be left undone, if you have striven after those first and foremost matters among your people, and obtained what St. Paul is here speaking of,—*righteousness, and peace, and joy in the Holy Ghost: for he who applies himself to the acquisition of these, is acceptable to Christ and approved of men.*

But let us return to the Apostle, who concludes: *Let us therefore follow after the things which make for peace, and things wherewith one may edify another.*[1] And let us not dispute with one another about every earthly matter, with mean and narrow minds, as though things of such a kind had any concern with Christ and his Church. *For meat destroy not the work of God;*—destroy it not, that is, through strife and contention: for these are as a plague-spot and eruption in the Church, which is the work of God. *All things indeed are pure unto the pure;* because they are such as is the recipient. To the bad all things are bad; to the dark all things are dark; to the good all things are good. *But it is evil for that man who eateth with offence*—with a feeling, that is, of being made to stumble.[2] By this he covertly implies that, if any shun certain kinds of meats too timidly, it is from their own uncleanness; because

Rom. xiv. 19.

Rom. xiv. 20; Tit. i. 15.

---

[1] The Vulgate has for the second clause of this verse, *et quæ ædificationis sunt in invicem custodiamus.* Erasmus shows the *custodiamus* to be a later addition, and not needed.—So with the *in* before *invicem* since his time.

[2] Colet, it will thus be seen, applies the words "with offence" to the feelings of the weak-minded brother, who was led on to do what caused him inward misgivings, and who therefore was in ill case. They may, however, be taken in the sense of "offensively;"—so as to put a snare, that is, in the way of another.

nothing is unclean excepting to the unclean, in whom clean things are unclean; because in fact everything is received by every one according to the nature of the recipient, and when received becomes of such sort as the recipient himself is. *It is good*—that is, it is better—*neither to eat flesh nor to drink wine,* although it may be lawfully done, when there results from it offence, stumbling and injury. For things that in themselves are good and lawful, are not good and lawful everywhere, and with all persons. Whereas what is serviceable and useful for others, and what preserves an harmonious agreement in the Church, is at all times lawful.

xiv. 22. *Thou* perchance, being stronger and endowed with greater faith, *hast faith to thyself,* and art conscious that thou canst do many things. But *have it* at the same time *before God,*[1] openly and avowedly in the Church along with thy brethren, united with charity. Otherwise thy faith cannot be pleasing to the divine sight, and before God. *Happy is he that judgeth not*—praiseth not, that is,[2] *himself in that thing which he alloweth,* and thinketh that he doeth right; but rather waits for his praise from God, and so acts as to be praised by God.

If he eat—that weaker one, namely—*he is condemned;* he has committed a sin worthy of condemnation, as acting not by faith, but beyond the limits of faith. And therefore what he has done cannot turn to good for him. Loving faith alone is the vital force of the soul that digests all things, and turns them into wholesome nourishment for the soul. Should it prove too scanty, and the soul grow chill through any distrust, then the eater becomes unable to digest; and this indigestion of the soul, arising from defect of faith, is a disease and sin. Wherefore he adds: *Whatsoever is not of faith,* but is done with want of faith, *is sin.*

---

[1] The Vulgate has: *Tu fidem habes? penes temetipsum habe coram Deo,* which may be read in various ways according to the punctuation. The construction favoured by Colet, in making a pause after *temetipsum,* is not approved of by Erasmus; and his interpretation of the words "before God," disagrees with that of most commentators.

[2] See note above, p. 108.

Because want of faith, of itself, cannot turn what has been received into what is good.

CHAPTER XV.

WE must therefore take a kindly account of the weak, and beware of laying any burden upon them. But rather let us have compassion on them; following the example of Christ, whose will it was to have compassion on us, that he might make us victors over our passions. And we must ever strive after agreement, which is the soundness of the Lord's body, and the health of the Church; that so, by souls conspiring together, God may be worshipped and adored; for this is the object of the Church's assembly and congregation, and of the Christian Society. *Wherefore receive ye one* xv. 7. *another to the glory of God*, dutifully and kindly, *as Christ also received us*[1]; who despised not those that were unlike himself, nor looked down upon the weak, but drew men to himself from among both Jews and Gentiles. And they, being thus drawn and established in Christ, ought mutually to welcome and love one another, even as they were welcomed by a loving Christ; the Jews in *truth*, the Gentiles in *mercy*. On either hand indeed there is both the mercy and the truth of God. For God is both true and merciful, and mercifully true and truly merciful.[2] But, inasmuch as God mercifully promised to the forefathers of the Hebrews that Christ should come, and at length did truly fulfil what he promised, therefore it was by a kind of true mercy that the Jews were received unto salvation through Christ, who ministered unto them salvation. Hence St. Paul calls Him *a minister of the* xv. 8. *circumcision*; that is, of circumcised Jews. And inasmuch as, though not promised to the Gentiles, He yet had mercy

---

[1] In the Vulgate, *vos*, "you;" which agrees with the best Greek text.
[2] This is explained by what follows: God's *truth* being conspicuous in the redemption of the Jews, and his *mercy* in that of the Gentiles. See also above, p. 69, note 3.

on them, he may therefore be said to have received them in a kind of merciful truth; so that, in the calling of the Jews, what is noteworthy in his mercy, is his *truth* in the promise and fulfilment; whilst in the invitation of the Gentiles we may chiefly observe God's *mercy* in truth. For it was of mere mercy that Christ offered himself to them, being in no wise promised. Since, although the prophets foretold it, God *promised* not that this should be; and Christ himself, who came, said that he was not come, save to the lost sheep of the house of Israel.

Hence St. Paul says *that Jesus Christ was a minister of the circumcision,* and ministered salvation to the circumcised, *for the truth of God, to confirm the promises made unto the fathers;* that is, that what was promised to the fathers might be seen to be true; that the Jews might adore God for the calling promised to them, *and that the Gentiles might glorify God for His mercy.* Of this mercy both David and Isaiah are witnesses. The former[1] says, *Rejoice, ye Gentiles, with his people:* the latter, *There shall be a root of Jesse, and he that shall rise to reign over the Gentiles; in him shall the Gentiles trust.*

Deut. xxxii. 43.
Is. xi. 10.

Seeing therefore that God in his truth and mercy drew unto himself both Jews and Gentiles, and embraced them as a Father; assuredly both Jews and Gentiles ought in turn to embrace one another as brethren, and link themselves together in mutual charity.

xv. 15.

There follows next in St. Paul an apology for his boldness in having written to the Romans; as to which they might perhaps have been wondering, and surmising the reason of St. Paul's having written to them, seeing he had never been among them. It was possible they might pronounce it a bold thing to do. Accordingly St. Paul gives them a reason for his act. He says that the cause was, that the evangelizing of the Gentiles had been especially committed to him; that from every place, so far as possible, he

---

[1] The quotation is really from Deuteronomy; that in the preceding verse being from the Psalms. It is somewhat curious to note that Aquinas errs in quoting the same passage; citing it (as Erasmus points out) from Isaiah xxxv.

ROMANS XV.

might by the preaching of the gospel gather together an offering for God. Among these Gentiles the Romans held the first place. And therefore, by right of his office and ambassadorship, he might teach them as well as other Gentiles. Yet he modestly declares in this passage that he is not *teaching*, but *putting them in mind*. His words are: *I have written the more boldly unto you in some sort, as putting you in mind;* the point of which is, "not teaching things unknown," but "reminding you of what is known." And this is agreeable to what he says in his first Letter—I mean, in the first part of this Epistle: *For I long to see you, that I may impart unto you some spiritual gift, to the end ye may be established.* The purport of which is : Ye are sufficiently taught, but need perhaps some brotherly reminding and confirming.

Now the Romans had received their first information and news of Christ, from Pontius Pilate himself,[1] who presided at His execution. From his despatches Tiberius Cæsar learnt what wonders He had wrought among the Jews ; and, had the senate allowed it, he would have enrolled Him among their Gods.[2] But, of the Apostles, the first who brought the tidings to Rome concerning Christ was Barnabas, as is testi-

i. 11.

---

[1] We need not do Colet the injustice to assume that he is here quoting as genuine the documents now extant under the name of *Acta Pilati.* The fact that Pilate would in due course transmit to Rome some account of the Crucifixion, is quite independent of the value of what now purports to be such an account.—See this well brought out in Bishop Pearson's *Minor Theol. Works*, i. p. 343.— Colet probably took the statement from Ivo's Chronicle (see note below), where what professes to be Pilate's letter is given. Or he might have found it at the end of *Liber Ysidori Contra Judeos*, printed at Rome about 1490.

[2] Tertull. *Lib. Apolog. c.* v.—" Tiberius ergo, cujus tempore nomen Christianum in seculum introivit, annuntiatum sibi ex Syria Palæstina, quod illic veritatem illius divinitatis revelaverat, detulit ad senatum cum prærogativa suffragii sui. Senatus, quia non ipse probaverat, respuit : Cæsar in sententia mansit, comminatus periculum accusatoribus Christianorum." See also the striking passage in *c.* xxi., " Sed et Cæsares credidissent super Christo," *etc.*; and the debate between Bishop Kaye and Mr. Woodham as to whether Tiberius, equally with Pilate, was secretly disposed to believe in Christianity.

fied by the History of Clement of Rome,[1] sent to St. James, Bishop of Jerusalem. This Clement, a follower of the teaching of Barnabas, came afterwards to St. Peter at Cæsarea, having been recommended to him by Barnabas. Then Peter, after spending eleven years in teaching in the East, came into Italy, and to Rome; and settled there for five and twenty years. This was about thirteen years before the arrival of St. Paul. And after being trained and instructed by that great Apostle, the Romans may perhaps have felt some disdain at being taught anew by St. Paul. On this account that wise Apostle, who would be thought to do nothing unadvisedly, gives a reason for writing his Epistle; saying that this office had been committed to him, and this burden laid on him by Christ, namely, that in every nation, so far as he could, he should help to increase men's faith. *I am debtor,* he says in the first part of this Epistle, *both to the Greeks and to the Barbarians; both to the wise and to the unwise. So, as much as in me is, I am ready to preach the gospel to you that are at Rome also.* And after long desiring to do this in person, but being unable, he attempted it, so far as was possible, in his absence; *that he might have some fruit among them also, even as among other Gentiles.* For *from Jerusalem, and round about unto Illyricum,* he spread the gospel of Christ; not in his own strength, but by the grace of God; not following the track of others, but taking other routes, and visiting those places where Christ was not before named; that, as Isaiah foretold, they that had not heard of him might understand.

In this extended and remote journeying through the provinces of the empire, he was not able, as he had long before

---

[1] This is related in the *Recognitions,* i. 7-11; and somewhat differently in *Homil.* i. 8 *sq.,* where it is said that the arrival of *another* Christian teacher at Rome excited Clement's interest, and caused him to make a journey to Alexandria, where he met with Barnabas.—See p. 163 of R. A. Lipsius' *Disquisitio de Clement. Rom. Epist. Priore* (1855).—Grabe (*Spicilegium,* 1700, i. 275) remarks how rich the Bodleian Library is in Clementine MSS.; but whether any connection can be traced between Dean Colet and any one of these, I have not had the means of learning.

intended, to proceed to Rome; but only after his second visit to Jerusalem, whither he was now about to go. His object in this was partly to give an account there of what he had done. For it was an established custom in the early Church, as Clement relates,[1] for every one to render up to St. James in Jerusalem an account of the management of his department. He partly went there also, to relieve the brethren, suffering and afflicted through famine, by means of the alms collected from Macedonia and Achaia. For the famine, the approach of which had been foretold by Agabus at Antioch, was then raging in all its severity. Moreover the Christians in Jerusalem, being hated by all, and shut out by the Jews from all supplies, were sore pressed by the extremity of want. To assist them, in the way appointed him by the Apostles, was St. Paul's object. And since, during his preaching in Greece and Macedonia, he had stirred up great liberality on men's part, he wished to bring in person to Jerusalem, as a common offertory, whatever had been so collected. This done, he purposed to journey through Italy into Spain. But whether he ever went thither or not, I am not aware. Ivo, Bishop of Chartres, a man of considerable learning, asserts in his *Chronicle*[2] that St. Paul did journey into Spain;

---

[1] Dicebat enim [Petrus] mandatum se accepisse abs te [Jacobo], ut per singulos annos, si qua essent a se dicta gestaque, ad te transcripta transmitteret." *Recognit.* i. 17, quoted by Grabe (*Spic.* i. 282), who remarks that the writer evidently took the hint for such a statement from *Acts* xxi. 18, 19.

[2] This will be found in the *Corpus Francicæ Historiæ*, Hanoviæ, 1693. In all the printed editions of Ivo's works that I have seen, the only *Chronicon* given is the short one (occupying but two or three pages) of the Frankish kings. The reason is, that the large Chronicle, extending from Ninus to St. Louis, of which the middle portion only is printed in the Historical Collections above mentioned, has been proved to be the work of Hugo Floriacensis, and not, as used to be supposed, of the Bishop of Chartres.—See Ivonis .... *Opera omnia*, Paris, 1647, p. 305.—The mistake arose from Hugo's custom of sending his compositions to Ivo, and other learned men, for their revisal. In Lambeth Library are two manuscript *Excerpta Ivonis Chronica* (Todd's Catal., Nos. 355 and 440), which might have been used by Colet.

The passage quoted in the text is at p. 28 of the *Corpus Franc.*

leaving Trophimus at Arles in France, and Crescens at Vienne, to preach in those regions the divinity of Christ. It is certain that from the second year of Nero's reign,[1] before he had come to Rome, he survived for twelve years longer, and that he set out towards the West. But how far he proceeded I am unable to affirm on any good authority; unless we listen to what St. John Chrysostom writes in his book *De Laudibus Pauli*, in the last Homily,[2] wherein he relates that he journeyed into Spain.

After saying, then, that Macedonia and Achaia had shown real and effectual liberality in succouring the poor, St. Paul then adds: *It hath pleased them verily; and their debtors they are*—bound *to minister unto them carnal things* (such, that is, as are necessary for subsistence) in return for their *spiritual things*. But we must observe his expression, *it pleased them*. He uses it to show that *debts* may be exacted; while at the same time it *pleases* men to pay and discharge them;—such debts, that is to say, as consist in alms to be applied for the food and clothing of spiritual persons, and which may be received, so far as it pleases the givers to bestow them. For although men are bound to support the spirituality, yet we are bound also not to exact more from them than they are pleased to give. Since it were better for them not to give, than to give unwillingly; because whatever is not voluntary in the Church is full of mischief. Therefore men are to be admonished, not so much to give, as to give willingly. A ready will must be elicited by kindly teaching; not money extorted, under the name of tithes and oblations, by harsh exaction. For it was not tithes and oblations that St. Paul demanded, but men's voluntary liberality alone; and this only for relieving the necessity of the poor. *Having food and raiment*, he writes to Timothy, *let us be therewith content. The love of money is the root of all evil*. And so he admonished Timothy to flee that hankering

---

Hist.—"Inde quoque postmodum Dei providentia relaxatus Hispaniam adiit. Et Arelatæ Trophimum, Viennæ vero Crescentem, discipulos suos, Gentibus ad prædicandum reliquit."

[1] See note above, p. 95.
[2] *Edit. Savil.* (1612), vol. viii. p. 59.

after things which we call covetousness, and to *follow after righteousness, godliness, faith, love, patience, meekness.* 1 Tim. vi. 11.

In like manner in this our generation must priests be admonished to follow the same things, and by their own example infuse these qualities into their parishioners also; and make them righteous, godly, meek, faithful, patient, charitable, by the pattern held out in themselves; and then will the liberality they demand follow readily, aye even more abundantly than they desire, if they themselves covet not more than they ought. If you have taught men to imitate what is good, not by words alone, but by your life as well, then it is quite certain that, even though you say not a word, there will be as much bestowed as is necessary for your livelihood;—and why we are to exact more than this, in accordance with the doctrine of Christ, I for my part do not see. Even St. Paul himself would not receive anything from willing offerers, but rather laboured with his hands, earning a subsistence by his occupation of a tentmaker, that he might neither raise any suspicion of covetousness, nor put any stumbling-block in the way of the gospel. For others, however, especially the brethren in Jerusalem, he did exact what was needful for subsistence, so far as men were willing to give of their own accord; teaching them that they were bound to supply bodily necessaries for those, from whom they had received what was necessary for the welfare of the soul.

He then asks the Romans to pray to God for him, as he was now about to go to Jerusalem, into the midst of enemies of the name of Christ; that he might have a journey safe from foes, and welcome to the brethren. And this was a matter that needed to be prayed for, since this last journey of his to Jerusalem proved by no means a safe one for St. Paul. For as soon as he was received there, he was harassed in a thousand ways by the unbelieving Jews, as the prophet Agabus had foretold. But that great-hearted man, great in faith and the love of Christ, *was ready not to be bound only, but also to die at Jerusalem for the name of the Lord Jesus.* And when he was come to Jerusalem, after being received and welcomed by the brethren, he reported to St. James and the Christian council there all that he had done in spreading

Rom. xv. 30.

Acts xxi. 13.

K

Acts xxi. 26.   Christianity, in due order. By them he was bidden to purify himself in the temple for seven days, after the manner and custom of the Jews, shaving his head and making offerings. Thereupon it was brought as a charge against him, that he persuaded the Jews not to circumcise their children; meaning that since the coming of Christ circumcision was of no account:—though in fact circumcision continued among the Jews in Jerusalem side by side with Christianity, as regarded their own race. He was then seized by the unbelieving Jews and dragged out of the temple to be murdered. Nor would he have escaped this fate, had not Claudius Lysias, the chief captain of the band, rescued him from the hands of the Jews; protecting him with difficulty against their lying in wait and their attacks. It was in prison that St. Paul then heard from

Acts xxiii. 11.   the Lord the words : *Be of good cheer, Paul; for as thou hast testified of me in Jerusalem, so must thou bear witness also at Rome.*

By the chief captain St. Paul was sent to Felix, at that time the governor of Syria and Judea; and in his keeping he remained two years at Cæsarea. He was then left to Porcius Festus, who succeeded Felix during the reign of Nero. By him he was sent to Rome, after defending himself before King Agrippa, and came there as a prisoner, and spent two years there in " free custody."[1] He survived ten years after that; and it was at this time that he is thought to have gone into Spain, as related by St. John Chrysostom in his book *De Laudibus Pauli*, and after him by Ivo, Bishop of Chartres.[2] If this were so, then he returned again to Rome in the thirty-sixth year after the death of Christ, and thirteenth of Nero's reign, and was at length put to death in the first persecution of the Christians.[3] Now he appears to have written this Epistle to the Romans four years before his coming to Rome, and in the twentieth of his own ministry. For in the collection of alms from Macedonia and Greece, and

---

[1] That is, not in a common prison, but placed in charge of some private person, who was held responsible for his safe keeping.—See, for an example, Sallust's *Catil.* c. 48.

[2] See note above, p. 127.

[3] For the chronology here followed, see note above, p. 95.

in travelling to Jerusalem and encountering the Jews, and finally in the journey to Rome, four years appear to have passed away.

And so at last he came to Rome, to the brethren there most welcome; to whom he was not afraid to write before, bidden as he was by every means to increase the faith of Christ.

CHAPTER XVI.

THERE are finally in this Epistle commendations of friends, both men and women, and greetings of the most loving kind, that spring from the great charity of St. Paul.

Phebe (a woman) appears to have gone with this Epistle to Rome. The rest, whom he wishes greeting to, whose acquaintance he made in other places, either lived at Rome, or had business there. Aquila, a Jew, with his wife Prisca (whom St. Luke in the Acts of the Apostles calls Priscilla), came to Corinth when all the Jews emigrated from Rome upon the edict of the emperor Claudius, and entertained St. Paul as his guest when he came to Corinth from Athens. Andronicus and Julia he calls *of note among the apostles;* xvi. 7. whence it appears that all who were sent to preach the Gospel were called by right apostles.[1] The others whom the Apostle next salutes we may gather to have been distinguished either by their virtue or their works; and St. Paul would encourage them in their virtuous course by his mention and praise. For even if men are running the race of virtue, they are stimulated by the notice and praise of divine men.

He next bids them *salute one another with an holy kiss,* and xvi. 16. stand firm in loving embrace, and be on their guard against false men and seducers. For such were sowers of discord and causers of offence; by cozening speeches beguiling the simple; seeking their own gain and not the gain of Christ;

---

[1] Hence we see that Colet understood the expression *of note among,* &c., to mean, not "respected by the Apostles," but themselves distinguished Apostles.

serving not God but their belly. Afterwards he admonishes them to be *wise unto that which is good, and simple concerning evil;* with knowledge to think and act well, not ill. For the knowledge of this, namely, how to act ill, is ignorance.

xvi. 19.

Last of all, he wishes them grace; the efficient cause, author, and preserver of all the good that either is or can be among men. By virtue of which grace I have said whatever I have well said, in writing upon this Epistle. And I pray the reader to take it in good part, and to mean well by me, whose wish it has been to mean well by St. Paul; and whose endeavour it has been, so far as by the help of divine grace I could, to express his true meaning. How I have done this I confess I do not know. But the best will to do it I have had.

The End of the Exposition on St. Paul's Epistle to the Romans.

Oxford.

IOANNIS COLETI A.M.
ENARRATIO IN EPISTOLAM B. PAULI AD ROMANOS.

EPITOME.

IN Epistola quam apostolus Paulus scripsit ad Romanos, hominibus illic Christiani nominis pacem suadet et concordiam.

Nam in illis tres erant contentiones. Una judeorum cum gentibus; secunda Christianorum cum paganis; tercia in ipsa Christianitate fortiorum in fide cum infirmioribus. Gentes enim et Judei mutuo se accusabant, et vicissim alter alteri se preferebat arrogantius. Verum insolentia Judeorum erat et major et superbior; qui magni se existimabant ob legem eis datam a deo.

Quamobrem Paulus se ponens medium, ut tantam litem dirimat, quanquam plurima afferat que premant gentium superbiam, tamen in Judeos se vertit maxime, confertque in illam partem sermonem suum et copiosiorem et acriorem. Erat enim Judeus durioris cervicis, jugo humilitatis semper reluctantis. Utrumque et Judeum et gentilem conatur Paulus trahere altius supra omnem gentilitatem et Judaismum, ac locare ambos et figere in uno Christo Jesu; qui unus sufficit, qui est omnia, in quo solo salus est hominum et justificatio. Ex quibus (Judeo scilicet et gentili) pariter quum constituerit ecclesiam, tum describit quenam illa Christianorum ecclesia sit; et quibus officiis et actionibus.

Christiani autem Romæ quomodo se gerant erga paganos, in quorum medio tunc erant, et vivebant sub potestate illorum, videlicet quatenus eos ferant injuriantes, et quousque tributum pendant exactum, multa erat multorum altercacio. Paulus ergo in hac parte prudenter docet pacem et obedienciam.

In tercio dissidio et contentione quæ erat in ecclesia

Christianorum, fortiorum in fide cum infirmioribus, ubi infirma conscientia timiduli dedignati sunt audaciam fortiorum, audaces vero freti opinione conscienciæ suæ infirmos despexerunt :—Discordia autem erat in escarum degustacione, quousque liceat progredi in ciborum generibus. Judeorum ritu vetita erant multa. Idolotita quidem, id est, immolata idolis, quamplurimi exhorruerunt. Fuerunt tamen qui quod arbitrati sunt sibi licuisse in hac re fecerunt audacter, degustaveruntque passim quod libuerit eis ; homines parum prudentes, parum considerati ; cum magno scandalo et offensione infirmorum. Hic ergo Paulus tradit piam rationem infirmorum habendam, et audaci facto, etiam in eo quod liceat, non esse percellendam mentem imbecillioris et constantiam, vitandum scandalum, querendam edificationem, pacem servandam compositis litibus ; in quarum prima suadet humilitatem, in secunda pacientiam, in tercia charitatem.

Postquam reddiderit rationem scriptarum litterarum, et promiserit se venturum aliquando ad Romanos, concludit tandem epistolam cum commendationibus et salutationibus.

CAP. I.

PRIMUM salutat Paulus Romanam ecclesiam. In qua salutacione per gratiam se assumptum esse dicit in apostolatum, ut nomine Jesu Christi proficiscatur legatus ad omnes gentes, tum Judeorum, tum aliorum quorumcunque.; ut eis denunciet ut obediant fidei, credantque Deo, in hoc scilicet quod Deus dispensavit modo et egit de filio suo pro hominum sanctificacione et salute. Qui filius Dei, deus et homo, secundum carnem traxit originem ab Abraam ; secundum vero spiritum sanctificacionis, quo homines sanctificat, præcestinatus et ostensus est in terris præpotens filius Dei, resussitans mortuos a peccatis sua ipsius resurrectione.

In quibus resuscitatis et retractis a peccatis, dicit eos quoque esse ad quos scribit Romæ, ut Jesu Christi sint nunc deinceps, et ad eum solum pertineant. Quapropter

eis gratiam optat et pacem concordiamque *a Deo Patre et*   i. 7.
Domino Jesu Christo.
Deinde gaudet de fide devulgata Romanorum, optatque
visere eos, ut fidem eciam cum eis communicet et doceat.
Non enim *se pudere evangelii* dicit, quæ virtus est credenti-   i. 16.
bus, et revelacio justificationis hominum per fidem ; siquidem in evangelio fides docetur. *Justus enim ex fide vivit* et   i. 17.
vero Dei cultu. Quod si vel gentes vel Judei Deum
negligentes idola coluerint, uti certe coluerunt, ii profecto
impii hoc facto et detestabiles fuerunt, et tales qui nequiverint se excusare, quandoquidem Deum in suis creaturis plane
agnoscere potuerunt. Qua propter deserti omnes ejusmodi
gentes Judeive, et relicti omnino a Deo, in ignoranciam et
improbam voluntatem, et in omne denique scelus, misere
corruerunt.

CAP. II.

UNDE concludit Paulus, neminem eorum, Judeorum
genciumve, alium accusare debere ; sed quemque proprium suum peccatum agnoscere, et properare ut se suæ
impietatis peniteat, nec abuti paciencia Dei, qui pro sua
clemencia tam diu distulit justam ultionem, ut interea
homines resipiscant. Qui etiam pro sua equitate et justicia
reddet unicuique secundum opera sua ; bonis et veritatem   ii. 6.
sectantibus, vitam eternam ; malis autem et adherentibus
falsitati, perpetuam mortem, sive hii Judei, sive gentes sint.
Quoniam non est selector Deus, et acceptator personarum,
nec (uti putaverunt Judei) habet eos, ob legem eis datam
peculiarem, sibi quam reliquos gentium multo graciores.
Sed in quaque gente ipsa eorum facta et spectat et laudat.
Quod si gentes sine data lege recte vixerint, eis non habere
legem non nocuit. Item Judei quoque si sub lege male,
ipsis tum habere legem nihil profuit. Res et laus hominis
tota est posita in actione ; quam bonam et justam qui exer-
cuerit, eciam si nullam habuerit sibi legem datam, is tamen
a Deo censetur recte secundum legem vixisse.

Verum in hoc loco animadvertendum est, Paulum non significare gentes, ullumve gencium sine lege recte vixisse, quum ejus est proculdubio sentencia neminem nisi ex fide Christi recte vivere, et justum esse posse. Sed ut infringat illam vanam spem, quam Judei in mosaica lege habuerunt, secundum id quod præ se fert in cortice, non secundum quod intus et in medulla continet, utque ostendat bonam hominis vitam, ex sancta mente profectam, id esse solam quod Deo placet, asserit eciam gentes quæ sine lege data fuerint, si modo recte vixissent, tam Deo gratas et acceptas fuisse quam Judeos ; quibus fuit data lex ut ad virtutem præparentur, circumcisionemque animi et mentis purificacionem præ se ferrent; in qua sola consistit hominis justificatio. Quod ignorantes Judei nichil gentibus præstiterunt, quatenus scilicet ad justificacionem attinet.

CAP. III.

SI vero quid prestiterint, hoc fuit solum quod eloquia et archana Dei oracula eis credita et commissa habuerunt. Quæ etsi non omnes intellexerint, tamen eorum stulticia sapienciam Dei non fefellit. Novit enim ille quid dederit et quamobrem, et quid esset tandem eventurum ; et Judeorum insipienciam improbitatemque despexit et providit. Quorum tamen stulticia, error et iniquitas non ideo accidit quidem, ut Deus sapiens et verus et justus videatur ; quod homines facile arbitrantur, quum audiunt Dei scienciam falli non posse, idque evenire tandem certo quod Deus futurum esse prospexit. Quare Paulus id ipse sibi objiciens, inquit

iii. v. *secundum hominem dico.* Verum quia homines peccant, non idcirco putandus est Deus verus, neque vero quia vere cernit, existimandi sunt homines peccare. Sed quodque ex sua propria causa procedit; peccatum ab ipsis hominibus, præsciencia Dei ab ipso Deo ; quæ una concurrentes ita simul comeant, ut quod committat homo, id necessario præsciatur, quodque eciam præscitur fore in peccatis, id committatur necessario ; tamen nec sit præscientia et veritas

Dei causa cur peccetur, nec peccatum, tametsi præscitum, causa sit ullo modo cur præsciencia Dei vera esse videatur. Hinc Paulus infert, *Alioquin quomodo judicabit Deus hunc mundum*, si vel falsitas hominis Deum verum, vel veritas Dei hominem falsum efficeret? Tunc enim esset locus dicendi, *Faciamus mala, ut veniant nobis bona;* quorum damnacionem dicit apostolus justam esse. Sed Deus judicabit hunc mundum justeque dampnabit impios. Quo fit ut neque veritas divinæ scienciæ sit causa peccati, neque peccatum sit causa cur Deus vere scisse videatur. iii. 6.

iii. 8.

Itaque Judei non intelligentes divinos sermones, atque ob id causæ non credentes, Dei propositum non frustraverunt, neque vero eo quod non crediderunt Dei præscienciam veram effecerint. Sed ipsi ex se ipsis falsi et peccatores agniti sunt, pariter se habentes cum ceteris gentibus, tum ad justam dampnacionem, tum ad salvacionem graciosam. Quia, ut cecinit David, *Non est qui facit bonum, non est usque ad unum.* Et, ut Paulus ait, ad graciam non est distinctio gencium. Judei igitur non habent quod confidant in observacione legum, more et ritu eorum, quæ non tollunt sed judicant peccatum. Ritus enim ille et ceremoniæ non purificant animam, nec hominem justificant. Neque vero imperata et vetita servari poterant sine gracia.

Ps. xiii. 3; Rom. iii. 22.

Quamobrem docet Paulus hoc unum restare quo homines justificentur, ut confidant Deo, agnoscantque Dei dispensacionem et graciam quæ opportuno tempore oblata est universis per filium suum Jesum Christum, cujus morte et interitu redempcio est hominum a potestate diaboli, et Deo reconsiliacio. Hoc salutare misterium qui agnoscit et credit et colit, ex quocunque sit hominum genere, eum censet Paulus salvum fore, atque ut salvus sit, eundem hoc firmiter credere oportere. Itaque coequans Judeos gentibus, atque impietate et sceleribus utrumque populum parem ostendens, omnia contrahit apostolus ad unam fidem in Christo Jesu, quo Judeorum legem significat spectavisse.

CAP. IV.

NAM circumcisio Abraæ, amputacioque illius pelliculæ quæ glans dicitur, quidnam sibi voluit aliud quam omnis diffidenciæ amputacionem a mente, ut nuda hominis et integra fides Deo appareat? Quæ fuit in Habraam ad magnam ejus laudem et justificacionem, antequam preputii circumcisio fuit adhibita, que circumcisam mentem et sine omni diffidencia Deo credentem significat. Quæ fuit in Abraam tanta, ut vel visa impossibilia hominibus, modo Deus promiserit, ea fore confisus est indubitanter, et ventura expectavit. Unde et apud Deum habitus est justus, et mundi heres cum suo semine destinatus, id est, semine et progenie fideli: quæ fidelibus promissa hereditas magnam Abraæ fidem et quasi vultum mentis illius representat; ut ex imitacione fidelitatis proles ejus existimetur. Cujus certe est hereditas et mundus, id est, Deus ipse, qui verus est mundus. Qui ex sua gracia se impartit credentibus sibi et confidentibus, quos idem ipse exemit et abstraxit ab infidelitate ad fidem, ut ei soli confidant, credantque plane nulla se alia racione nisi divina gracia justificari posse. Quoniam lex, in qua speraverunt Judei, peccatum indicat, terminos præscribit, transgressoribus minitatur; non tollit quidem delictum, non trahit hominem ab augustiis, non graciose fovet et sustinet. Quod quidem divina gracia et fortiter et suaviter facit, ut soli Deo possit confidere. Quæ gracia attigit et attraxit et justificavit Abraam, promisitque illi quamplurimos, et ad numerum eciam stellarum, pariter ac similiter homines justificatos fore, qui ejus filii censerentur, partim (ut modo dixi) ex quadam representacione, partim et maxime quod parens et secundus propagator fidei, Jhesus Cristus, secundum carnem originem esset tracturus. Qui fuit filius et semen promissum; ad cujus propaginem divina promissa Abraæ spectant.

Propago autem et quasi proles Christi fidelitas est multitudoque fidelium, undecunque ex quibusque quumque sunt vocati a Deo; qui, ut ait Paulus, *vocat ea quæ non sunt*

iv. 17.

tanquam ea quæ sunt. Quam dispensacionem ignorantes Judei, quorsum sua lex tendit non intellexerunt, sed humilibus operis a lege discriptis adherentes, quasi operarii mercedem felicitatis poposcerunt; non animadvertentes testimonium justiciæ Abraæ fuisse ante operas et ritus legis institutos, ut doceatur plane justificacionem non esse operancium sub lege, sed fidem Abraæ imitancium ; qui facile Deo et divinæ dispensacioni adhibent fidem, sicuti Abraam ille quondam adhibuit: tametsi quæ promisit Deus longe humanam racionem transgressa sunt.

Ita eciam in hoc quoque tempore qui confidit Deo, et credit illum tum posse, tum voluisse, tum egisse cum suo filio quod egit ; videlicet quia incarnatus, mortuus, resuscitatus erat, pro humani generis redempcione et reconciliacione Deo ; qui, inquam, illud ineffabile misterium et sacramentum credit firmiter et jugiter colit, eo solo habet satis quo justificetur, salvusque fiat.

CAP. V.

QUAPROPTER concludit Paulus justificatos ex fide et soli Deo confidentes, per Jesum reconciliatos esse Deo, restitutosque ad graciam, ut apud Deum stent, et maneant ipsi filii Dei, et filiorum Dei certam gloriam expectent, pro qua adipiscenda interim ferenda sunt omnia pacienter, ut firmitas spei declaretur ; quæ quidem non falletur. Siquidem ex Dei amore et gracia erga nos ingenti reconciliati sumus. Alioquin ejus filius pro nobis eciam impiis et contrariis Deo non interiisset. Quod si alienatos a se dilexit, quanto magis reconciliatos et diligit et dilectos conservabit? Quamobrem firma et stabili spe ac leticia esse debemus, confidereque Deo indubitanter per Jesum Cristum, per quem unum hominum est ad Deum reconciliatio. Nam ab illo ipso primo homine, et diffidencia, impietateque et scelere ejusdem, totum humanum genus disperiit, sic ut neque lege naturæ, neque vero lege mosayca ad vitam potuit restitui.

Quod si ea vis fuit in peccato, et unius hominis peccato,

ad interimendum, multo tum major sit vis oportet et potencia in gracia, in vivificandos homines, et in eosdem ad integram et stabilem salutem restaurandos. Quod vel ex eo licet cernere, videlicet, quod quicquid ex uno peccato crevit ad interitum (crevit autem peccatum multiplex et infinitum), id totum quum consummatum fuit, et quasi vigor morbi efferbuit, simul tum omnipotens gracia sua prepotenti et mirifica vi discussit, et omne peccatum delevit. Fuit enim potencius consummatum malum tollere quam inchoare. Ita fit ut Dei amore et gracia apprehensi et tracti ad Deum, si sperant, forcius et firmius sustinebuntur conservabunturque ad vitam ab ipsa prepotenti gracia, quam a peccato detrusi et depressi ad mortem fuerint; tametsi peccatum quiddam violens et impetuosum est. Verum magnificæ potestati dulcis et suavis graciæ, quæ molliter mirabiliterque, et vi quadam latenti ac mirifica agit, nihil potest resistere. Quapropter credendum est longe plus posse in mundo graciam reconciliantem Deo, quam peccatum a Deo alienans. Quo fit ut multo plus possit justicia et obediencia Christi ad revocandos homines, qui revocandi sunt, Deo, quam peccatum et inobediencia Adæ ad eosdem a Deo avocandos. Nam proculdubio vivificacior est virtus multo quam peccatum est mortificans, et auctor virtutis longe potencior est quam peccati causa. Verumtamen tantum valuit, ut a lege naturali mosaycave vinci non potuit. Immo potius hiis legibus peccatum exauxius factum ad majorem hominis perniciem operatum est. Siquidem exorta luce primum naturalis et deinde mosaicæ legis, transgressiones antea non deprehensæ nec notatæ, tunc manifestissime apparuerunt, hominesque agnoscentes suam miseriam et errores, et ex seipsis ut ad viam redeant impotentes, quodammodo scienter peccavere.

v. 20. Quare ait Paulus, *lex intravit ut abundaret peccatum*: hoc est, post introductam legem, ab hominibus multo gravius peccatum fuit, non lege quidem id efficiente, sed hominibus ipsis, pro sua eorum imbecillitate sine gracia, aliter non potentibus facere quam peccare. Itaque aucto aggravatoque peccato, fuit necesse ad hominum curacionem, ut salutaris gracia tunc multo plus aucta habundaret; ut ea justificati homines ad vitam eternam per Jesum possent pervenire.

EP. AD ROMANOS V.

Sed hic notandum est, quod hæc gracia nichil est aliud quam Dei amor erga homines; eos videlicet quos vult amare, amandoque inspirare spiritu suo sancto; qui ipse est amor et Dei amor; *qui* (ut apud Ioannem evangelistam ait salvator) *ubi vult spirat*. Amati autem et inspirati a Deo vocati sunt; ut accepto amore amantem Deum redament, et eundem amore desiderent et exspectent. Hæc expectacio et spes ex amore est. Amor vero noster est quia ille nos amat; *non* (ut scribit Ioannes in secunda epistola) *quasi nos prius dilexerimus Deum, sed quia ipse prior dilexit nos*, eciam nullo amore dignos, siquidem impios et iniquos, jure ad sempiternum interitum destinatos. Sed quosdam quos ille novit et voluit, Deus dilexit, diligendo vocavit, vocando justificavit, justificando magnificavit. Ioan. iii. 8.

1 Ioan. iv. 10.

Hæc in Deo graciosa dileccio et caritas erga homines ipsa vocacio et justificacio et magnificacio est; nec quicquid aliud tot verbis dicimus, quam unum quiddam; scilicet amorem Dei erga homines eos quos vult amare. Item cum homines gracia attractos, vocatos, justificatos, et magnificatos dicimus, nichil significamus aliud quam homines amantem Deum redamare. In quo amore et redamore consistit hominis justificacio. Hæc redamacio in nobis est cum spe, et debet esse firma, quæ non falletur. Quia amamur a Deo, ut eum speremus redamantes. *Quia* (ut sunt verba Pauli) *caritas* et amor *Dei diffusa est in cordibus nostris;* id est, quia amamur, Deum redamamus per spiritum sanctum, qui datus est nobis; id est, per amorem acceptum, qui impertitur nobis ex divino amore, hoc amore accepto amamus Deum, Deo confidimus, Deum speramus. A quo amore, quæ nostri est justificacio, valde nos admonet ne avocemur, quum suadet ferenda esse omnia adversa et vexancia, in eisque letandum, ut aureus noster erga Deum amor comprobetur, ostendaturque fides et spes firma, quam amor gratiaque Dei non fallet, quum eam amor gratiaque Dei in homine excitavit. v. 5.

Sed redeamus ad Paulum; a quo tamen hiis verbis non multum discessimus.

CAP. VI.

QUI deinde in hac epistola argute docet, non rursus peccandum esse iis qui sunt a peccatis gracia liberati. Quod fortasse calumpniose dicent aliqui, occasionem capientes ex illis verbis Pauli, quæ loquens modo de infirmitate legis, et meremento peccati addidit dicens: *Ubi autem habundavit delictum, superhabundavit gracia.* Ne inquam ex eo loco cavillarentur ac dicerent, *Maneamus in peccato ut gracia habundet,* occurrit apostolus, subtiliter arguens et demonstrans homines amore graciaque Dei solutos a peccati vinculis, nichil habere amplius unquam quod cum peccatis agant; qui, quatenus ad peccatum attinet, prorsus interierunt, ut secundum eam vivendi rationem nichil omnino deinceps appareant. Qui quidem sunt quasi *complantati* et mortui et *sepulti* cum Christo, ut resurgant, renascantur et reviviscant cum eodem Christo; qui mori voluit pro hominibus salvandis, ut ipsi simul reputent se interiisse.

Mori autem voluit, ut ejus magnifica morte deleantur hominum delicta, pro quibus homines ipsi interiissent; utque deposita persona peccatrice ac solita consuetudine peccandi omnino abolita, homines ii qui vocati sunt, quales fuerunt deinceps non appareant, sed sint quasi simul mortui cum Christo; qui quodammodo crucifixerunt veterem hominem pristinamque illam vitam peccabundam, ut perinde omnino ac mortui et sepulti postea in peccatis personaque peccatrice nusquam extent nec agnoscantur; sed in novam condicionem et statum renovati, et cum Cristo resurgente in novam vitam exorti, exhibeant se semper et perpetuo novos, longe a pristino eorum statu differentes; ne, cum eo si quid commercii habere voluerint, cum Christo non mortui fuisse nec cum eodem resurrexisse videantur. Quod si quasi ex mortuis moribundaque vita surrexerint in vitam vivificantem, in ea sane eis sollicite standum est et permanendum; ne, si rursus peccatum fuerit, salutaris mors, qua aboleantur peccata, una altera non reperiatur. Siquidem Christus iterum non morietur, *nec mors illi ultra dominabitur.* Semel mortuus fuit pro peccatis, ut iis qui sequuntur Christum peccata intereant. Quod si reviviscant, ubinam erit mors qua tollantur? cum Christus non iterum morietur.

Hoc loco videtur Paulus subsignificare, sola morte Christi peccata hominum oblitterari posse, et qui deposuerunt peccata, si iterum ad eadem relabantur, talibus hominibus spem curacionis non esse; quandoquidem medicina peccatum tollens, mors Christi, non iterabitur. Sed caute circumspicienda sunt omnia Pauli, antequam de ejus mente aliqua feratur sententia. Nunquam enim censuisset revocandum ad ecclesiam fornicatorem illum, quem tradidit Sathanæ in prima epistola ad Corinthios, si peccatoribus post baptismum nullum penitendi locum reliquisset. Quamobrem existimandum est hic apostolum severius locutum fuisse, et adduxisse Christum non iterum moriundum, quo magis detineret eos a peccatis ad quos scribit, inducta quadam suspicione incurabilis morbi, si rursus peccarent, quo magis caveant ne peccent. Quia ut morbus non parit medicinam, sed eam habet ei adhibitam pro medici voluntate, ita peccatum non parit nec provocat graciam, sed semel pro voluntate Dei, ad peccati morbum curandum, data fuit medicinalis gracia in morte Christi.

Qua semel peracta ad interimendum peccatum, non est committendum iis qui secuti Christum peccatum in se necaverint, ut peccatum quasi a mortuis revocent, ut rursus sit necesse deletrix peccati mors Christi adhibeatur. Sed studiosissime agendum est, quum modo emerserint ex peccatis in virtutem, ex morte in vitam, ut virtute et justicia viventes peragant, ut eternam vitam assequi possint, stentque in gracia et amore Dei, quo sunt apprehensi; ne, si a Deo recidant, periculum sit vel maximum eos in amorem illius et graciam redire non posse. Quum negligentes ejus amorem verisimile est Deum tales tardius iterum amaturum. At redamare nisi amatus non potes; hoc est, sequi nisi vocatus, et ascendere nisi tractus. Quod si amantem Deum sepius neglexeris, profecto est tum timendum, ne ejus amore omnino destitutus, spe omni sublata, in perpetuum pereas, easque miser in mortem infinitam, quo tendit peccatum et negligentia Dei. Quamobrem gracia attractis, et ab amanto

1 Cor. v. 5.

Deo excitatis ut redament, in assidua redamacione permanendum est, ut sine intermissione a Deo amante amentur, quo divino amore graciaque salvi fiant, vivantque sine fine feliciter. Nam, ut ait Paulus, *gratia Dei est vita eterna;* quæ est prepotens ut sustineat te et salvet, si ei confidas. Quod ne lex quidem potuit; quæ magis ostendit morbum et irritavit, quam sustulit. Quare omnibus aliis rebus et medicinis posthabitis, homini qui sanus et salvus esse velit, in sola gracia amoreque Dei est conquiescendum.

Verum quia Judei ita tenaciter adheserunt legi mosaicæ, ut nulla fere racione ab ea develli potuerunt, iccirco Paulus prius hæc aliqua affert, ut solvat eis funem, utque inducat in mentes eorum nichil esse nunc periculi, si quasi a tergo relinquant legem omnino. Immo eciam id necessario faciendum esse, si ejus status volunt esse, quem nunc novum sub Cristo et gracia profitentur.

In qua re, ut Apostoli sermo melius intelligatur, est animadvertendum, quum homo constet ex anima, quam Paulus vocat interiorem hominem, et corpore senciente, quod hominis animal (uti Plotinus vocat) potest appellari, a privaricacione Adæ, qui volens inservire blandis sensibus a Deo se desciverit, animal hoc hominis in universo humano genere, præterquam in admodum paucis, quos Deus ad se ab illa miseria raptavit, in hominis statu, et (ut ita dicam) in humana republica, imperium tenuisse, ac sua stulticia et libidine omnia in homine gubernasse, detrusisseque omnia deorsum ad infelicitatem.

A cujus violencia et tirannide, anima homunculusque ille interior, propter infelicem illam ruinam Adæ invalidus et impotens, nullis conatibus se per se solvere et liberare potuit. Potuit quidem admoneri et excitari in nonnullam cognicionem miseriæ suæ et servitutis, ac deinde excitata parumper velle aliquantulum admonitorem sequi; verum id in re præstare, et bonis admonicionibus ac præceptis obsequi, non est passa animæ infirmitas.

Admonuit autem animam, et ei bene ac salutariter præcepit lex mosaica, bona sane et sancta, et, ut eciam vocat Paulus, spiritalis, quia aliquousque ad spiritum revocat. Spiritum eciam futurum denunciat. Sed hæc lex admonens, dumtaxat admonuit; et admonendo ac præscribendo terminos transgressiones indicavit. Vires autem, quo quispiam se a transcursu et deliracione contineret, nullas dedit. Itaque factum fuit ut per legem illaque bona præcepta pocius plus et gravius peccaretur, quam nichil peccaretur. Quandoquidem indicancia et ostendencia exorbitaciones, hominibus peccantibus et animadversionem delicti et scienciam attulerunt; ut, considerata hominis imbecilitate ac impotencia obediendi legibus, eis melius fuisset, si lex ipsis nunquam data fuisset.

Ut enim egrotis, quos diu perniciosus morbus infirmavit, quorumque vita desperata est, non expedit adhibere medicinam morbum propellentem, sed multo magis nocet, tametsi probatissima, quia eam ex imbecilitate eorum ferre non possunt; ita quoque Judeis non profuit Judaica lex; non quia ipsa non bona fuit, sed quia Judei mali fuerunt, et ob diuturnum morbum inobedienciæ inepti ut bonis preceptis obtemperarent. Et ut in egrotis, quos longus morbus omnes prope corporis vires exhauserit, si ulla sit spes salutis, oportet ea sola sit in dandis et augendis viribus, ut roborata natura a morbi vinculis exeat, ita Judeis, deprehensa eorum imbecillitate per leges, per quas excitati se sanare et justos facere non poterant (ita enim ab Adam deinceps magis atque magis invaluit morbus, et lues ac feda contagio mali ita alte pervasit, ut humanis viribus nulla potuit esse curacio) ; in ea, inquam, tanta infirmitate, Judeis ea fuit sola reliqua spes, ut per graciam vires eorum augerentur, auctæque et roboratæ a malis evolarent, hominemque illum interiorem a mala et servili condicione in libertatem et bonitatem raperent. Ac denique præterea, ut neque medicus ille, qui bonam et congruentem adhibuit medicinam,† non † est accusandus, nec existimandus imprudens, quanquam sua medicina non sanaverit, nec medicina contemnenda, quanquam sanitatem non restituit, homine ex se existente insanabili, sed potius et laudandus est medicus et probanda medicina, quæ magnitudinem morbi et periculum indicavit, ut ea admonitus homo ad periciorem medicum confugiat; sic eodem modo certe nec Deus nec lex mosaica incusanda est, quanquam ea homo non recuperavit pristinam bonitatem et justiciam; sed agendæ sunt graciæ Deo et legi, quod per eam admoniti fuerint homines ut ad efficaciorem medicinam et ad Deum ipsum confugiant, illiusque graciam, per quam tandem liberati et ad sanitatem restituti in ipsa sola salutari gracia conquiescant; de lege autem, quæ spectavit ad personam peccatricem, modo ea est per graciam deposita, non plus cogitent, nec ad se eam plus pertinere putent, quam putat ille egrotus quisquis sit, qui modo mirabili arte restitutus ad sanitatem, ad se pertinere illam medicinam, quam pro sua ipsius imbecilitate impotentem sibi et inefficacem expertus est esse. Solutus enim ab ea condicione propter quam excogitata fuit medicina, non habet preterea quod cum medicina agat, quum alia via et racione quod voluit medicina assecutus est.

Ita similiter Judei justificati tandem per admirabilem Dei et mirificam graciam, qui per legem justificari non poterant, causam habent nunc nullam cur pendeant ex lege. Immo vero cur non pendeant ex lege, curque eam omnino negligant, eis est causa vel maxima, quum ea nunc sint condicione per graciam ut minime lege egeant. Quod si adhuc velint contendere se lege egere, seque adhuc ad legem pertinere, tunc est necesse confiteantur graciam in ipsis nihil valuisse, seque adhuc in peccatis esse, de quibus ut admoneantur lex fuit opportune data. Quod si arbitrentur gracia se esse apprehensos, et personam peccandi omnino deposuisse, tum simul oportet plane secum statuant, nihil ad eos spectare legem; causamque esse nullam, cur, quid lex vel vetat vel jubet, animadvertant; quum quidem nunc sunt per graciam facti justi; cujusmodi hominibus non datur lex, sed peccatoribus.

Fuit autem data lex Judeis indicandæ eorum iniquitatis causa; ut Judei aperte agnoscentes et quanto morbo laborarint, et ipsi quoque ex se ipsis quam imbecilles fuerint, tandem sanati per graciam omnia graciæ tribuant, manifestissimeque sensiant se sola gracia salutem et vitam recuperasse. Vult enim Deus ut sua benignitas misericordiaque et beneficium totum ex se et aperte profectum cognoscatur; ut homines non habeant locum nec superbiendi nec cavillandi; sed agnoscentes nihil ex se ipsis, sed omnia ex Deo

v. 11. esse, *in solo Deo*, ut jubet Paulus, *glorientur*.

CAP. VII.

At nunc ad Paulum redeamus. Is ostendit Judeis Christum sectantibus, et gracia a regno animalis et sensus absolutis, atque secundum peccandi statum omnino quasi mortuis, nihilque in peccatis apparentibus, ejusmodi, inquam, Judeis, quorum persona peccatrix crucifixa, mortua et sepulta est cum Christo, ostendit legem nullum habere respectum, nec ad eos ullo modo pertinere, quum deposuerint condicionem propter quam sub lege fuerint, condicionem videlicet peccatoris, cujus gratia data fuit lex. Quapropter, quatenus ad eos spectat, potestas legis et lex ipsa frustratur, et potest dici interiisse.

Quibus quum interierit lex, propterea quod afflati spiritu sancto reformati sunt in alium statum, ad quem lex nihil pertinet, est eis libera potestas sine periculo tradendi se alii legi, et quasi mortuo priore viro cum alio se viro in matrimonio collocare. Mortui autem est eis lex, quia ipsi legi sunt mortui, quum non appareant nec sint qui fuerunt, sed ob reformacionem in alium statum et quasi in aliam civitatem translati, nec leges pristinas agnoscere, nec ab illis agnosci debent; sed soli novæ legi, tanquam novo viro caste adherere ; ne, si ab eo desciverint, violasse matrimonium et adulterium commisisse videantur.

Quum vero ait Paulus, *Quum essemus in carne, passiones* vii. 5. *peccatorum, quæ per legem erant, operabantur in membris nostris, ut fructificarent morti ;* significat per legem gravius et perniciosius peccatum fuisse ; eo quod, monstrante lege transgressiones, quodammodo scienter fuit peccatum. Quum addit, *Nunc soluti sumus a lege mortis*, istam eandem legem vii. 6. dicit quam supra; quam vocat *legem mortis*, quia indicans et aggravans peccatum magis et miserius mortificat. A qua lege mosaica, mortificante magis ob ineptitudinem hominum quam vivificante, quum quasi ex mortuis renati homines et reformati spiritu soluti et liberi sint, profecto non est committendum ut aut rursus descendant ut humili ea lege implicentur, aut novi et spiritales non sectentur eam formam doctrinæ, quæ nova est et spiritui accommodata. Hæc doctrina est Dei et Christi graciæ et amoris; ut redament amantem Deum, et Deum expectent, et Deo soli confidant.

Deinde Paulus docet quam fuit impotens lex, quamque non sustulit peccatum, sed indicavit; quamque eciam, quanquam ipsa in se bona et ad bonum tendens fuit, tamen hominibus malis pro malicia eorum fuit mala. *Accepta enim sunt cuique omnia pro modo accipientis.*

Omne autem malum homini, ei suboritur ex inferiori sua parte, quæ animal, ut supra dixi, et hominis bestia potest vocitari; quæ tradita fuit interiori homini et animæ, ut ab ea regatur. Sed postquam homo se a Deo impietate et diffidencia solverit, in corpusque deciderit, hominis statu sic mutato et everso, bestia nostra prorupit foras statim petulanter et insane, et in homine regni gubernacula occupavit; animam ejus stulticiæ et libidini misere subjecit; secundum judicium sensuum omnia tractavit. Viguit tunc in homine respublica tota quasi popularis et plebeia, judicio et decretis sensus administrata, intellectus et racionis auctoritate nulla interposita, quæ ceca et subjecta fuit, quodammodo coacta ut regnantibus sensibus prope (ut ita dixerim) sua sponte inserviret. Quam miseram et perditam hominis condicionem et animæ dolendam servitutem hic Paulus deplorat, et de injusticia ac tirannide sensientis corporis graviter conqueritur; dicens se nescire sub ea servitute quid agens agit; velle bonum sed non posse persequi; agnoscere legem admonitricem justiciæ, sed non posse obedire. Ita urget et instat et blande imperat, et falsis deceptiunculis nostra bestia astringit animam, et sibi devincit, ut quonam pacto se exolvat, nisi divina gracia succurrat, non videt.

Itaque Paulus exclamans, et ad hunc modum interrogans, *Infelix ego homo, quis me liberabit de corpore mortis hujus?* id est, sic me mortificante et ad sempiternum interitum rapiente; respondet et concludit, *Gratia Dei per Jesum Christum dominum nostrum.* Hoc est, gratia et amor Dei, quem erga homines ostendit, quando Verbum suum voluit incarnari et mori pro humano genere, ut homines a justa morte salvi essent. Nam si Jesus Christus non interiisset pro sufficienti rerum satisfactione et recompensacione pro peccatis, tum sine dilacione homines ipsi omnes impii, quisque pro suis delictis interiisset, ad sempiternamque mortem et supplicium raptatus fuisset. Sed unus Jesus passus est id sibi inferri injuste quod in universos juste illatum fuisset, ut misericordia, et quadam simul decenti justicia, quos velit omnium sibi a morte reservaret; illa inquam infinita, in quam corruissent homines ipsi, si peccatores interempti fuissent. Morte ergo Christi pro universis peracta retinentur homines in vita, mirifica Dei gracia, ut morte Christi perinde ac sua ipsorum propria deletis peccatis, in tota reliqua vita ad virtutem contendant et ad Deum aspirent.

Ita factum est admirabiliter quadam misericordi justicia et justa misericordia, ut hominum peccata tollerentur ex mundo, non ipsorum morte ad sempiternum deinceps interitum, sed reservata vita, ut si velint hic vivant ad eternam vitam apud Deum possidendam. Quod ut faciant, qui voluit pro omnibus mori ex amore in eos suo singulari, quum alienati fuerint, idem dabit vires necessario, et eos conservabit, præsertim quos revocatos ad se sibi et Deo reconciliavit. Quod Paulus significat dicens, *Multo magis nunc justificati in sanguine ipsius salvi erimus;* et paulo post, *Multo magis reconciliati erimus in vita ipsius.* v. 9, 10.

Ita vere delere peccata, ac purgare homines, et reconciliare Deo lex Judeis data non potuit, tametsi illuc et ad eum finem tendit, et justiciam sectandam multis et variis modis admonuit. Veruntamen animæ nec dedit nec auxit vires, quibus se eximere a servitute et e corporis carcere evadere potuit. Ad tenue quoddam lumen et scienciam boni excitavit animam; verum eam intime non incendit eciam amore boni et Dei, ut tota ardens, quasi rapta in flammam, umbrosum corpus relinqueret et Deo se soli applicaret. Hunc calorem, vitam et robor præstitit Deus homini per Jesum Christum, ut dirruptis peccatorum vinculis liber exiret, et apud Deum viveret; nec legem amplius spectet, quæ spectavit ad peccatum, nec corpus ipsum peccabundum, peccati causam, formidet, Deo confisus, in Deo sperans, solum Deum amans; sed denique quicquam dampnacionis extimescat, modo, secutus Christum, ad exemplar magistri quoad potest se effingat, Christique formam referat.

viii. 1. Quoniam, ut ex superioribus concludit Paulus, *Nihil est dampnacionis iis qui sunt in Christo Jesu*, qui sunt abducti omnino a carne, et contracti in spiritum, apprehensi et rapti gracia, ut in spirantem Deum respirent, et in vivificante Deo vivant, et roborante valeant.

Quoniam ejusmodi (ut docet deinde Paulus) Deum habent amicum, adjutorem et conservatorem sui; ut cum sint certi se nec a Deo nec ab ejus filio vel dampnatos vel accusatos fore, quem habent sibi amantissimum patronum ac defensorem et liberatorem Jesum, eciam morte sua ipsius propria, qui voluit mori salvandi humani generis gracia :—

CAP. VIII.

QUUM, inquam, id certum et exploratum habent, profecto hii magna spe pendentes a Deo, nihil est præterea quod extimescant, nec, quum Deum auxiliatorem tenent, quicquam sibi adversari et periculosum esse posse putent, sed amplexi Deum, immo pocius a Deo amplexati, omnino tutos et salvos se esse in Deo confidant. Hii sunt, ut tradit Paulus, quos prescripsit divina mens ad se sua gracia vocandos, ut justificentur, quos arbitraria inspiracione sic agitans reformavit ad imaginem filii sui, et ab humana ac solita affectione tractos ad quendam novum vitæ statum et divinum sic transtulit, ut nihil qui antea fuerint videantur deinceps, sed quasi regeniti ac prorsus renati denuo, in omni eorum vita et actione, quoad patitur humana obscuritas, Deum in se ipsum representent.

vii. 14. Hii sunt vero qui (ut scribit Paulus) *spiritu Dei aguntur*, *ut sint filii Dei*, qui in se Dei et Christi spiritum possident; qui sunt, vivunt, sensiunt, sapiunt, volunt denique omnia

Gal. v. 25. spiritu, et (ut apostoli verbis utar) *spiritu ambulant*, aguntque omnia; qui ardente spiritu et amore Dei omnes fluctuantes corporis affectus exciverint, qui leve et obediens rationi corpus effecerint, qui firma et stabili spe ac exspectacione gloriæ filiorum Dei perseverant, qui omnia pocius vel acerbissima paciuntur quam vel a spe decidant, vel ab amore Dei avocentur. Nihil est enim quod debeat a nobis putari tanti, ut nos a Deo abstrahat. Qui, inquam, sunt tanto spiritu afflati et amore erga Deum et spe tanta tenti, et tam magna paciencia virtute et justicia prediti, ii revera, ut inquit Paulus, sunt Christi, id est, Christiani, filii et *heredes Dei*, et *coheredes Christi*, nunc notati et quasi insigniti spiritu sancto, ut adoptivi post hanc vitam in domum magni et supremi Patris introducantur, fruanturque eterna illa et felici hereditate, Deo videlicet ipso. Quem ut possideamus, interea dum hic sumus et manemus in hac vana et umbratili vita, hoc fumoso corpusculo obfuscati, omnia sunt pacienter ferenda nobis, et spe summa standum ; quam eciam spiritus ipse qui eam genuit, si confidimus, languere non sinet, nec pacietur quidem ut velimus aliud quam quod conveniat spiritualibus viris Deoque placeat. Quia spiritualibus hominibus et *diligentibus Deum omnia cooperantur ad bonum.*

Hiis racionibus conatur Paulus ecclesiæ Romanæ persuadere ut magna et immobili spe sint ; atque, tametsi adversitate devexentur, tamen fixi in Deo maneant ; a quo sunt vocati, ut ei confidant et in eodem sperent. Quod si fecerint, a fideli Deo non decipientur. Sin vero negligentes Dei amorem et tractum, aut a corporis illecebris alliciti aut vi aliqua depulsi a Deo deciderint, rursusque secundum carnem carnalesque affectiones vixerint, quæ sunt contrariæ et inimicæ Deo, ipsisque hominibus pestiferæ—proth scelus, si hæc nephanda impietas in homine fuerit, quem Deus tantopere dilexit, jure tum certe destitutus divina gracia preceps corruet in longe miseriorem condicionem quam antea fuit. Quocirca summa fide standum est in Deo et Christo suo, et indubitanter expectanda quæ filiis Dei ostendentur; et Deo ipsi maxime ac Jesu Christo tanquam stabili stabilientique saxo, flagrantissimo amore adherendum.

Quem suum amorem Paulus significat erga Deum Christumque, tam de se bene meritum, tantum esse et tam magnum ac vehementem, ut nihil nec esse in tota rerum universitate nec excogitari quidem potest in quocunque genere tam violentum et efficax, ut possit eum *a charitate* amoreque *Dei, qui est in Christo Jesu, separare.* Hoc affert de seipso Apostolus, ut exemplo sui ipsius quam ardentissimi amoris ecclesiam Romanam in amore Dei confirmet, stabiliatque in spe expectacioneque eorum quæ Deum caste amantibus constituuntur, dummodo sunt vocati divina gracia ad id libertatis in hoc mundo, ut possint amare Deum, et ei confidere, ac illius liberalitatem expectare.

viii. 14. Sed qur Paulus in hac parte scribit, *Qui spiritu Dei aguntur, eos Dei filios esse,* ac deinde non multo post ingentissimam suam charitatem erga Deum ostendit, de primo hoc animadvertendum est: spiritum Dei, qui Deus est ipse, ubique esse, omnibusque adesse, non tamen inesse illuminareque omnes, sed eos duntaxat qui sunt mente divina predestinati ut illuminentur. Eos quidem, id est, eorum summas mentes suaviter et dulciter agitat spiritus, ac mirifice quasi calefaciendo inspirandoque primum aliquantulum amoris emollit et extenuat, et, si sic liceat loqui in talibus rebus incorporeis, quodammodo rarefacit, ut intus et intime luceant valde et concaleant.

Lux autem hæc infusa fides est, qua misterium verbi incarnati cernitur et creditur ad salutem. Amor vero una cum fide simul animam occupans, et eam (ut ita dicam) rarefaciens ac amplificans, est id quo, quantum ab homine fieri potest, Deus et ejus Christus capitur et colitur. Hæc duo, ut mihi videtur, ita inter se differunt, non re quidem sed quadam racione reciproca : ut fides minus unitus et quasi sparcior amor, contra amor coactior et unitior sit fides. Quo fit ut amor sit vi et potencia fide multo prestantior, et ad efferendum hominem in sublime ac cum Deo copulandum 1 Cor. xiii. longe efficacior. Hinc illud Pauli ad Corinthios : *Major* 13. *eorum charitas.* Hæc autem mirabilis et divina lux fide pulchre lucens, amore vehementer ardens, apprehendens animam hominis, eam afficit, disponit et format ; ut quiddam novum ex ipsa anima tanquam ex materia, et spiritu complectente tanquam ex forma, compositum divinitus extet. In quo multo magis spiritus ipsi animæ quam format, quam anima, quod format, corpori antecellit. Atque ex anima et spiritu longe magis unum fit, quam ex corpore et anima ; quod minus resistit anima ut cum spiritu coeat, quam corpus ut cum anima copuletur. Nam dimensiones quibus corpus distenditur videntur maxime unicioni adversari.

Itaque hæc perbella et performosa persona hominis spiritualis, tandem divino spiritu genitus, ex tribus constat naturis, corpore et anima et spiritu; ut Christum, in quo fuit Deus, anima et corpus, trina compositura referat; et qui eam personam induerint, a trina relacione Christiani ac quodammodo quidem Christi vocitentur. Quo spectat illud Pauli : *Quos predestinavit conformes fieri filii sui, ut sit ipse primogenitus in multis fratribus.* viii. 29.

Sic patet parumper quonam modo spiritu aguntur homines, et qua racione a Paulo filii Dei nuncupantur. De charitate vero illa a qua nulla se racione dimoveri posse Paulus dixit, hoc est deinde quod dicamus ; quod scilicet charitas et amor idem est ; quodque amor Dei in nobis ex amore erga nos Dei excitatur, et ab amante nos Deo in nobis gignitur. Hinc illud Joannis in epistola : *Charitas ex Deo est: et paulo post addit, In hoc est charitas, non quod nos dileximus Deum, sed quod ipse prior dilexit nos.* Itaque, Deo nos amante, ipsum redamamus. viii. 35. 1 Ioan. iv. 7.

Quam autem hæc redamacio nostra et charitas erga Deum ejusque Christum est nobis ante omnia salutaris, ex Marcilii Ficini platonici verbis de Dei amore, positis in suo quarto et decimo libro de platonica theologia, plane constat ; quæ sunt ferme ad hunc modum :

Homini, videlicet, per suam excellentissimam animæ partem, quæ mens est, duos esse excellentissimos actus, circa objectum excellentissimum ; Dei cognicionem et amorem. Sed Dei amorem in hac vita longe cognicioni prestare ; quoniam Deum hic nemo vere cognoscit, nec potest quidem. Amare autem potest; et amat Deum quoquomodo cognitum is qui Dei gracia omnia spernit et contemnit. Item, quanto deterius est odisse Deum quam nescire, tantum melius est certe Deum amare quam nosse. Adde perscrutacionem Dei admodum anxiam et difficilem, et denique cum modico lucro, et in longo tempore esse ; contra, amorem in perbrevi plurimum fructus adipisci, facereque ut appropinquemus Deo citius, et eidem firmius adhereamus. Est enim amoris vis in unione magis, cognicionis in distrectione. Unde necessario amor magis vehemens et efficax est, et ad assequendum bonum citacior, quam cognicio in vero deprehendendo ; plusque eciam necessario possidet bonum quam cognicio verum. Quineciam proculdubio ipsi Deo multo est gracius amari ab hominibus quam prospici, et coli quam intelligi. Nam intuendo Deum nichil ei tribuimus ; amando vero quicquid sumus aut possumus aut habemus, ei damus. Scrutando eciam videmur nostrum lucrum querere, amando lucrum Dei ; unde illud ab apostolo est dictum, *Charitas non querit quæ sua sunt.* Et idem ipse totus amor fragrans non sua sed quæ Jesu Christi sunt, quem tantopere dilexit, conquisivit. Quapropter amantibus Deus seipsum tribuit pocius quam scrutantibus. Hinc est quod Paulus dicit: *Diligentibus Deum omnia cooperantur ad bonum.* Quia talibus Deus se ipsum dat ; cui pro sua ineffabili bonitate omnia sunt bona, eciam ipsa mala, quæ ab illo ad aliquid boni vertuntur ; ut, qui diligunt Deum Deumque possident, est necesse, quicquid accidat, ii in bonam partem accipiant, referantque quicquid in malis numeratur ad bonum finem ; ut, quanquam id malum ipsum in se sit malum, tamen ipsis diligentibus Deum, quia boni et divini sunt, bonum esse possit.

Sed addamus reliqua de amore, cujus natura et vis admirabilis est. Quam vel ex eo licet cernere quidem, quod amore Dei male uti nullo modo possimus : sciencia certe possumus ; videlicet ad arroganciam et superbiam. Quod testatus est Paulus in epistola ad Corinthios prima, quum dixit: *Sciencia inflat, charitas autem edificat.*

Item amor Dei mirum in modum jucundior est quam scrutacio ut sciatur ; amantesque Deum longe plus voluptatis quam perscrutantes percipiunt ; fiuntque tandem homines multo meliores amando Deum quam exquirendo. Et denique, ut non is qui videt bonum, sed qui id vult et appetit, evadit bonus ; ita animus quoque non ex eo quod considerat Deum, sed ex eo quod amat, divinus efficitur. Sicuti quod igni apponitur, non ex eo quod lucet, sed ex eo quod intime ardet et flagrat, ignis factus esse indicatur. Preterea est homini magis honorificum, et divinæ majestati eciam sane magis congruum, ut statim ametur pocius ab homunculis, quam aliquatenus exquisicius cognoscatur ; quod contendentes ut cognoscamus Deum, conamur eum ad nostræ mentis humilitatem et angustiam contrahere quodammodo, et quasi devertere; at vero amantes, ad Deum ipsum nos attollimus, et ad immensam illius bonitatem nos ipsi amplificamus, ut magni et excelsi eam capiamus quoad possumus; nos illi non illam nobis accommodantes. Unde multo conveniencius est et Deo et hominibus ut diligatur Deus, quam perscrutetur a nobis ut cognoscatur. Noscunt enim homunciones quantum Dei capere possunt, quod est admodum exiguum. Amant vero non modo quantum noscunt et intuentur, sed eciam quantum vaticinantur divinæ bonitatis superesse, quod cognoscere non possunt. Non est enim amor sienciæ finibus contentus, sed pro sua excellenti vi longius progreditur, et lacius vagatur, nec ei satisfactum est, donec est nactus primum illud immensum et infinitum bonum in quo solo conquiescat. Hic amor sublimis, amplus et amplectens Deum, atque strictim ei adhærens, et arcte hominem Deo copulans, verus Dei est cultus et religio, qua hominum mentes cum Deo colligantur.

Hæc tradidimus de amoris excellencia, Marcilium secuti, sed nostris verbis nostroque scribendi modo maxime pro nostro arbitrio usi; non quod putamus nos aut aptius aut lucidius quam Marcilium (quo nihil in philosophia potest esse eloquencius) ea exprimere posse; sed quod, libertate loquendi usi, habuimus facultatem inter scribendum inserendi quæ voluimus, et dirigendi sermonis eo quo nostro proposito maxime conveniret; quod totum huc tendet; ut minime miremur si Paulus tanto Dei amore captus, tam ardenti spiritu et oracione tam ampla et grandi asseruit, nihil prorsus esse potuisse, quod eum ab amore Dei et Christi avocaret. Minime eciam miremur, si homo totus divino amore flagrans et flammeus, atque in se expertus charitatis mirificam vim, tantum in eis epistolis maxime ad Chorinthios scriptis, tribuit Charitati; sine qua affirmat nihil, quantumcunque habetur in bonis et potentibus, tamen, inquam, nihil prorsus sine charitate valere posse.

Sed unde sumus digressi aliquando revertamur, pergamusque in enarrando argumento hujus epistolæ ad Romanos sicuti a principio instituimus.

In qua quum modo ostendit in Judeica lege vim esse nullam et facultatem sanandi hominis, sed spem salutis omnem esse positam in fide, ut homines soli Deo confidant, et in spe ut ipsum Deum expectent, et in amore ut amantem Deum ardentissime redament, et hoc quidem in Verbi sui incarnacione, ac tota reliqua illa ineffabili et graciosissima dispensacione de Jesu Christo, pro humani generis revocacione ad Deum, ut ex Christo et in Christo et per Christum et propter Christum Deum maxime ament, et ex eo omnia expectent, et eidem soli confidant:—et preterea quia in superioribus significavit ex proposito Dei et voluntaria predestinacione, et quasi decreto immobili, qui credant et confidant Deo ab ipso Deo vocatos esse ;—

CAPP. IX. X.

HINC deinde nunc vehementer desiderat, et valde quidem optat, ut Judei eciam (tametsi vocari recusarint) in numero tamen aliquando vocatorum, et eorum qui confidant Deo, per divinam graciam habeantur. Id quidem optat ex ingenti suo amore erga illos. Immo eciam ea lege et condicione ut, modo illi salvi sint, ipse anathema fiat, ac oblacio pro eis et hostia, quæ ad placandum Deum immoletur.

Hoc enim anathema grecum significat. Nam anathematizo, ut Joannes Carmelitanus interpretatur, tum detestor, tum divoveo significat; quod est dico et consecro. Unde anathema (ut idem docet) oblacio est cui astipulatur; quod divus Jeronimus scribit ad Algatium, dicens se animadvertere crebro in sacra scriptura anathema occisionem denotare. Etenim pecudes occisæ et mactatæ ad faciendum Deum hominibus propicium fuerunt immolatæ.

Ita immolari et offerri voluit Paulus, ut Judeis Deus, quibus jure erat infensus, propicius redderetur, utque divina benignitate et gracia ad fidelium numerum adsciscantur. Ad quos (ut Paulus significat) maxime pertinuit ut accersiti vocantem Deum et Christum sectarentur; quandoquidem eos, ut ita dicam, peculiari quodam studio Deus testata apud illos sua voluntate, et data lege, diu ante quasi effinxit ad suum Christum et graciam capessendam; quem etiam Christum ex illorum patribus nasci, et graciam apud eos exoriri voluit. Attamen ita fuerunt ceci, et vocati a Christo ita obsurduerunt, ut ad commoda eorum quæ antegressa sunt, tradita a Moyse, nihil processerunt. Veruntamen consilium et Dei propositum propterea nihil falsum nec deceptum fuit; qui providit quorsum Judei voluerint, quidque de sua in eos exhibita gracia tandem eveniret. Nec ea certissima et infallibilissima providencia rebus ejusmodi dedit exitus; sed quid fuit futurum quodque ex sua causa, et homines propriis quid essent et suis voluntatibus facturi pervidens Deus, simil quod sibi videtur agendum esse agit, et eterna sua concilia in tempore explicat, atque omnia dirigit ad eos fines quos vult et novit ipse solus, qui *attingit a fine usque ad finem fortiter, et disponit omnia suaviter.* Sapient. viii. 1.

Quod ineffabile concilium et disposicionem rerum incognoscibilem nos homunculi venerari debemus jugiter, non perscrutari; existimareque a Deo omnia esse facta sic ut nihil possit esse sapiencius, nec justius, nec utilius, nec ex omni parte congruencius. In qua sua providencia, ordinacione et disposicione rerum, omnia, undequumque sint profecta, sic concinnantur in universo et quadrant, et benigna Dei justicia et justa benignitate sic pulchre et dulciter temperantur, ut, quum undique et in omni parte mundi appareat equitas simul cum misericordia, nihil sit in rebus quod de Dei facto jure conqueri possit; sit vero eciam simul quod de Dei misericordia et gracia tum ipsum tum totum universum sibi gaudeat et gratuletur.

Itaque Judei magni gubernatoris illius propositum et voluntatem minime fallere potuere. Et quanquam non eo pervenerint tandem quo aliquousque Mosaica lex et prophetica doctrina eos contendit promovere, quoque etiam postremo Christus ipse eosdem trahere attemptavit, videlicet ad quandam spiritualitatem in vita et divinitatem, a corporeis imaginibus et humanis affectibus valde absolutam, tamen in hiis conatibus propositum Dei frustratum non fuit; qui tot racionibus manifestissime voluit ostendere in una gente illa Judaica quod de toto humano genere perdiscatur, quam scilicet homines ex peccatorum pondere, quo pressi nequiverint se levare, duriter et difficulter in altum trahuntur. Quod si aliter atque evenit evenisset, Deus tunc quod voluit non assecutus fuisset. Voluit quidem aperte monstrare necessitatem divinæ graciæ; hoc est, quam fuit necessaria divina et raptans gracia, ut homo servili et misera condicione qua fuit liberetur. Quod si Judei levioribus tractibus ex se sua ipsorum improbitate non restitissent, magnifica potencia salutaris graciæ ostensa non fuisset. Non tamen fuit necesse, nec coactio fuit ulla quidem, ut Judei tractibus reluctarentur. Sed amplo suo conspectu cernens omnia Deus, quod Judei malum sua sponte essent facturi et tandem fecerint, id pro sua infinita bonitate, quomodo maxime conveniret humano generi, et utile esse possit, traduxit ad eum exitum, et finem dirivavit, ut (quanquam causa mali non fuerit) tamen ex malo mirificus auctor boni extaret; qui *malis nostris*, ut ab Aurelio Augustino præclare est dictum, *bene utitur, sicuti nos suis bonis male.*

Itaque Deus improba Judeorum facta ad bonos fines convertit; non ipsis quidem bonos, qui male dictum sequentes ipsam miseriam in mali finem juste devenient; sed toti universo, et quasi communi rerum reipublicæ bonos; ut, cum pro Dei justicia singuli et hii qui mali sunt non habeant cur accusent Deum, curque de eo conquerantur, tamen simul mirum in modum, pro beneficentissima Dei gracia, ordo rerum et totus mundus habeat de quo et gaudeat sibi, et Deum, quem etiam in ipsis malis tanta esse bonitate agnoscunt, summopere glorificent.

Sed nunc vagamur a Paulo, et, disserentes de providencia Dei, plura sane loquimur quam videtur ille nos velle facere; qui pondere auctoritatis suæ occludit ora hominum, et quasi vetat ne de tanta re tamque inscrutabili disputemus; *O homo,* inquirens, *quis es qui respondeas Deo?* verum quia homines non facile liberare se admiracione rei possunt, ne forsan ammirantes aut turbentur secum, aut impie de Deo cogitent, hæc paucula duximus dicenda esse; ut eis, quorum mentes intentæ in rem tam reconditam hebescunt, nostro hoc sermone aliqua ex parte satisfiat.

Paulus autem ipse succincta et simplici oracione omnia in mera Dei voluntate et arbitrio collocat; ut illi accedant ad Deum soli quos ille vocat, quos prefinivit, proposuit, promisit, elegit et predestinavit. Est quidem pernotandum, apud Apostolum hæc verba proponere, promittere, eligere, predestinare, significare idem; et Dei propositum in hominibus, et promissum, electionem, et predestinacionem idem esse; et quos promisit se vocaturum, et quos proposito ac statuto vocavit, et quos elegit, et quos predestinavit ad suam domum et hereditatem, eosdem esse.

Cujus modi Dei voluntas et suum propositum uti ei placet, non solum est in eternis rebus ad hominum electionem ad eternæ felicitatis possessionem, sed preterea eciam in hiisce terrenis ad terrenam aliquam et temporalem felicitatem assequandam. Quod docet Paulus exemplis ex veteri testamento petitis, ut in ipsis ediscant Judei in quaque re, uti proposuit Deus, ita eventurum, suumque illius propositum falli non posse. Proposuit autem Deus et statuit Abreæ, repudiato Ismaeli, Isac heredem fore. Quinimmo, ut nullus sit cavillandi locus, utque Dei arbitrium et voluntas in rebus, uti ipse sicuti ei placet omnino velit eligere, manifestissime demonstretur, ex geminis uno partu editis, in ipsis nulla antecedente causa cur alteruter anteponatur, rejecto tamen Esu, Jacob sibi delegit, qui in paternis bonis et benedictione succederet. Quidnam sibi hæc velint aliud, nisi Deum scire quid promisit, atque quod promisit ipsum prestare; accessumque ad omnem hereditatem, tum temporalem, tum maxime spiritualem et eternam, ex promissione Dei et electione esse? Quod miranda racione simul sacra scriptura complectitur, ut in suis exemplis constat a Paulo introductis. In quibus qui traduntur electi, non solum ad paternas possessiones in terris, sed preterea multo magis ad eternam Dei possessionem in celis, fuerunt destinati; ut, utrum ex duobus sensum sequi velis, aperte videas providente et dirigente Deo res duci, atque ut ille velit in humanis fieri; non ex vi quidem aliqua illata, quum nihil est remotius a vi quam divina actio; sed cum hominis natura, voluntate, et arbitrio, divina providencia et voluntate latenter et suaviter et quasi naturaliter comitante, atque una et simul cum eo

Rom. ix. 13.
Gen. xxv. 23.

M

incedente tam mirabiliter, ut et quicquid velis egerisque agnoscatur a Deo, et quod ille agnoverit statuitque fore, simul id necessario fiat.

Statuit autem (ut non recedamus a Paulo) et apud se ipse decrevit, quinam hominum ejus essent filii futuri, quique eternam felicitatem assequerentur; ut Judei non potuerint nec debuerint, sicuti fecerint quasi jure hereditario, qui ab Abraam traxere originem, sibi auctoritatem et locum apud Deum vendicare; quum ipse quoque Abraam et Israel nihil suo jure poterat exposcere; sed si in filiis Dei numerari velint, id ex divina electione debent expectare. In quo Dei propositum falli non potest. Quia quod ille statuit et promisit fore, non ex hominum voluntatibus, sed ex sua potestate et arbitrio pendet. Quod Paulus docens Judeos, inquit: Non omnes qui sunt filii Abraæ sunt filii Abreæ, nec ex Israel nati omnes Israelitæ. Sed promissi et electi Dei arbitratu: siquidem Isac et Jacob, Ismaeli et Esu repudiatis et rejectis; quod vel ad ipsa temporalia licet cernere. In qua tamen re gesta electioneque ad terrena, pro ratione instituti sui, sacra scriptura altius Dei propositum et modum accedendi ad celestem hereditatem depinxit, cujus participes Abreæ filios et Israelitas vocat. Ii sunt qui Abreæ fidem, quæ tam grata fuit Deo, et Israelis visionem Dei assecuti sunt. Ii quidem sunt deinde quos ipse Deus decrevit fideles et credentes, id est, videntes fore. Hii vero sunt veri filii Abreæ, et, quia ad Abreæ fidem electi, filii Dei, et vere Israelitæ, quod Deum per fidem vident. Hii sunt denique quos promisit Deus et proposuit et predestinavit Abreæ filios fore, id est, representatores fidei Abreæ; et Israelitas, id est, Dei visores; qui vocantur filii promissionis et electionis Dei; nati certe, immo renati potius ex semine promisso, Jesu videlicet Christo, cujus figuram Isac promissus gerebat.

Hinc Paulus illud meminit Genesios: *Sed in Isac vocabitur tibi semen;* in Isac scilicet promisso et præelecto: et continuo exponit, non filii carnis ex Abraam nati omnes, nec quisquam certe eo quod natus ex Abraam fuit, hii filii sunt Dei; sed qui filii sunt promissionis, id est, promissi et electi, estimantur in semine, id est progenie divina, quæ ex Christo, spirituali Isac, propagabitur. Ita docet promissione et arbitraria electione Dei omnia acta esse hominibus, ipsis cur eligantur nihil conferentibus, ne Dei concilium et propositum ex hominis voluntate et factis pendere videatur; quo spectat illud quod affert apostolus de geminis uno pene momento editis; de quibus eciam antequam nati fuerint, *non ex operibus sed ex vocante Deo*, dictum fuit: *Jacob dilexi, Esau autem odio habui; et major serviet minori; quum adhuc nihil boni malive egerint; ut secundum electionem propositum Dei maneret;* qui quod vult proponit et promittit, et quod promisit ipse electione prestat, ut homines integrum Dei beneficium et ipsum eo totum agnoscant; ut, si quid glorientur, in Deo solo auctore gloriæ glorientur. ix. 13, 11.

Hæc est apostoli Pauli de racione assequendæ celestis hereditatis verissima et sanctissima et divina majestate dignissima sentencia; ut, quicquid sit de hominis beatitudine, id totum in Dei proposito, voluntate et gracia ponatur.

Quod hoc quam est verum, et justum, et Deo et hominibus c ngruum, quanquam homo pro sua cecitate nequeat decernere, tamen profecto ea parva ingenii vi quam habet, in tanta et tam sublimi materia abuti non debet, vel solicitius perscrutando, vel temere aliquid senciendo, vel quod nequit videre contemnendo, vel denique, extimescens et exhorrens potestatem Dei et voluntatem, de se desperando. Hæc enim quisquis facit, indigne sane et misere abutitur ingenio suo, quod est ei datum ut confidens Deo subjiciat id ei, ut a cecitate in lucem, et a stulticia in sapienciam, hoc est, a diffidencia et disquisicione ad fidem et rei ac veritatis inventionem, per graciam possit attolli.

Quapropter consideret quisque qui de divina illa et arbitraria electione hominum ad celestem vitam quasi cecutiens cogitat;—consideret, inquam, imprimis, quanta est sublimitas et celsitudo divinæ majestatis, quamque non modo homunculis, sed prestantissimis angelis quam longissimo intervallo antecellit, ut ne ipsi quidem illi omnium supremi spiritus omnia quæ sunt Dei cognoscunt, *qui inhabitat lucem,* ut inquit Paulus alibi, *inaccessibilem.* Consideret deinde humilitatem et vilitatem suam; quam sua mens longe abest a Deo, tum per se, tum quod detruditur in grave et hoc cali- 1 Tim. vi. 16.

ginosum corpus, quo ita eccecatur anima, ut non modo celestia suspicere (ne dicam ipsa divina) sed ne presentia quidem et ante oculos posita omnia sine fallacia valet intueri. Hæc considerans secum, et quieta mente colligens, nil miretur si a divinissimis hominibus, quibus Deus revelavit, ea dicantur et tradantur de Deo divinaque mente, ad quæ obstupescat ipse, et ex sua infirmitate exhorreat magis in principio quam admittat, quamque ea vere dicta esse sentiat. Immo magis miretur si in tam humili et ima condicione ipse, et in corpore eciam tam umbroso et feculento, tam alta et pura et luculenta possit aspicere. Majus enim esset miraculum certe posse illa ab homunculis conspici, quam non posse.

Verumtamen ab optimo et pientissimo Deo quæ apud ipsum consulta, decreta et facta sunt pro hominum salute, non ita quidem sunt facta, nec ipsa Deus sic a se fieri et in homines conferri voluit, ut ab ipsis hominibus nullo modo cognoscantur. Sed certe sic sunt exhibita, et in hominum oculis (ut par est, quum a Deo profecta sunt) talia et tam miranda apparent, ut facile admoneantur homines primum a se ejusmodi, quæ tam longe transcendunt humanam mentem, aspici non posse; deinde, si aspicere velint, ab ea condicione qua sunt, in aliam omnino, videlicet divinam, se transmutari oportere; et pati ut ad ea quæ velit cognoscere attrahatur, non agere quidem quicquam ipsum ut ad se illa contrahantur.

Quæ si homo conatur trahere ad se, et ex natura ac facultate suæ mentis examinare, profecto statim, quasi degenerancia a sua veritate et dulcedine, pro facilitate et ineptia humanæ mentis, ei falsa quodammodo et insipida evadent necesse est; ad eundem ferme modum quo egrotis salubria insalubria, et febricitantibus suavia amara, et item quo solis radius per rubeum vitrum transfusus rubet, et aliquis bene olens liquor in fetido vase positus fetet. *Nam quodque evadit ejusmodi uti illud est in quod recipitur.* Unde propheta Esaias execratur eos, qui sua sorditate labefactant et inquinant omnia; dicens, *Ve illis, qui dicunt bonum malum et malum bonum, dulce acerbum et acerbum dulce.* Hoc est, execrandi sunt illi et valde detestandi, qui ex natura et viribus suæ mentis omnia metiri et diffinire volunt; maxime vero divina, quæ omnes humanæ mentis limites excedunt. Quæ si ab homunculis recte et pro eorum dignitate intelligantur, oportet tum sane ii ad illa tollantur; non illa ad eos deprimantur: oportet, inquam, impietas et superbia humilitati et gratiæ cedant. Ex impietate enim et nepharia arrogantia divina ad nos trahimus; ex humilitate autem nostra et divina gracia nos ad divina trahimur, et amplificamur ad capienda illa; quod magis convenit quam ut illa cogantur in angustius ut a nobis capiantur. Itaque summittendus est homo Deo divinæque inspiracioni, si velit aliqua ex parte sapienciam divinorum consiliorum intueri. Et ut materia prima, ut formetur, nuda est, ne quicquam in ea sit quod formacioni adversetur; ita est necesse homo exuat omnes suas vires et subjiciatur Deo omnino paciens, si inspiracione ad divina intelligenda illustretur; ne, si ipse ex se quicquam agat, divinam actionem et reformacionem sui impediat.

Quod sapienter Paulus docuit quum scripsit ad Corinthios: *Si quis videtur inter vos sapiens esse in hoc seculo, stultus fiat, ut sit sapiens.* Hoc est, agnoscat stulticiam suam, et senciat apud se, se nihil sapere, nec ex se posse quidem; deponatque omnino omnem sciencæ opinionem, confisionemque sibi et viribus suis, quæ nullæ sunt vires, sed debilitates pocius; ac totus subjectus Deo soli Deo confidat, expectetque a Deo reformacionem sui, et vim et facultatem recte omnia cernendi et judicandi. 1 Cor. iii. 18.

Quod qui fecerit humilis et supplex, simul pie et assidue deprecans ut ex tenebris in lucem attollatur, is profecto non frustra se cum Deo egisse sensiet, nec inutiliter cogitacionis lumen petiisse; sed divino radio et gracia ab humili in altum, et vacillante racione in certam sine dubio et stabilem fidem attrahentur; quod lumen est quoddam a divino sole infusum in humanam animam, quo certo et indubitanter divinæ veritates revelari cognoscuntur; quod tam prestat lumini racionis, quantum certum incerto, et quantum solis lumen coloribus. Atque ut in certitudine non est incertitudo, nec in lumine coloracio, ita similiter in fidei luculencia umbratilis ratiocinacio apparere non debet; quæ si introducatur, labefacta est fides. A qua humili, errabunda, et inquieta racione, ac nunquam reperiente in quo conquiescat, quum ad rectam fidei viam veritatemque Christi reduceris, cave delires unquam plus ea, et racionare, videareque tibi sapiens, putesque racionis viribus quicquam te veritatis assequi posse; quod esset perinde ac in tenebris lucem quererc, et in ipsa stulticia velle sapere. Siquidem omnis humani ingenii vis cecutit et ceca est, ad Dei divinarumque rerum lucem. Quod testatus est Paulus quando dixit, *Sapienciam hujus mundi stulticiam esse apud Deum.* Quod quidnam aliud est dictu, quam qui putat se sapientem esse, eum divina cernere non posse? Hinc illud apostolicum eciam est quod modo dixi: *Si quis existimet se sapere, stultus fiat ut sit sapiens.* Est enim principium sapienciæ apud Deum, scilicet ignoranciam agnoscere et confiteri. Ac nihil est certe quod tam discutit divinam graciam, quam alta de te ipso opinio, et existimacio quædam aliquid in te sapienciæ esse. Quo animo et mente qui est, plane is statuat secum, quamdiu in ea opinione manserit, tamdiu se divinæ graciæ participem esse non posse.

Fit ergo ut, qui vult videre quam sunt vera et bona et justa et Deo digna, et hominibus congrua, et denique toti universo conveniencia et conquadrancia ea omnia, quæ Deus ineffabili quodam modo et gracia dispensavit de Filio suo, Verbo incarnato, ad revocacionem eorum ad se et restitucionem ad pristinum statum; immo eciam supra illum statum qui fuit Adæ in paradiso; longe in altius tractionem quos inscrutabilis illa mens ex omni hominum genere ad tantam dignitatem et graciam prescripsit, *eciam* (ut ad Ephesios scribit Paulus) *ante mundi constitucionem,* esse attrahendos et secum copulandos:—qui id, inquam, vult et cupit videre, ac preterea in eo hominum delectu qui sunt prefiniti ad supplementum angelorum, quam simul est Deus, vel eligens vel repudians, mirabiliter et justus et misericors, ut sine querela cujusquam sit multorum gaudium:—hæc, inquam iterum, qui cupit videre et cernere, oportet prorsus se exspoliet et nudet, deponatque omnes mentis cogitaciones, quas solitus est habere, quibusque opinatus est se aliquid scisse; ac subjectus Deo et in Deum suspirans in primis agnoscat stulticiam et vilitatem suam, agnoscat errores, deploret peccata, imploret graciam, offeratque se patientem, purum et simplicem Deo; ut a simplici et puro divino radio graciaque attingi, agitari, affici, et in novum hominem, spiritualem videlicet et divinum, reformari possit; ut deinceps non animæ humilis cecum intellectum et crassam voluntatem, sed eam voluntatem et intellectum habeat, novum et talem, cujusmodi formam spiritus consequitur; ut ex nova forme, vi, voluntate et actione ipse totus homo novus esse videatur.

Intellectus autem spiritus est fides Deo; voluntas vero ejusdem est charitas et amor Dei. Hæc gignuntur in animo hominis benifico Dei radio; qui ipse in se mirifice tum lucet, tum calet; quique nactus lautum et tersum et nitidum animum, eum apprehendens simul suavissime et calefacit et illustrat. Calor autem et hæc quasi clara flamma in anima genita charitas est. Illustracio vero et lumen infusum, quo intime anima in se luceat, et quasi foras verissime videat, fides est. Hæ sunt novæ vires et veræ et potentes, ex nova hominis et spirituali forma exortæ, quibus homo preditus omnino novarum actionum et operum auctor et effector est; hujusmodi videlicet in quibus omnibus sua fides Deo et Dei amor, ut in effectibus causa, eluceat; ut, quicquid aut egerit aut dixerit aut cogitaverit secum, id totum ex animo tam fideli et amanti proficiscatur, ut nihil apud eum aliud valere demonstret, quam fides et amor Dei. Ad hanc prestanciam et perfectionem quum homo, tum sua humilitate tum vel maxime divina Dei gracia, pervenerit, tunc, quasi emergens in lucem, et se et Deum et divinam graciam et divina mysteria, et denique Jesum Christum ac salutarem hominum electionem e vestigio et perspicaciter fidei oculo videbit, colet et venerabitur, desinetque in perpetuum ratiocinari de ea re quæ longe omnem racionem supergreditur, et sublimatus, atque in alta fidei specula constitutus, et fragranti Dei amore, libentissime in eo et dulcissime conquiescet, fructum fidei et amoris sui et fidelium ac amabilium actionum et operum constantissime expectans. Quam expectacionem firmam et spem bonus et fidelis Deus non fallet; quandoquidem ipse prior nos diligens eam in homine excitavit.

Sed longe modo aberramus a Paulo nostro, non potentes cohibere nos, quin ex levissima occasione prorumpamus in multum sermonem, quotiens est nobis aliquid loci, ut de predestinacione Dei et hominum de ea judicio dicamus. Quod quia solet in plerisque vacillare et titubare, iccirco ex quodam nostro studio et pietate in homines oracionem fundimus longiorem; non tam verentes legentium fastidium, buam cupientes confirmacionem infirmorum et vacillantium.

ix. 20. Sed nunc ad Paulum redeamus; qui vetat hominem de Dei consilio disputare, inquiens *O homo, tu quis es qui respondeas Deo!* id est, potes aliquid respondere ad defensionem tui, si Deus velit conqueri, et te (uti potest) severiter accusare? Quasi diceret, nihil potes respondere; sed tuam ipsius impietatem et iniquitatem agnoscens, mutus et elinguis stes necesse est, non aliter quidem atque fictilia vascula coram figulo. Quibus si esset sensus, non rogarent opificem cur ex eadem mole ad varia et diversa officia et usus effinguntur; nec, ad viliora ministeria destinata, de ea sortione sui conquerentur. Ita neque est hominis, figmenti Dei, vel conqueri, vel percontari quidnam sit causæ cur eligantur alii ad gloriam, alii deserantur? Id enim esset racionari cum Deo, quo nihil potest esse magis impium et detestabile. Quod si curiosius vestiget curnam salvantur alii, alii vero condempnabuntur, nullam aliam reperiet causam, nisi salutis esse graciam, damnationis vero esse hominis improbitatem; indignissimosque salute divina benignitate et gracia esse salvos, dignissimos morte juste et

ix. 22. peccati jure esse damnatos. *Quid si Deus* (ut addit Paulus) *volens* fuisset *ostendere iram, et notam facere potenciam suam?* Legatur interrogative, et est ex vehementia loquendi imperfecta et suspensa sentencia; cui subaudiatur: *Profecto tunc Deus antehac diu universos disperdidesset.* Ideo subjungit Paulus, clemenciam Dei et graciam ostendens, *sustinuit*; et subaudias *sed,* legasque, *sed sustinuit* et passus est *vasa iræ apta ad interitum,* id est, damnabiles, durare in mundo, ut

ix. 23. *ostenderet divitias gloriæ suæ in vasa ire*; id est, ut manifestaret graciam in eos quorum voluit misereri, *quosque in gloriam preparavit.*

Nam quum ex perdito et profligato mundo, quem totum sua scelera condemnaverunt, delegit sibi Deus quos voluit ipse justa damnacione liberare, ita manifeste declaravit graciam suam, ut nemo vere nisi ex gracia possit dicere se salvum esse. Hanc salutiferam graciam impertivit ut libuit communiter ad omnes gentes, tum Judeorum tum aliorum.

Quia Deus unius personæ et qualitatis hominum non est
acceptator. Sed ex quaque gente uti velit, et quos velit,
trahit et sibi acceptos facit. Quod probat testimoniis prophetarum Oseæ et Esaiæ; quorum hic *quasdam reliquias* Es. x. 22.
Israel, id est, apostolos et discipulos Christi, et reliquam
apud Judeos ecclesiam; ille autem, Oseas, ex aliis locis et
gentibus eciam accitos fore ad Deum, vaticinatus est. Os. ii. 23.
Quoniam, ut predixit Esaias, fuit Deus aliquando proposi-
turus universis hominibus doctrinam quandam, non cujusmodi fuit Judeorum, multiplex, longa et imperfecta, sed
quandam brevem, simplicem et perfectam; quam facillime
discere homines, et uno fere verbo exprimere possint. Quam
tunc, quum Paulus ad Romanos scripsit, proposuit Deus per
filium suum, et in terras exhibuit. Quæ doctrina est fidei,
ut credant et confidant Deo, et suo nuncio Jesu Christo,
suamque fidem verbis confiteantur. Quam doctrinam vocat
Esaias *verbum consummatum et abbrevians;* quoniam in ea Es. x. 23.
summatim omnis doctrina, sapiencia, virtus, et virtutis pre-
mium felicitas, continetur. Siquidem qui crediderit Christo,
et ex ea fide quæ a Christo sunt tradita coluerit, indubitanter salvus erit. Hæc autem doctrina fidei, reconciliatio
hominum, vita, salus, est tandem a benigno Deo oblata
universis, sicuti angeli cecinerunt pastoribus illis : *Gloria in* Luc. ii. 14.
excelsis Deo, et in terra pax hominibus bonæ voluntatis. Pax
enim et reconciliacio est credentibus Jesu Christo nuncianti
veritatem, et viam salutis demonstranti; quod ipsum evan-
gelium est; *Dei virtus,* ut vocat Paulus alio loco, *in salutem,* Rom. i. 16.
omni credenti, Judeo primum et Greco. Quod evangelium,
bonum nuncium, et brevis fidei doctrina, fuit ante oculos
hominum, et quasi in omnium ore posita, ut credentes
cernant veritatis et fidei nuncium, Jesum Christum, et x. 8.
eundem confiteantur. Nam is denunciatus fuit sic per
universum orbem, et apostolorum voces fuerunt, ut David Ps. xviii. 4.
precinit fore, ita in omnes terræ fines, ut qui apostolorum Rom. x.
predicacioni crediderint, ii Christo ipsi et Deo justissime 18.
cencentur credidisse. Non enim poterant Christo credere, x. 14.
nisi de eo audiverint, nec audire, nisi fuissent qui nunciassent,
nec nuncios fuisse, nisi missi fuissent. Qui ergo missis et
apostolis crediderint, ipsi Christo crediderint.

Ejusmodi deductionem adducit Paulus, ut probet necessario adhibendam esse fidem apostolis et legatis Christi. Quorum opera et industria quum voluntas et disciplina Christi fuit devulgata, id est, lex et ratio fidei, ut homines ubique soli Deo confidant, et per Christum se salvos esse credant, non fuit cuiquam locus dicendi se de Christo et salutifera fide nihil unquam audivisse, quandoquidem sermo de ea et predicacio per apostolos affuit, sicque presens cuique fuit, ut preter voluntatem ipsorum hominum qui audiverint, quod ad eorum salutem pertineat, videatur nihil defuisse. †Fidem adhibuerunt. In quibus qui non adhibuerint fidem imprimis et maxime Judei fuere; quod probat Paulus interrogans ad hunc modum: Sed dico, numquid Israel non cognovit? Hoc est, numquid Israelitæ sunt ex hiis qui non cognoverunt? ‡ Unde Paulus verba Moysis legislatoris Hebreorum affert, quæ habuit ille quondam, ut in Deuteronomio scribitur, ad ipsos Hebreos, post conditas et scriptas et traditas leges ac sepe eis promulgatas; quibus admonuit, modo leges in manibus habuerint, et totam vivendi normam, non aliunde exquirant regulam vitæ, virtutis et religionis, nec interrogent quisnam vel ex celo, vel ex aliquo remotiori loco adducat doctrinam et legem qua recte religioseque vivi potest, quasi ejusmodi non haberent; sed plane ante oculos positam et frequenter in aures eorum inculcatam legem agnoscant eique inserviant. Quod si non fecerint, modo lumen habent presens quo monstratur recta vivendi via, eis accusatio culpæ nulla esse potest. Verba autem Moysis hæc sunt: *Mandatum hoc quod ego precipio tibi hodie, non supra te est, nec procul positum nec in celo situm, ut possis dicere, Quis nostrum valet celum ascendere, ut deferat illud ad nos, ut audiamus atque opere compleamus; neque trans mare positum, ut causere et dicas, Quis ex nobis possit mare transfretare, et illud ad nos usque deferre, ut possimus audire et facere quod preceptum est? Sed juxta te est sermo valde in ore tuo, et in corde tuo, ut facias illum.* Quibus verbis aperte constat eum admonuisse hebreos, modo data eis et presens lex fuit, prevaricacionis excusacionem nullam esse posse.

Deut. xxx. 11-14.

---

† ‡ Locus hic perperam insertus ex sequentibus.

Quod autem de illa lege dixit Moises, videlicet quod palam et prope fuit, ut non potuit quidem non cerni, id idem nunc de lege Christi, quæ lux et ratio est fidei, commode dici potest; quum denunciata per apostolos et devulgata in conspectu omnium est. Atque, quia finis Mosaicæ legis est Christus, quiaque quicquid Moises scripsit, istuc ad Christum spectat, videtur loquens de sua lege simul vaticinatus esse de lege Christi et fide; ac quum habuerit illa verba de lege sua quæ ad Christianam legem venturam pertinuit, eadem simul videtur habere vates de ipsa lege Christiana et fide, quam prospexit non minus presentem fore universis quam suam Judeis. Quapropter Paulus illa verba afferens Moisis, ea exponit de Christo et ejus lege. Qui Christus quum modo venerit, et per suos apostolos tum se tum suam fidelem doctrinam et legem universo mundo fecerit, jure potuit dici, sicuti Paulus dicit Mosaicis verbis: *Prope est verbum in ore tuo*—cuique scilicet —*et in corde tuo;* x. 8. hoc est, *verbum fidei quod predicamus;* quod credulitatem exposcit, sicut Judeorum lex observanciam; ut, quemadmodum legem Mosaicam servantes tuto sub ea et sine morte corporis, suppliciove vixerint, ita credentes evangelio Christi et confidentes Deo, et fidem quam habent Christo et Domino confitentes, hac scilicet fide pergentes, tum animo tum corpore semper vivent, et eternam felicitatem assequentur.

Sed non omnes predicato Dei evangelio fidem[1] adhibuerunt. In quibus qui non adhibuerint fidem in primis et maxime Judei fuere, quod probat Paulus interrogans ad hunc modum: *Sed dico, numquid Israel non cognovit?* Hoc ix. 19. est, numquid Israelitæ sunt ex hiis qui non cognoverunt? id est, Christo et evangelio non crediderunt. Nam adverte in hoc loco, credere, et obedire evangelio, et evangelium cognoscere, apud Paulum idem significare. Itaque quum interrogavit, Numquid Judei ex illis fuerint qui audientes non cognoverint Christum, neque ei crediderint, quasi significans certe illos in primis tales fuisse, idem tunc probat testimoniis prophetarum Moisis et Esaiæ, qui suis oraculis plane testati sunt quam semper ad fidem Deo gens Judaica

---

[1] Vide sup. p. 170 *n.*

tarda esset futura; quamque aliæ gentes ad capescendam fidem veritatemque essent Judeis multo propenciores. Hinc est quod Paulus vicem eorum tam graviter doluit, optavit-

Rom. ix. 3. que se immolari, modo illi reconciliati Deo essent, retractique fuissent ad lucem et intuitum veritatis; quos significat crassitate mentis et ignorancia oblatam veritatem repudiasse, et recalcitrantes ad lapidem offensionis lesisse se, non sinentes ut Christus, petra scandali, id est, petra objecta labentibus in profundum, viciis eorum obstaret; sed calcitrantes, et quasi pedibus petentes lapidem, ut e via tolleretur, ne suum precipitem casum ad mortem impediat, ita graviter se offenderunt, et sibi ipsi tantum volnus inflixerunt, ut fuit necesse, ad magnum argumentum suæ stulticiæ et impietatis, diu id malum in ipsis postea restaret.

CAP. XI.

VERUNTAMEN, ut postea patet in contextu oracionis, Paulus agitatus prophecia, et divino spiritu instructus, vaticinatur fore aliquando ut Judei per divinam graciam cum Deo in graciam redeant, resipiscantque et agnoscant Christum, ac totum illud Dei salutare misterium de Christo admittant et venerentur, et Deo denique, uti debent, confidant. Quod suo more Paulus Esaiæ prophetæ testificacione

Es. i. 18. comprobat. In cujus vaticiniis est, videlicet, per Christum labem eorum delutam et peccatum deletum fore; qui statim post ejus adventum purgavit, et suo spiritu pergit purgando

Ioan. iii. 8. quos vult, donec rursus redierit. *Spiritus enim*, ut Jesus ipse apud evangelistam Joannem dicit, *ubi vult spirat*. Itaque Judeos spiritu Dei purgatos fore vidit Paulus et predixit: quod quando erit, et qui et quot eorum accersientur, ut ait Origenes, solus Deus novit. Quoniam non omnes accersientur, sed pro portione eorum copiosior multitudo quam ceterarum gentium, ad supplementum predestinatorum.

Quam illorum vocationem Paulus sapientissime tandem adjunxit, ut afferat Judeis spem graciæ, provocet eos ad graciam capescendam, utque desercione eorum gentes non

superbiant, nec se efferent de habundancia graciæ, quum
Judei quoque tanta, si velit Deus, abundare possunt. Quinimmo eciam ipsas quoque gentes ostendit facillime a gracia
recidere posse, nisi caverint, cauteque et humiliter incedant,
agnoscantque non ex se ipsis gracia stare, sed quod ab
auctore graciæ sustinentur. Qui omnia sua misericordia
metitur et pensitat fidelitate, atque, ut summittentes se et
incipientes credere confidereque Deo, graciose apprehendit
et attrahit, ita similiter superbientes insolentius ac con-
versos in se et desinentes Deo confidere Deus ipse e vestigio
deserit, ac omni gracia destitutos relinquit. Quod in sua
epistola testatur Petrus apostolorum princeps; dicens, *Deus* 1 Pet. v. 5.
superbis resistit, humilibus autem dat graciam.

Ita Paulus mira prudencia et arte temperat oracionem
suam in hac epistola, et eam quasi librat tam pari lance, et
Judeos et gentes simul ita coequat, ut utravis pars agnoscere possit nihil in se esse cur se alteri anteponat; quo
maxime tendit apostoli tam varius et diffusus sermo, quo
ostendit primum Judeos et gentes impietate pares fuisse, et
etiam infirmitate pares, et ad resurgendum pari impotencia.
Deinde quum tradidit sola gracia Dei hominum revelacio-
nem esse posse, ad eam pariter et similiter tum Judeos tum
ceteras gentes se habere demonstrat, omnes preterea pecca-
visse ad damnacionem, omnes egere gracia ad salutem; in
humilitate et fide reconciliacionem hominum Deo esse positam; humiles illos et fideles esse quos Deus sibi subjecit et
fideles fecit; quos autem vult ex toto perdito humano genere
ad se revocare, ut sibi inserviant et credant, qui non vocantur, vocari posse, qui vocantur eciam posse repudiari; mira
dispensacione rerum Judeos passos ut aberrent a Deo, ut
justa occasione gracia ad gentes deferri possit; gentes credidisse, ut eorum exemplo Judei ad fidem provocentur : ex
Judeis tandem Deum, ut patribus eorum promissa prestet,
tametsi inimici evangelio fuerint, quot videbuntur satis,
tracturos : illum agere in elargienda sua gracia (sicuti decet)
ut ipse velit maxime et sibi placet : illum in arbore fidei,
cujus radicem posuit Christum in Judea, ut illic cresceret,
quos vult, ramos inserere, quos vult, defringere; denique
ex universo orbe hominum et multitudine quos et quando

et quomodo vult, deligere; et, quod prescivit et predestinavit de salute hominum et fidelium numero, id totum, uti sibi melius videbitur, et quando maxime conveniet, consummaturum.

Hæc quum Paulus ostendit, quumque divina de salute hominum in Dei potestate, sicut proculdubio ponenda sunt, posuit, et de Dei ineffabile et stupendo consilio multa disseruit, tum postremo præ admiracione tantæ et tam inscrutabilis rei et dispensacionis, exclamat secum hiisce verbis:

xi. 33-36. *O altitudo divitiarum sapienciæ Dei: quam incomprehensibilia sunt judicia ejus, et investigabiles viæ ejus. Quis cognovit sensum domini? Aut quis consiliarius ejus fuit? Aut quis prior dedit illi et retribuetur ei?* Quasi diceret, Nemo consulit Deo, nec quicquam est eo prius. Quia *ex ipso* vero primo, qui est in omnibus, *et per ipsum solum*, sine adjutore, *et in ipso*, quo nihil est amplius, qui continet omnia, omnia promanarunt, sunt, et conservantur.

Ita hactenus produximus argumentum hoc quod in hanc partem solum hujus epistolæ ad Romanos instituimus scribere, quæ illa admirandi Pauli sentencia concluditur. Quod hoc argumentum profecto in multo longius crevit quam initio statuimus. Sed brevitas simul et quasi in augustum coarcta fecunditas Pauli poposcit a nobis quandam ampliorem explicacionem. Verum arbitror neminem omnia explicare posse. Tantus est enim thesaurus, et tam copiosa supellectilis sapienciæ et divinitatis in Pauli sermone recondita, ut quicquid erueris et deprompseris, semper tamen restabit infinitum, quod a te sapientiore depromi possit.

Nos autem quicquid in hoc argumentum contulimus, quanquam non tam aliis quam nobismet ipsis scripsimus, tamen si fortasse hæc nostra, quæquunque sunt, aliquando in aliorum manus inciderint, quicquid in hiis legent, eos precor ut boni consulant, tribuantque soli Deo si quid repererint quod recte dicitur. Sin vero aliquid sit quod eos offendat, qui meliori sunt judicio, id redargui, repelli, et in me rejici non recusabo. Agnosco enim infirmitatem meam; agnosco eciam omnia omnibus ex gracia esse; ut possumus et debe-

2 Cor. iii. 5. mus illud apostolicum dicere, *Non sumus sufficientes ex nobis, sed tota nostra sufficiencia a Deo est.*

FINIS.

Sequitur reliqua enarratio et argumentum in reliquam partem hujus epistolæ Pauli ad Romanos, a Joanne Colet conscriptam.

At quanquam decreverim mecum non enarraturum me plus in hanc epistolam a divo Paulo ad Romanos scriptam, quam quod modo narratum est a nobis, et productum ad eum usque locum, in quo Apostolus suam oracionem, qua Romanam ecclesiam conatus est totam ad Deum convertere, suadereque ut nihil sibi ascribat, sed omnia Deo tribuat, soli Deo confidat, a Deo omnia expectet, hiisce verbis concludit: *Quoniam ex ipso, et per ipsum, et in ipso sunt omnia: ipsi gloria in secula seculorum. Amen;* tamen certe, multum ac diu rogatus a quibusdam amicis, et eiisdem interpretantibus nobis Paulum fidis auditoribus, quibuscum, pro amicicia, quod in superiorem epistolæ partem scriptum est a nobis communicavi, adductus fui tandem ut promitterem, quod est ceptum modo me perrecturum, et in reliquam epistolam quod reliquum est enarrationis adhibiturum.

xi. 36.

Quod quidem nunc faciam, Pauli vestigia sequens, sicuti supra fecerim. Etiamsi nonnunquam vagatus fuero abieroque a proposito, quatenus clarius exponendi ratio exposcet, revocabo me tamen, et sic ad viam redibo, ut a Pauli semita tandem nihil videar dissessisse. Itaque quæ reliqua sunt ad hunc modum exordiamur.

CAP. XII.

SCRIPTIS ab apostolo quam plurimis ad Romanos illos quidem, qui emendationem vitæ, et Dei ac Christi cultum professi sunt, quæ omnia eò contenderint ut arrogantiam et superbiam tollant, unde in hominibus omnis discordia nascitur, utque persuadeant soli Deo confidendum esse, unde ad homines quicquid in bonis est proficiscitur; ideo deinde nunc obsecrat, obtestaturque omnes, ut contrahant se et componant; hoc est, abducant se omnino a sordibus hujus mundi, et corpus astringant in obsequium animæ et racionis, et quasi aptam et expurgatam materiam se divinæ reformacioni subjiciant; ut quisque, divina gracia apprehensus, divinoque spiritu afflatus, totus novus et divinus fiat; utque ex omnibus innovatis nova Dei civitas et celestis construatur in terris et extet; ut, sicut in celo, quod in dominica oracione petimus, sic eciam in terra aliquando Deus regnet, et in ipsis hominibus imperium habeat; ut nihil nec appetitum nec actum sit a quoquam, quod non ex Dei ipsius voluntate actum esse videatur.

xii. 2. Id est quod hic Paulus jubet, videlicet ut Romani reformentur in novum sensum rerum et judicium, ut probent et ostendant factis quid Deus velit, quidque bonum et perfectum et Deo est placens, non quid sibi; ut non deinceps nunc propriam, sed divinam in se voluntatem habere ostendant, Deumque in ipsis regnare, quæ ipsa est bonitas ipsa et perfectio, quæ facit ut omnia bene et perfecte agant, utque tota societas et ecclesia bona et perfecta existat. Hoc quidem fiet pulchre, si aversi a Deo homines ad Deum revertantur, omniaque quæ sunt hominis sursum spectent, sursumque, quoad possint, contendant; corpus ad racionem, racio ad Deum; ut illud animæ et racioni inserviens quodammodo racionale, racio autem ipsa et anima humana, Deo subjecta et dedita, divina evadat, presencia quidem certe divini spiritus, a quo novum et longe supra se excellencius illustramen capit.

Quod quamdiu tenet, quasi nova tum forma effigiatus ad imaginem Dei expressius, non tam homo quam Deus videtur esse. Tenet autem, vel tenetur potius (nam superioris amplecti et tenere est) quamdiu sua ipsius anima corpus cohibet, et sursum in obsiquela sibi sustentat. Quod si neglexerit, sique corpus effluere in libidines siverit, e vestigio tunc simul a sustinente spiritu negligetur ipsa et deseretur, totusque homo deorsum pronus et preceps ad terram et mortem miserrime corruet. Nam quo fertur una hominis pars, vel corpus vel anima, illuc statim totus homo trahitur; sic ut totus aut sursum aut deorsum tendat necesse est. Illuc si sursum tendat humilis et confidens Deo, apprehensus a spiritu trahetur altius, et supra se quadam in divina condicione sustinebitur, anima divino spiritu, corpore animæ jugiter serviente. Sin vero deorsum corporis sensuumque et cecorum et petulancium tractum sequatur, quid multis? (brevis dico) una cum corpore anima infelix destituta a sui conservatore spiritu, ad sempiternum interitum delabetur.

Quapropter Paulus per misericordiam Dei rogat Romanos, ut sua corpora rationi obsequentia reddant; ut deinde ipsi facile spiritales et divini effingantur. Nam corpore reformato anima, factoque (ut ita dicam) *animali*, id est, quatenus ejus crassitas patitur, simili naturæ animæ, statim ipsa deinde anima, si confidat Deo, Deumque amet, divina gracia et spiritu reformatur, fitque spiritalis et naturæ Dei similis, totusque homo pulchre redigitur sursum in statum divinum, quum anima in Deum, corpus in animam incumbat, extatque in terris plane quidam Deus, quandoquidem *qui adheret Domino, ut est in Epistola ad Colocenses, unus est spiritus*. Hinc David *sibi adherere Deo dixit bonum fuisse*, et quidem juste, quum nihil preterea est quod hominum bonum facit, aut facere possit, quum solus Deus est bonus; et quicquid bonum est, id est bonum illius bonitate.

Rom. xii. 1.

1 Cor. vi. 17.

Ps. lxxii. 28.

Quod autem hortatur Paulus hoc loco, Exhibeant corpora sua hostiam viventem, latenter carpit sacrificia eorum omnium qui peccora mactarunt et immolarunt; maxime Judeorum, qui, ut Aristeas scribit, septingentis ministrantibus soliti sunt festis diebus cesis pecudum millibus facere victimas et offerre, ac totum templum opplere sanguine; existimantes eo facto se valde Deo placuisse. Unde Esaias in persona Domini exclamat: *Quo mihi multitudinem victimarum vestrarum? Plenus sum holocausta arietum, et adipem pinguium, sanguinem vitulorum agnorum et hircorum nolui. Incensum abhomminatio est mihi. Manus vestræ sanguine plenæ sunt. Quis quesivit hæc de manibus vestris?* Quocirca addit propheta: *Lavamini et mundi estote. Auferte malum cogitacionum vestrarum ab oculis meis*. Hoc enim est sacrificium quod placet Deo, et hostia pinguis ac immaculata; homo videlicet a malis purgatus. Quo Judeorum sacrificia spectant, ut signa et monumenta; et mactacio illa pecoris significat pecuinas appeticiones in corpore enecari oportere, ut corpus purgatum et sanctum vivat et obsequatur racioni et placeat Deo. Nam revera Deus non mortuis

Es. i. 11. 16.

sed vivis hostiis delectatur, nec quicquam in pecudibus exposcit, sed in ipsis hominibus. In quibus velit quasi mactari omnes beluinas appeticiones, et easdem igne divini spiritus incendi, ut ab omnibus viciis purgatum corpus sanctum et sine labe vivat animæ et Deo.

Quapropter obsecravit Paulus Romanos, ut corpora sua exhibeant hostiam sanctam, viventem, obsequentem racioni ; hoc est, revocet quisque et contrahat suum corpus in obsequium animæ et racionis, ut libera abduci ab hoc mundo et subjici ac tradi Deo possit ; ut ab illo reformata, et divino vigore roborata, et firmius secum constet, et forcius immodestum et excurrens corpus coarceat. Hæc autem vis impertita animæ cuique, quæ est substrata Deo, qua fit vigorosior, est quædam spiritualis vita, luce constans et calore spirituali. Nam, ut corpus luce et calore vivit, vigetumque est lucido calore et calida luce, quæ ab anima in ipsum diffusa est, quæ ipsa corporis vita dicitur, qua sentit, appetit, et agit omnia ; ita ferme eodem modo ipsa quoque anima vivit, viget et valet quadam vita, quæ spirituali luce et calore constat, quæ in eam defusa est ab omnium animarum anima, Deo. Cujus radio est unus, qui et lucens et calens mirifice unita, illustrata et calefacta anima, sollide secum constat, et vere sentit, et bene agit omnia. Ab unitate enim solliditas et potencia ; a luce veritas et rectitudo ; a calore bonitas et proba actio. Ex unione in Deum, ab uniente gracia et radio, regignitur anima et est denuo. Esse enim nihil est aliud quam unitas. Ex illuminacione confidit Deo creditque, ac credens cernit clarissime, et cernens credit. Ex calore denique amat et desiderat Deum, divinaque omnia propter Deum.

Ita voluntas sua, qui est divino spiritu regenitus in Deum, amor est Dei et divinorum: intellectus, visio Dei divinarumque rerum fide: esse, unitas et constantia est in statu, in quem contraxit et rapuit illud mirificum et prepotens, quod vel divinum spiritum, vel radium, vel vim, vel influxum, vel graciam possumus appellare. Hæc constancia et esse, ut mihi videtur, spes est, qua sumus et stamus. Nam spe vivimus, sumus et stamus ; sicuti contra desperacione solvimur, defluimus et cadimus. Et ut hæc non reperit in quo consistat, ita spes habet in quo se figat et conquiescat; ut animæ ipsa stabilitas in Deo videatur esse spes; luculencia et claritas, fides; ardor et efficacia, charitas. Et concludamus ergo, spe nos esse, fide sapere, charitate bonos esse; hiisque tribus animæ vitam constare et vigorem, qua vivit, et est, et sapit, et amat Deum; qua stat, et se conservat et sustinet; qua etiam astringit corpus, et in obsequium sibi devincit; qua denique totus homo bonus, pulcher et felix fit.

Quam quidem vitam felicitatemque non a se ipsa anima, sed aliunde ex alto habet, et *desuper ab illo patre luminum;* a quo, ut scribit Jacobus, *omne donum perfectum est;* qui condidit mundum et humanum genus; qui passus est scelera juste multorum; qui misericorditer revocavit paucos; qui lege astrinxit aliquos, hebreos videlicet; qui crebro eosdem per prophetas monuit; qui postremo immensa quadam clemencia et benignitate voluit totius humani generis misereri tempore opportuno, ac modo et racione mirabili; quandoquidem suum ipsius proprium filium ei coeternum et coequalem, ac substancia essenciaque penitus idem, tantus ille et tam indulgens pater voluit hominem fieri; ut per eum homines revocati ad Deum dii efficerentur. Hic filius Dei et hominis, Deus et homo, qui grece *theonthropon* dicitur, Jesus est Christus, mediator Dei et hominum, in se ipso utrumque extremum mire copulans; ut hoc ineffabili medio commode et gratiose extrema inter se illa copularentur. Verbum caro factum est, et Deus filius hominis, ut caro ad verbum habeat accessum, et homo filius Dei fieret. Deus induit humanitatem, ut homo divinitatem indueret. Deus se humiliavit, ut homo exaltaretur. In Christo humanitatis et divinitatis unitio, ut homines cum Deo co-unirentur.

O extremorum medium mirabile et mirificum, omni cultu colendum et adorandum! *Nec est aliud nomen* quam hoc sacrosanctum Jesu *sub celo* (ut recte scripsit Joannes) *in quo oporteat homines salvos fieri.* Hic, ut verissime de se ipse testatur, *via est* et *hostium;* et, ut scribit Paulus, *Dei virtus in salutem omni credenti, Judeo primum et Greco.* Hic consilio dispensacioneque inestimabili venit apparuitque in terris in carne in hominibus, ob hanc quidem maxime causam,

Iac. i. 17.

Act. iv. 12.

Rom. i. 16.

immo solam, ut homines sibi superbe confisos ad humilem Deo fidem convertat; ut qui sibi suisque viribus, quæ nullæ sunt, confisi sunt arrogantius, versi in Deum humiliter soli Deo confidant; nihil sibi, sed omnia Deo tribuant; nihil ex se sed ex Deo omnia expectent; denique nihil se sed Deum solum ament et desiderent.

Hic enim finis, hoc propositum fuit incorporationis incarnationisque Christi, ut mundus confidat credatque Deo, qui ante Christi adventum sibi est confisus et credidit. Unde omne genus mali miseriæque exortum est. Nam revera quum mundus in se versus ac sibi confidens magnifecit seipsum, ex hoc cecitas, improbitas, libido, perversitas, arrogantia, ambitio, avaricia, invidia, odium, bellum, rapina, homicidium, luxuria, gula, fornicatio, negligentia Dei, contemptus hominum, ubique violatio juris tum humani tum divini, ac preterea quicquid in malis est, ita aliud ex alio crevit ad totius mundi perniciem, ut jure communis perditionis radix possit dici ea hominum sibi ipsis confidençia, quæ revera odiosa superbia est. Hinc tot testimoniis sacra scriptura superbiam detestatur. Sed nunc uno illo concionatoris illius contenti volumus esse, qui *odibilem coram Deo et hominibus* dicit *superbiam;* et paulo post omnis *peccati inicium* vocat superbiam. Hoc est quia hominibus illi inique confidunt, qui *terra et cinis est;* qui sunt nati ut sursum spectent, expectentque sibi omnia a Deo, ex Deo pendeant, Deo se soli credant, Deo fidant, in Deo conquiescant: quod donec fiat, finis malorum esse non potest. *Est enim hic mundus* ita *totus positus in maligno,* ut ejus innumerabilis malicia nisi ab infinito bono vinci non potest; nec homines unquam malis carebunt, nisi vi quadam longe super se a malorum turba rapiantur, nisique ab ipso bono boni fiant, ut in bono malum vincant. Nam bonitas est sola quæ malum vincit, hominesque bonitate prediti sunt soli potentes qui discutiant malum, malumque exsuperent. Hæc quidem bonitas a Deo bono diffusa ad malos, et qui mali erant benefaciens, est ea vis quæ fortem reddit animam et victricem malorum; quæ counit, sistit, stabilit, illuminat, illustrat, incendit, inflammat. Quæ quidnam est aliud quam gratia Dei, et Dei charitas, et Dei donum? qui ipse (ut Augustino placet) spiritus est sanctus.

Qui unus unit divisa, constans sistit vaga, clarus illuminat obscura, ardens incendit frigida, dispersa congregat, dissidencia conciliat, dissoluta componit, inordinacione difformia coordinat pulchraque facit; qui denique ubique, in quibusque residet, efficit sua salutari presentia, ut mirum in modum ubique unitas, pulchritudo et bonitas appareat.

Hunc autem spiritum et graciam donumque Dei ut afferret in terras proponeretque hominibus, venit pius Jesus; spiritum scilicet primo homines Deo, deinde ipsos inter se homines, conciliantem. Quod nato Christo testati sunt angeli, cantantes pastoribus : *In terra pacem hominibus bonæ* Luc. ii. 14. *voluntatis;* pacem videlicet et reconciliacionem tum Deo, tum inter se ; si docti a Christo velint Deo confidere. Quæ confidencia Deo est humilitas ; sicuti contra illa tibi ipsi confidencia, superbia. Nam ut tibi confisus te effers, ita Deo confidens subjicis te Deo. Quæ humilitas certe est maxima hominis altitudo. Nam quid altius quam subjici altissimo, subjectioneque prope ad altissimum accedere ? Contra quoque quid humilius, dimissius et dejectius est, quam versione tui in teipsum averti, discedere et distare a Deo ? Quo fit ut nihil tam humile et depressum est quam superbia, nihil etiam tam erectum et altum quam humilitas ; hæc enim tendit sursum ad Deum, illa deorsum ad hominem. Hæc decessus est hominis a se et accessus ad Deum ; illa accessus ad hominem est, immo ad inferius homine, et a Deo longe dissessus.

Quæ superbia, ut sæpe dixi, nihil aliud est quam hominis suis ipsius viribus arrogans confisio, quæ primum angelos, deinde homines prostravit. *Ascendam*, dixit ille lucifer Es. xiv. 14. *superbius, et ero similis altissimo.* Attemptavit etiam ille Adam primus homo gustare vetitum, ut Deo similis fieret ; quæ superbia fuit abiitio a Deo longe, et in imum prostratio. Qui vero minime sibi confisi, Deo subjecti, confidant Deo, hii confidentes in altum trahuntur ; quod diffisi sibi Deo confisi sunt, et quod agnoscentes suam infirmitatem, suisque viribus diffidentes, recognoverint magnitudinem et potenciam Dei, eamque ammirati sunt et amaverint, et illi se crediderint, in illaque sola posuerint spem, quam Paulus asserit *non confundere*, id est, non fallere et decipere Rom. v. 5. hominem. Quia Deus sperantes amat, et facit sperantes redamare ; qui diffundit suam charitatem per corda hominum, per spiritum sanctum quem dat hominibus.

Verum, ne noster sermo versetur in equivocis, verba quibus utimur distinguamus. Quoniam, quum tradidimus tria quibus anima nova vita et divina constat, spes, fides et charitas, spem in unione posuimus et esse; fidem in illuminacione et sapere; charitatem in ardore et amore. Atque etiam, quia modo disserentes de confidencia Deo, quam vocabamus humilitatem et subjectionem, hæc verba confidere, confisum et reliqua dirivata a fidere usurpavimus; ne quispiam ex hoc capiat, fidem illam quæ in lumine consistit, humiliationem esse, et primum unde hominis salus exoritur, volumus ut hæc legentes sint admoniti nos aliquando per confidenciam spem significare; hæcque duo verba sperare et confidere confundere, quod latine loquendi mos patitur, quum qui sperant, confidere dicuntur, et qui confidunt, sperare. Nec id eciam ab usu sacræ scripturæ abhorret, modoque loquendi Pauli. Siquidem ad Corinthios scribit: *Habentes spem, multa fiducia utimur;* et ad Hebreos, *Si fiduciam et gloriam spei usque ad finem retineamus.*

<small>2 Cor. iii. 12. Heb. iii. 6.</small>

Quæ spes inicium est humanæ profectionis in Deum, quæ est collectio animæ et counitio ac contractio in Deum ut illuminetur et incendatur. Nam divisa et dispersa per corpus, nec lumen tenere nec calorem servare potest. Primum ergo est ut a multiplici diffidentia cogatur in unam spem, ut unita illuminetur, illuminata ardeat; cogatur quidem in unum, contractu spiritus sancti, ut uni Deo speret, ut sperans credat, ut credens diligat, ut amor ex fide et ex spe fides possit proficisci.

Sunt quidem hæc tria, fides spes et charitas, a Dei spiritu uno bono et pulchro simul eodem momento in animam infusa. Verumtamen, si nihil prohibeat quin in momentaniis ordo excogitari possit, et primum, secundum et tercium statuere, profecto ratio exposit ut fides charitati, spes fidei antecedat. Quandoquidem spes unitione, fides lumine, charitas ardore consistit. Quod si rerum ordo exigit ut prius quodque sit unione quam luceat, prius luceat quam ardeat, profecto tum necesse sit, ut primum locum teneat spes, quæ est quædam unitio et stabilitas animi; secundum fides, quæ illustratio mentis et Dei cognitio; tercium et ultimum charitas, qui amor est cogniti Dei et desiderium. Quæ tria, si tria sunt distincta racione, eum arbitror habere ordinem. Sin vero unum quiddam dumtaxat est, quod fortasse eciam potest non absurde putari, quum radius unus est et omnino individuus, sique non est differentia in re, sed in phantasmate quædam discreta apparitio; hoc sua crassitate false unum et simplex quodque dispartit in se et dividit: utquunque est, si pluralitas statuatur, sique sint tria distincta, ea sentimus ad ordinem quem modo diximus succedere oportere, sitque prima spes confidentiaque Deo, secunda fides revelatorumque visio, tercia charitas creditorumque amatio; quarum trium virtutum tametsi hic cogitatur ordo, tamen ita sunt connexa, et tam arcto vinculo colligata, ut nec spes potest esse, nisi luculenta et ardens, nec fides nisi sperans et diligens, nec denique charitas, nisi cum summa spe et claritate.

Hæc una et pulchra bonitas, et bona ac pulchra unitas, et una ac bona pulchritudo, ipsa vita est animæ, reddens eam fortem, formosam et beneficam; quæ unitas est firma spes, pulchritudo splendida fides, bonitas ardens charitas. Supra terras *exortus est sol justiciæ,* unus pulcher et bonus Christus, Mal. iv. 2. *in quo sunt omnes thesauri sapienciæ et scientiæ absconditi.* Col. ii. 3. In quo *inhabitat omnis plenitudo divinitatis corporaliter;* qui Ib. 9. potens, splendidus, et suavissime calens, mirifice coegit hominum animos in spem, illustravit fide, incendit amore. Hic sol hominum animos irradians, eorum videlicet qui sibi ipsis confidere desinunt, quique contracti facile incipiunt confidere Deo, id est, sperare, simul eos counit in robur, attollit in lucem, arripit in flammam; ut fortissime secum constent sperantes in Deo; clarissime videant quam plurima, credentes revelatis; vehementissime ardeant desiderio, Deum divinaque misteria amantes.

Hic Christus *splendor paternæ gloriæ,* lux mundi, vita Heb. i. 3. hominum, caput ecclesiæ, anima humanæ societatis, mirabiliter, ut decuit, ex virgine depromptus est inter homines, ut homines tum Deo tum eos inter se reconciliaret; constitueretque in terris civitatem, cujus ipse sit dominus; construeretque ex hominibus quasi corpus, cujus ipse sit caput;

a quo, tanquam a fonte, vita, id est, unitas, lux, et calor spiritalis per membra pulchro ordine dirivetur; ut quisque participet, quantum sua sinit capacitas et sibi satis est; utque omnes coeant tanquam membra unius corporis in unam communitatem, in qua quisque teneat locum suum, et agat pro modulo suo, nec plus attemptet quam vires paciuntur, nec omittat ullo modo facere quod vires concedunt, sed acceptum referat Christo, et impertitam graciam, quoad possit, conferat in communem utilitatem; semper memor se corporis Christi membrum esse, et accitum non ut sibi vivat soli, sed corpori; immo eciam pro corporis salute, si sit necesse, moriatur.

Oportet enim hujus sanctæ societatis, quam in unum cogere voluit Christus, omnes partes integrum ac sanum corpus corporisque portes imitari. Quæ quanquam multæ, variæ et diversæ sunt, tum forma, tum viribus, tum officiis; tamen certe natura et vita conciliante, a corporis capite in omnia membra et artus profecta, omnes partes ita inter se coherent et ad unum constudent, et pro viribus mutuo tam se inter se sedulo coadjuvant, operis ultro citroque collatis, ut in toto non plures, sed ex pluribus partibus unum quiddam totum confectum extet, in quibus nulla privata sit racio, nulla proprii commodi cura, sed ubique et ob omnibus, tacita docente natura, communitatis et unitatis ac totius corporis salutis mirum studium; ut quodvis membrum videatur confiteri tunc se maxime valere quum totum corpus maxime valeat; idque, quod in communionem corporis confert, † se † sentire in semet ipsum se conferre; nec meliori racione, immo nulla alia, sibi vitam et vires querere posse, quam agere quoad maxime possit ut totum corpus vigeat et valeat, quum ex totius corporis salute et robore suam ipsius bonam valetudinem videt dependere; ac, nisi in totius corporis bona valitudine, se ullo modo valere posse.

Hoc naturæ exemplar, quæ optima rectitudinis materia est, ut modo dixi, Christianum corpus, quod ex Christo capite et Christianis fidelibus, tanquam membris, constat, oportet valde imitari. Christus ipse autor naturæ propositum habuit in hominibus ipsam naturam exprimere, et ad naturæ ordinem et pulchritudinem quæ ab ordine deciderint redigere, reformareque humanum genus, quod erat morbis et transgressionibus totum deforme, fedum et detestabile. Quod fieri non potuit sine prepotenti aliqua vi et vita, quæ plena in uno ab ipso uno in multos fundaretur; quæ pergens, revocans, restituens, reconcilians, restauraret pristinum statum hominibus, hominesque ipsos inter se aliquo justo ordine componeret, reformaretque omnia in melius; ut non amplius malum et iniquitas in hominibus, sed in omnibus bonum et equum esset; et ex omnibus ordo ac concensus, et in unum et ad unum conspiratio, commune studium, mutua voluntas, benignitas, benificencia, misericordia, et subsidium vicissitudinarium, leticia et meror communis, detrimentum et lucrum, denique omnia communia, privatum autem nihil prorsus neque in bonis neque in malis, sed in prosperis congratulatio et congaudium, in adversis compassio et condolentia; ut ex pluribus et diversis mutuo et intimo concensu ac concordia unum quiddam ac quasi penitus idem esse videatur.

Id studium est capitis in quoque corpore, unde vita manat, in quæ manat et dirivatur, ea in communionem unitatemque conciliare; vi scilicet vitæ ejus quæ una defunditur, quæ unifica ubique contendit ad unum et simplex, ipsamque unitatem et simplicitatem certissimum suæ presentiæ prestat argumentum; quam sanitas in toto corpore et validum robur et vivax color suapta natura consequitur. Hæc quidem vita in corpore est lucidus calor et calida lux, profusa sane ab illa intima et summa anima quæ est caliditas et lux verior et purior, siquidem spiritalis, non sensu quidem sed a cognoto sibi intellectu agnita. Cujus in corpore sentitus calor et lux, quam vitam corporis voco, posterior et crassior illius antiquioris vitæ et purioris ymago est; illam ruditer et pinguiter in sordida et inepta materia referens. Quæ vita in corpus ab anima est invecta, per quedam congrua media, quæ utrumque extremum in se unum,[1] quæque constant ex superiori et sinceriori corpore, et ex anima humiliore et (ut ita dicam) concretiori. Quos vitales spiritus medici appellant, quæ sunt luculenta cor-

---

[1] *Leg.* uniunt.

puscula ex sereniore corporis parte et animæ dimissiore ac quodammodo obscuriori composita, quæ, media inter summam animam et humile corpus, faciunt et corpus referre animam, et animam corpus agnoscere. In anima ipsa calor et lux est intellectus et voluntas; in hiis mediis spiritibus sensus et appeticio; in hoc denique corpore lumen et fervor sensibilis.

Sic ordine promanant et commeant hæc duo a summo ad imum; lux videlicet et calor; quæ ut succedunt deorsum et degenerant in deterius, ita diversis nominibus sortiuntur. Sed quocunque deducuntur, id laborant ut se tutentur quoad possint, utque multiplicem et sparsam materiam in quam illapsæ sunt contineant in unum, in unitateque conservent. Et superioris cujusque gradus ea est assidua cura, ut inferiorem, cui est vicinior, sustentet unicione. Est etiam cujuslibet ad superius se sollicita obsequela, ut ab illo ipse quoque in unitate et vita sustineatur. Nihil enim in tota rerum universitate seorsum et in se omnino absolute vivere potest, preter unum illud primum, quod nullius indigum sibi soli sufficit. Quicquid vero preterea est in mundo, cum egens est, nec sibi satis est, oportet, ut sit et bene sit, cum aliis vivat. Quapropter nihil nec naturæ rerum congruentius, nec Deo gratius, quam quum singula per se egent, in copulata societate sufficienciam quererе, in quam mutuis auxiliis cuique egenti fiat opitulatio. Quoniam nihil potest dicere vere *quod non eget;* nihilque est quod non ab alio potest et debet adjuvari; non modo inferiora a superioribus, sed forsan etiam multo magis ab inferioribus superiora. Quandoquidem mundi machina ita est temperata ut nihil alio carere potest. Ita est sapientia et amore Dei et creata et conjuncta, ut nihil possit tam placere Deo quam sapiens et amabilis et mutuo inter se amans omnium rerum societas. Quam primum in magno mundi corpore et, ut Plato vocat, *animali*, sancte servatam, secuta omnia deinde animalia obnixe servant, non solum in se quodque sua ipsius compositura, sed, quod mirabilius est, occulta impellente natura, quæ generis ejusdem sunt, ordinem inter se querunt et societatem. Omnium autem quæ sunt racione predita in hoc spectabili mundo, solum genus hominum nescio qua infirmitate et per-

1 Cor. xii. 21.

versitate exorbitant, plane defectu conciliantis et continentis vitæ, id est, sapientiæ et amoris. Quapropter *Dei sapientia et Dei virtus* Jesus Christus descendit, ut humanum genus ad viam, ordinem, et societatem sapientem et bonam reduceret, infundendo in homine sapientiam et virtutem ut concaleant et colluceant in vitam, in unumque congregati arcto federe amoris colligentur contrahanturque in Deum unde exierint. Nam ut diffusa corporis vita ad animam tanquam ad fontem reducitur, ita hominum omnis vita quidem, qua una se continent et conuniunt,[1] id est, sapientia et bonitas, Deo unde prodiit referenda est. Etenim[2] Deus hominum anima, non aliter quidem quam corporis sua cujusque anima; vivitque et bene valet quæque societas Deo, ut corpus anima. Is idem in homine voluit esse, et incarnari, et quasi quodam in capite esse, ut funderet in omnes homines vitam; et quasi sibi conficeret puriorem hominum partem, id est, simpliciorem, delegit quos afflavit spiritu; et quasi† quodam in capite esse† vitales spiritus sibi et ceteris hominibus fecit, qui a se in totum mundum et humanum corpus lucem et vitam ferrent. Hinc illud evangelicum: *Vos estis lux mundi* et *sal terræ*. Fuerunt enim apostoli, *quorum sonus in omnem terram exivit*, vita lucida vehicula et calida, instar vitalium spirituum, illuminantia homines et calefacientia. Sermo ille illorum apostolorum fuit evangelium; sermo et oratio lucida et calida ab igneis hominibus profecta, quæ discussit ignoranciæ tenebras, et peccatorum ac impietatis frigus superavit, fecitque quos apprehendit sapientia et amore Dei perlucere. Ignis ipse, ipsa anima hominum in Christo capite, id est, divinitas, illustravit incenditque apostolos. Hii deinde angeli et ministratorii spiritus inter caput et corpus illuminaverunt ac pietatis calore vivificaverunt corpus, id est, reliquam hominum multitudinem; eam videlicet quæ vitæ radios admittere et eis commoveri potuerint. Hii quidem erant quos divina providencia fecit idoneos. Ex hiis vocatis et tractis per vitæ radios conficitur unum corpus, cujus caput

1 Cor. i. 24.

Mat. v. 14, 13.
Rom. x. 18.

---

[1] Fortasse *convivunt*.   [2] *Leg.* Est enim.

est Christus, cujus anima est divinitas, cujus membra divina inspiracione et gracia viventes sunt homines.

In quibus pro varia imperticione spiritus, variæ sunt vitæ status et condiciones. Alii enim se habent in hoc corpore ut spiritus intus vitales, qui internuncii sunt expediti et celeres, ut ubique et omnia membra vivificent. Verum in hiis spiritibus est longus ordo, aliique ex eis plus lucent, alii minus. Summatim tamen omnium est officium ut purgent, illuminent et calefaciant, vivificent et roborent. Quod quidem faciunt alii ad phantasma in corpore et communem sensum; alii ad visum; alii ad auditum; ad odoratum alii; alii ad gustum; alii ad expeditionem linguæ; alii ad promptitudinem manuum; ad celeritatem pedum alii. Ita presencia animæ et irradiacione spiritali, varia efficiuntur membra in corpore pro porcione spiritus, et ad diversa destinantur officia.

Sic eodem modo presentia Dei in hominibus et in Christo capite vigente, spiritalis et divina irradiacio est hominum a Deo anima, primum in homines simplices, apostolos, deinde in alios ordine, in quemque scilicet pro sua capacitate, et ut anima eum effinxit idoneum, a simplicioribus ad multipliciora pergens, et progressu degenerans, quanto in materiam delabitur crassiorem. Prima creatio et constitucio spirituum est, qui ipsi exoriuntur varii et dissimiles pro materiæ varietate. Nam anima eis insidens et animans ac illustrans penitus una et eadem est. Sed ut corporea pars dissimiliter se habet in crassitate et sinceritate, ita luminosæ animæ et vitæ dissimilis et varia est participatio, diversique in primis constituuntur spiritus vitales. Et hoc quidem alta animæ providencia factum est in corpore, ut quum in corpore sint varia et diversa membra, sint eciam varii agentes et illuminantes spiritus, ut sit quod cuique parti corporis accommodetur. Ita pariter divinitas in Christo capite, summa illa humanæ societatis anima in capite vigens, primum simpliciorem sincerioremque humani generis partem se impertivit, et quasi vitales spiritus composuit, qui ipsi quoque inter se ita differunt luminis et divinæ vitæ participacione, ut apprehensi a lumine sensiuntur inter se simplicitate et multiplicitate differre. Ut enim se habet crassitas et subtilitas in corporibus ad lumen ab anima diffusum, ut corpus vivat, ita simplicitas sane et multiplicitas in animis se habet ad radios divinitatis. Atque, ut quisque est simplex vel multiplex, unus vel divisus, ita plus minusve est deificatus; hoc est, animatus et reformatus divino spiritu, ut spiritalis vita sit, vel spiritus vitalis. In hoc hominum genere, qui se habent magna illustracione ut spiritus, sunt apostoli, quos Christus vocavit mundi luces. Et Joannes in Apocàlipsi plane *spiritus* vocat Dei, *angelos* et *stellas*. Apoc. iii. 1.

Qui ipsi apostoli varie illuminantur quidem, ut magis conveniat locis ad quæ mittantur; ipsique eciam humilius et crassius corpus, id est, reliquam ecclesiam et mundum varie illuminant, faciuntque ut varia extent in crassa materia lumina, vel colores potius, ut quisque tam appareat bonus et pulcher, et sit eciam, quam est particeps lucentis et calefacientis graciæ; quod Paulus significat cum dicit; *Unicuique secundum mensuram fidei*; sintque aliqui in quibus sit quasi quidam candor lucis, ut in humilioribus rebus facile quid album quid nigrumque sit decernant; id est, quid bonum quid malum; aliique eciam sint qui absurda et consona fidei judicent, qui sunt quasi aures Cristiani corporis; aliqui olfaciunt quid bene spirat beneque olet in sensum Dei, de humanis actionibus; in hiisque eciam quid male olet et fetet; aliqui qui doctrina quavis apposita notant statim quid bonum et suavem saporem habet, quid amarum; aliqui qui facile palpant in hominibus quid calet in Deo, quid friget. Communis sensus et phantasma hæc omnia facit, et supra phantasma racio modo excellentiori; racio inquam spiritalis. Mens autem christianæ ecclesiæ, et ipsa intima divinitas longe maxime et certissime; quam nemo latere potest; qui est Deus *scrutans corda et renes;* quo quanto dimissius itur, eo officia ad particularia magis contrahuntur, et ex profluxu et degeneracione nascitur ordo in hominibus, et series virtutum ac membrorum corporis Christi, sic mirum in modum, ut cum vilitate necessitas et utilitas major excrescat, ut recompensacio fiat, et adequacio membrorum; ut quanto quodvis pulchritudine superet, tanto idem ab aliis necessitate superetur. Rom. xii. 6. Ps. vii. 10.

Quod sapientissime Paulus notavit et docuit in prima

1 Cor. xii. 22.	Epistola ad Corinthios, dicens: *Multo magis quœ videntur membra corporis infirmiora esse, necessaria sunt.* Et addit:
Ib. v. 27.	*Vos estis corpus Christi, et membrum de membro;* quo agnoscitur profusio membrorum, et degeneracio et varietas simul cum recompensacione; ut fiat coequatio et counitas ex pari prestancia, si omnia numeres et equa lance perpendas.
Ib. v. 24.	Hinc in eodem loco Paulus ait: *Deus temperavit corpus, ei, cui deerat, abundanciorem tribuendo honorem, ut non sit scisma in corpore, sed in ipsum pro invicem sollicita sint membra.* In quo est valde animadvertendum quidem Deum tale, et ex talibus ex quibus ille vult hominibus, corpus ecclesiamque sibi construere, quos ipse non solum inspiravit reformavitque in parte suo corpori digna, sed preterea effecit ut ad reformacionem apti essent, et divinæ formæ vitæque capaces; ut non solum reformacio cujusque et quod is locum habent in Dei ecclesia tribuendum sit Deo, sed eciam certe ipsa cujusque habilitas, formæque capacitas. Quoniam habilis et idoneus (si Pauli doctrinam sequamur, quæ ante omnia sequenda est) ut cogatur in unum et illustretur fide, nemo esse potest, nisi quatenus benigna Dei gratia ipsum habilem fecerit; qui novit quos vult eligere, et eligit notos, et notos effictioni formacionique suæ adaptat. Nam, ut Joannes
Ioan. iii. 8. 1 Cor. xii. 18.	evangelista testatur, *Spiritus ubi vult spirat;* et Paulus ad Corinthios, *Nunc,* inquit, *posuit Deus membra, unumquodque eorum in corpore, sicut voluit.* Is enim effingit aptos et aptat fingendos. Is materiam et format et disponit. Ab eo Deo est proculdubio tota hominis vivificacio et salus; ut homo in se de quo glorietur nihil habeat prorsus, sed agnoscat ex
Ps. xxiii. 10.	Deo esse omnia, Deoque soli, qui *rex est gloriæ,* omnem gloriam deferendam.

Verum nunc aliquando ad Paulum nostrum revertamur, qui ecclesiam velit corporis constructionem imitari, ordine, copulacione, connexu, mutuis officiis et virium moderacione. Quoniam ex modestia, ordine et amore pulchre secum constant omnia. Immodestia autem et excursio, disturbacio ordinis, et dissidium, labefactat et deturpat omnia: vis autem in servando ordine et unitate consociatorum est maxime posita in tenenda modestia et temperancia; ut nemo supra se contendat, nec fines impositos transgrediatur, sed agnoscat vires, et intra suarum virium terminos se contineat. Ita facit quodque membrum in humano corpore, quamdiu sanum permanet. Nec est insanitas et morbus aliud quidem quam excursio membri a vita et forma sibi ab anima tributa, et quasi dirupcio vinculorum continentis formæ, et membri in se solucio; unde infirmitas, deformitas et morbus nascitur, ac apparet in corpore, quod est interitus inicium. Nam nihil est aliud tocius corporis mors, quam ejusdem a sustinente forma casus et solucio. Ex forma et contencione corporis in unum, robor et valitudo corporis est; ex lapsu vero in se, in suam ipsius multiplicitatem, suboritur imbecillitas et egritudo, quæ pergit ad mortem. Ut ergo totum corpus valet et viget, quamdiu firmiter a tota animante forma continetur, ita quodvis membrum ejus similiter tenet vigorem suum, quamdiu intra terminos suæ particularis formæ tenetur; a qua si exilierit, egrotat, et ex imbecilitate fervet et ardet immodestius. In forma vero dum continetur, calet mollius et suavius, vitali spiritu dulciter fovente; a quo quum discesserit, in seque ceciderit, tum crassius et intemperatius ardet, et urit immoderatius; qui incastigatus ignis et inflammatio in membro morbus est. Sanitas ergo corporis in obsequio consistet materiæ formæ et vitæ datæ, inque observacione modi, et intra fines libenti permansione.

Ita quoque est similiter in Christiana ecclesia, in qua hominum animi spiritali vita a Deo fusa vivunt; quisque scilicet pro modo datæ et acceptæ vitæ. · Hæc vita, ut est modo a nobis sepe dictum, amans fides est et credulitas Deo. Quæ est quadam analogia et sapienti proporcione a Deo hominibus distributa, ut hii Deo credentes in Deo vivant, sintque fideles omnes varia fide, magnitudine et parvitate ad constructionem unius fidelis ecclesiæ, cujus caput sit Christus; in quo veritas ipsa et divinitas insidet; unde omnis fides et vita in hominum animos promanavit.

Quod si tota ecclesia et omnes ejus partes amanti fide vivit Deo et Christo, sique hæc fides est quasi vita coporis et ecclesiæ, tum profecto est necesse tam diu vivat et valeat ecclesia, quam diu ab anima, id est, a Deo, in una fide contineatur. Hoc quidem erit quamdiu homines obsequuntur et adherent modo suæ fidei, in ejusque finibus retineri se patiantur; quæ est mollis, suavis et clarus intellectus rerum, fovens et firmans animam, et eam in sanitate sustinens. Quod si quispiam deserens fidem delabetur in se in fervorem et insaniam ingenii sui, et quasi solutus a vinculis fidei defluat infirmiter ultra terminos credulitatis, contendatque sua infirmitate aliquid vel sentire vel agere, est necesse primum is amissa vita fidei animo egrotet, et deinde, quicquid attemptat, debiliter agat, nihilque proficiat. Hic casus a fide cujusque in suam ipsius infirmitatem et opinionem plane ipsius animæ insania est et stulticia, fervens et furens pene immodestius, et vagans in tenebris, quandoquidem a suavi et serena fide deseritur, quæ est dulcis animæ vita, lumen et stabilitas, animam serenans, et in unum continens, nec sinens eam ab unitate confidenciaque Deo defluere.

Itaque omnis morbi causa, immo morbus ipse quisque et dissonancia in ecclesia, est intemperies racionis, et a vitali fide exorbitacio, ac insolens transcursio finium, et discessus a *modo fidei;* quæ est unicuique, ut ait Apostolus, divisa ad mensuram et analogiam, ut ex pluribus et variis fidelibus pulchra et concinna proporcione quiddam unum conficiatur, ordine et modo ubique sancte et religiose servato.

Quapropter admonet Romanam ecclesiam, *ut nemo plus sapiat quam oportet, sed sapiat quisque ad sobrietatem;* hoc est, non excurrat modum fidei, sed quisque suam rationem fidei freno castiget, cohibeatque se intra terminos fidei, quos si sibi confisus intemperata racione exeat, tum plus sapit quam oportet, et sanam fidem deserens insanit et desipit plane, quum se putat sapere. Sicque sapere sine fide revera est minus sapere, et a vera sapiencia degenerare in humilius et deterius. Nam, ut membrum quod a vitalibus spiritibus et molli ac dulci calore deseritur, in se fervet et urit edacius, quando ipsum urere est minus calere; ita in Christiano corpore et ecclesia, qui discessit a fide et sibi confisus conatur sua racione uti, ex seque ipso sapere, is profecto a meliori sapiencia decidit, et sua ipsius sapiencia non tam sapit quam desipit immodestius, quum in se versus delapsus est in deterius, crassius et obscurius. In quo statu mentis nihil est nisi immoderatus error et petulans contencio, cujus exitus horrendum est tedium et confusio. Quo devecti fuerint omnes heretici ob nullam quidem aliam causam, nisi quia sibi suæque infirmitati arrogancius confisi sunt, volueruntque plus attemptare impotenti racione quam firma fide et efficaci. Castigata ergo racio et observatus fidei modus societatem ecclesiæ et unitatem conservat; quando singulus quisque nihil nec sentit nec appetit nisi ex fide Deo et amore Dei, neque plus aggreditur quam credit se suo facto placere Deo, neque vero eciam omittat ullo modo quo se Deo et hominibus placere posse putat. Nam non solum debemus cavere ne excedamus fidem, sed eciam curare diligenter ut assidue, quoad fides patitur, bene agamus, ne desidia torpescat vita, neve inutiliter a Deo donum et vires accepisse videamur. Ut enim in corpore nullum est ociosum et sine officio membrum, ita in ecclesia nemo esse debet qui non aliquid agat, aliquidque utilitatis in communitatem conferat. Præterea eciam, ut in humano corpore mira sollicitudine omnia inter se membra mutuis beneficiis ultro citroque collatis se coadjuvant, fovent, nutriunt et conservant; ita similiter in ecclesia esse debet, et inter omnes fideles, tam mutuus amor et studium, ut quisque suas vires quascunque sibi datas esse crederet ob eam solum causam, ut eas semper in subsidium aliorum et in reipublicæ emolumentum, conservacionemque unitatis et pacis exerceat. *Sumus enim* (ut inquit Paulus) *multi unum corpus in Christo;* et alius alii membrum est et minister; id est, omnes sumus vivificati fide in structuram unius corporis, ut quisque alium pro viribus fidei juvet et sustineat in salute; ut ex auxiliis vicissim prestitis mutua charitas possit apparere inter ipsos inter se homines, imago scilicet illius eximiæ charitatis, quæ fuit et est Christi erga ecclesiam; *ut invicem inter se diligant, sicut Christus dilexit ecclesiam.* Rom.xii. 5.

Eph. v. 25.

Ex presentia quidem Dei, diffusioneque graciæ, variaque impertitione fidei et amoris, varia quasi membra, vires, facultates, officia, actiones, et utilitates in hominibus nascuntur, quæ summatim et cursim commemorat Paulus; magis ut exemplum det et specimen quoddam, quam ut exacte omnia et vero ordine recensiat. Itaque ex fide *prophetiam*, et vaticinium rerum futurarum, et *ministerium* xii. 6. *sqq.*

quam dyaconiam greci appellant, et *doctrinam*, et *exhortacionem*, et *distribucionem*, et *præsidenciam*, et[1] *elimosinam* appellant; quæ facultates elucent in hominibus pro modo et racione impertitæ graciæ et fidei. Addit deinde (quæ debet esse in tota ecclesia) veram Dei *dilectionem, a malo fugam, bono adhesionem,* mutuum inter fideles et *fraternum amorem, anteposicionem in honore,* sollicitudinem et *diligenciam,* calorem vitæ, observacionem temporis, *gaudium in spe, in adversis pacienciam, instantem oracionem,* liberalitatem, hospitalitatem. Subjungit postea benificenciam perpetuam, eciam maledicis et malefactoribus, communem leticiam, communem dolorem, sensus et omnis voluntatis communitatem, humilitatem, inclinacionem, benignitatem, amorem, consensum, concordiam, unitatem, quæ nascitur ex mutua accommodacione et diversarum inter se partium conformacione. Arroganciam vero, superbiam, dedignacionem, altam opinionem, despectum aliorum, injuriarum ultionem, in hominibus detestabiles significat, et valde prohibet, ut seminarium pestis et perniciei. Vult enim Paulus ut omnis vindicta et ultio Deo soli relinquatur, qui in suo propheta dixit: *Mihi vindictam, et ego retribuam.* In membris Christiani corporis et ecclesiæ sentit fidem Deo esse oportere et rationem subjectam fidei, humilitatem, tolleranciam, constanciam in bono semper et sine intermissione, bonam actionem eciam male agentibus et nos lacessentibus injuria; ut quodque membrum, quoad potest, caput suum Christum representet; qui fuit ipsa humilitas, bonitas, paciencia, benignitas; qui bonum fecit malis, ut sua bonitate ex malis bonos faceret; imitans patrem suum in celis, qui *facit solem suum oriri super justos et injustos.*

Rom. xii. 19; Deut. xxxii. 35.

Mat. v. 45.

Nam nihil est quod vincit malum nisi bonum. Quod si contendas malum pro malo reddere, conerisque malum opprimere malo, tu ipse tum descendis in malum, et migras stulte in infirmius, et te ad confundendum malum reddis impotenciorem. Immo eciam exauges malum, cum te malis parem facis; quando vis, ipse malus, cum malis confligere. Non potes enim reddere malum pro malo, nisi in reddendo

---

[1] Deest aliquid.

male egeris. Etenim qui infert et qui refert malum, uterque in malo versatur. Uterque ergo malus. Quapropter omnino bonis cavendum est, ne pro malis malum reddant, ne hoc descensu ad malum boni desinant esse. Sed constanter perseverandum est in bonitate et confidencia Deo, ut, quod natura rerum exposcit, contrarium contrario vincamus, et malum bono; agentes videlicet bonitate et paciencia nostra, ut mali boni fiant.

Quæ sola sane est racio et via vincendi mali. Qui vero arbitrantur malum malo discuti posse, profecto stulticia insaniunt, quod res ipsa et experiencia docet. Siquidem humanæ leges, et inflicta pena, et suscepta bella, ac quicquid preterea sit quo homines laborant malum tollere, frustra eo contendunt, et quod volunt nihil assequuntur. Quum plane constat, quicquid homines suis viribus confisi contenderint, ob id tamen nihilo minus mundum plenum esse malis, et ea succrescere quotidie, multiplicarique vehementius (quanquam stulti id non vident), quanto magis homines suis conatibus eradicare ea attemptant.

Nam sit hæc firma et rata sentencia, malum nisi per bonum tolli non posse. Ut enim lux est quæ discutit tenebras, et calor qui frigus propellit, ita sane similiter sola virtus et bonum est quod malum superat vitiaque exterminat. Atque eciam si sol, ut abigat tenebras, se obscuraret, esset inefficacior, minimeque quod velit perageret. Ita profecto qui a bono decedunt, et quasi se obscurant, in malisque par pari referant, nunquam quod moliuntur acquirent. Nam oportet quam dissimillimum se faciat ei quod velit vincere, quicquid sit quod vincere velit. Nam a dissimili vincitur quodque, non a simili. Itaque quam maxime ad bonitatem contendere debes, ut malum vincas; et ad pacem et pacienciam, ut bellum et injustam actionem superes. Non enim bellum bello vincitur, sed pace et paciencia confidenciaque Deo. Etenim ea virtute videmus apostolos totum mundum superasse, et pacientes maxime egisse, et victos vicisse maxime, et denique mortuos vitam in terris maxime reliquisse. Est Christiani viri pugna proculdubio paciencia, et agere ejus pati est, et victoria ejusdem confidencia est Deo, ut ille malum aut juste paciatur aut ferat patienter. Quod quidem non facit malo, sed sua omnipotenti bonitate et misericordia, quando sua benefica gracia vult, qui sunt mali, bonos facere. Quem Deum patrem debet quisque bonus imitari, conarique constanti bonitate aliorum maliciam superare, quoad possit; et,

Mat. v. 44. quod docet bonitas ipsa, Jesus Christus, debemus *diligere inimicos, et qui nos oderunt, eis bonum facere, orareque pro persequentibus, ut possimus filii patris nostri esse, qui est in celis, qui pluit super justos et injustos.*

Huic consentaneum est quod hic apostolus, evangelii

1 Cor. ii. 16. explanator, et possessor *sensus Christi*, scribit et precipit,
Rom. xii. 16. dicens: *Nolite esse prudentes apud vosmet ipsos*, et arrogantes, confidentesque vobis; et *malum pro malo non reddatis*, quod non vincit malum sed auget. Sed estote boni, bonumque exerceatis constanter tum coram Deo tum coram hominibus; ut manifesta bonitate vestra improbi aliquando succumbant, et vestri similes se fieri cupiant. Non irascimini irascentibus, nec vim vi propellatis, sed pacem habitote cum omnibus, faciteque, quantum in vobis est, ut alii vos non ledant; hoc est, offendatis neminem, verum omnino cavete, quomodocunque serviant in vos homines, ut non commoveamini ipsi, neque reluctemini vosmet ipsos defendentes. Sed servate inviolatam pacienciam, et pacem in vobis saltem immotam tenete, ac date locum iræ. Sinatis Deum ulcisci injurias, qui non novistis quamobrem et ad quem finem mala patitur. Non interrumpatis vestra arrogancia, et confidencia viribus vestris, magnam et optimam Dei providenciam; quod quidem est alte sapere et prudentes esse apud vosmet ipsos. Sed sentite humiliter, et soli Deo confidatis, perstate in bonitate et patimini mala. Quæ si vestra bonitate vinci non possunt, tunc credite ob meliorem finem Deum sinere ad tempus et quasi ferre malum. Quare sublacionem illius relinquite Deo magna fide, vosque interea non facite finem bene agendi omnibus, ut bonitate vincatis. Pascite inimicos et sicienti adversario potum date, ac quicquid utilitatis conferre potestis, alacriter omnibus et libenter exhibete. Nam sic profecto solum vincetis malum, et homines eciam malivolos vobis amicos consilietis. Amore et benignitate vestra calefacietis algentes malicia et impro-

bitate, et mansuetudine duros ac rigidos emollietis. Nam ut homines dulcescunt bonitate et clemencia, ita contra malignitate et sevicia amarescunt et acerbi sunt. Verum mollis, suavis et efficax bonitas benignitasque coquit omnia tandem, et facit suo benefico calore ut dura mollescant, et dulcescant amara, ut asperi homines leves, ut feri mites, ut superbi humiles, ut mali boni, denique ut humani divini fiant. Hoc quidem est quod ait Paulus *congerere carbones* *ignis in capud ejus;* quod est calefacere hominem, ac crudam ejus maliciam coquere, et implacatam mentem demulcire; quod aut bonitate et suavitate facies, aut nunquam facies; quia non superatur quicquam nisi a contrario. Quod si malum te provocet ut malum reddas, a malo tum vinceris, ipseque incipis esse malus. Sin contra tua bonitas, mansuetudo, benignitas et beneficencia eos qui mali sunt allicit, et trahit dulciter in statum meliorem, tum tua bonitate malum devicisti. xii. 20.

Quo genere solo pugnandi cum malis primi illi in ecclesia milites sub Christi vexilla sunt usi, glorioseque vicerunt. Quam bonitatis vim et potenciam quum cernit sapientissimus Paulus, hoc aureum preceptum ad Romanos scripsit, scilicet, Noli vinci a malo, sed vince in bono malum. Quod est idem quod paulo supra dixit, Noli malum pro malo reddere; quum hoc est a malo vinci trahique in malum; sed perstate in bono; et coram Deo secrete, et aperte eciam atque audacter coram hominibus. In quos tam firmiter tenenda est paciencia, ut mori pocius debeat quisque quam pati eam in se labefactari; et prius contestari virtutem morte, quam vita vicium ulla ex parte augere. Quod martires fecerunt, de quibus illud dicitur: *Quam preciosa in conspectu Domini mors sanctorum ejus.* Quorum martirium nihil aliud fuit, quam paciencie et virtutis testimonium. Ps. cxv. 15.

Sed nunc quæ sunt reliqua et quæ sequuntur in hac epistola pergamus. In qua scribendo tantam frugem et fructum reperimus, et contemplando singula tanta voluptate tenemur, ut eciam cupientes certe in tam frugifero et ameno agro nequimus leviter preterire. Verum hoc non pretermittam, quum auditorio nostro verba Pauli de ecclesiæ partibus exposuerimus, nos dixisse prophetas fuisse illos ab apostolo dictos qui in unum et in altum contracti in ipsa eternitate veras rerum raciones ac rectam vivendi normam speculati sunt; doctores vero eos qui eam deinde populo concionibus tradiderunt; ministros medios fuisse illos qui acceperunt a prophetis quod doctoribus referrent.

Hunc ordinem existimavimus Paulum significare voluisse, propterea quod admodum congruit racioni, et imitacionem eciam habet illius celestis hierarchiæ, ubi primi ordines ardent et herent Deo continua contemplacione; ultimi huc spectant ad inferiora, et in assidua administracione custodiaque versantur; medii vero sunt intercurrentes ministratorii spiritus, qui accipiunt a superioribus vicissim et ad inferiores deferunt: quem ordinem representari in Christiania ecclesia voluit Paulus, esseque aliquos qui sine intermissione pendeant a Deo, quorum copula cum Deo tota reliqua ecclesia sustineretur, aliquos deinde qui divinum et vitalem liquorem haustum a primis accipiant sedulo, et tradant eis qui id diligenter et continuo populo distribuant. Hic tercii quidem doctores sunt, qui dant plebi quo firmi et validi esse possunt in Deo, unumque sentire et agere, ac cum charitate mutuo se juvare, et unanimiter ac sanctissime vivere et vigere in Deo in unum; ut ab uno Deo nasci et ali et sustineri in unum videantur, habereque radices suas positas in ipso Deo, qui sunt primi in ecclesia, et ab illis trahere et dirivare et decoquere divinum alimentum sapienciæ et bonitatis, in robor et nexum tocius corporis, tam arctum et firmum, ut in id ipsæ portæ inferi non prevaleant. Ad id enim tendit divinissima mens et intencio Pauli. Sed nunc tandem ad institutum revertamur.

CAP. XIII.

SEQUITUR in Epistola post hæc quædam sapientissima admonicio fidelium omnium, qui tunc Romæ fuerant, oportune sana adhibita, ut caute agant, et caveant omnino ne Imperatori et Romanis principibus adversentur, in eis presertim rebus quæ spectant ad morem et consuetudinem Romanæ civitatis, et leges quæ feruntur de tributis et vectigalibus exigendis; quibus (dum cogit necessitas) parere possunt et debent, religione non labefactata. Quibus si noluerint parere, sique exacta tributa solvere recusarent, contempnerentque Romanos Magestratus et illius civitatis et imperii sub quo vivunt auctoritatem, statim illos in iram et crudelitatem provocarent, facerentque ut ipsi partim necati partim ejecti essent a civitate. Quamobrem velit Paulus adhuc in nascenti ecclesia, maxime eciam illis Romæ, in tanta paganorum autoritate, omnia circumspecte, sobrie et pacienter fiant de re pecuniaria, vel quicquid aliud sit cujus mundus est avidus; nihil reluctentur; tributa et vectigalia exacta pendant facile; Romanos illos magistratus *timeant* eciam, et (ut mos est) *honore prosequantur*. Nam, xiii. 7. ut innuit Paulus, sinit et patitur Deus tales magistratus et infidelium potenciam ad tempus. Quamobrem autem et ad quem finem ille solus novit. Disponit enim ille omnia in hoc mundo, ut vult, et ordinat; quod si resisterent, Dei voluntati resisterent. Quocirca ferenda omnia, quæcunque sunt, latenter suadet Apostolus, et docet semper bono cum malo contendendum esse, malumque bono vincendum si fieri possit. Sin minus, tamen a bono nihil decedendum, nec reddendum malum malo, quod est a bono ad malum descendere, sed perstandum firmiter in bonitate et paciencia mali; ut petulans malum constanti bono, et contrarium infirmius revera demum a fortiori contrario superetur.

Fuerunt quidem filii Dei et fratres et Christiani Romæ undique circumsessi malis, et hostibus virtutis ac veræ religionis, quam illi Christicolæ professi sunt. Cum quibus hostibus et adversariis confligendum fuit nullis aliis armis quam contrariis. Non enim frigidum frigidum, nec tenebras tenebræ, nec denique simile simile (immo hoc auget magis); sed calidum vincit frigidum, et lux tenebras, et contrarium profecto contrarium. Ita similiter necessario solum bonum vincit malum; et superbiam, infidelitatem, falsam religionem, odium, injuriosas actiones, bellum, homicidium, et reliqua scelera, eis contraria, humilitas et fides Deo, verusque Dei cultus, amor, paciencia, pax, et mortis in boni constancia non recusatio. Hæc inquam arma lucis si pergant strenue, vincunt et superant et contraria illa longe discuciunt, et suis radiis tandem illustrant omnia. Hiis armis Christus et Apostoli, quos vocavit luces mundi, et depugnarunt et devicerunt. Hac via sola quicquid lucis in mundo est introductum est. Hac eadem via quoque sola introductum quodque vel lucis vel bonitatis servatur ab hominibus et exaugetur. A qua quanto disceditur, eo magis fumus, tenebræ et malum miseriaque in humana vita concitatur.

Quod qui non videt, quique arbitratur vim vi et bellum bello et malum malo repellendum esse, is misera cecitate nihil lucis videt. Qui quanto in errore est ex hoc clare agnosci potest, quod nullis conatibus unquam quod attemptat et cupit perficere assequetur, nec ea via proculdubio senciet aliquando finem malorum, sed mala ex malis exorta ita spisse, ut illa racione in exsolvendo se quanto magis laborat, eo magis in malis se implicabit. Atque adhuc in hoc mundo, qui totus *positus est in maligno*, quod tot malis circumvenimur et eisdem pene obruimur, nulla est quidem alia causa nisi quod stulti et ceci non querimus contrarium suo contrario vincere, sed volumus potius malum malo augere; non cernentes, cum malum malo rependimus, augere nos malum, non repellere. Vidit autem apostolus Paulus, a Christo doctus, illius evangelici precepti, Malum scilicet non reddendum malo, mirificam veritatem. Quod preceptum si sancte et constanter observatum esset, finem malorum haberemus. Iccirco id suis literis sepius et explicavit latius et in hac epistola ad Romanos de eo disserit copiosius, ut Romæ, ubi ex omni parte obstrepuere mala, Christi nomen colentes non malum ullo modo malo reddant, sed paciantur malum, ut constante bonitate tandem et innocencia importunum et procax malum juvante Deo prosternant, et neminem offendant, sed molliter, suaviter, sancte et innocenter incedant in civitate, et agant cum quoque cum nullius contemptu, sed reverencia cujusque, et cuique quod suum est reddant prompte et alacriter; ut ea bonitate simplicitateque vivendi bonum eciam malorum favorem sibi et graciam concilient, quietemque sibi comparent inter inquietos et improbos illius civitatis; ut sine turba et divexacione Deo et Christo inservire possint.

Fuit quidem hæc epistola scripta ad Romanos imperante

EP. AD ROMANOS XIII. 201

Claudio, in exitu sui imperii, circiter annum XXmum predicacionis Pauli. Ad quod eciam tempus, quantum conjicio ex historiis et ipsius Pauli epistolis, utraque epistola ad Chorinthios, et illa ad galathas data, scripta fuit; sed hæc ad Romanos post illas, non multo ante suam ultimam profectionem Iherusolimam. Nam quarto quintove anno post has datas litteras vinctus a festo prefecto Judeæ et missus Roman venit, qui annus fuit XXVus a morte. Christi et commissione Pauli, et neroniani imperii secundus. Post quod tempus adhuc ad XII annos vixit et docuit in Italia, et sub Christo duce a prima sui conversione annis triginta et VIItem usque ad mortem militavit. Interiit prima persecutione Christianorum sub nerone durante, anno illius neronis imperii XIIII° una cum petro in eodem die.

Hæc autem refero ut magna Pauli consideracio et prudencia animadvertatur; qui cum non ignoravit Claudium Cesarem tenuisse rempublicam, qui fuit homo vario ingenio et improbis moribus et repentinis institutis, quique (quod in illius vita scribit Suetonius) Judeos assidue tumultuantes impulsore Christo Roma expulit; propter quem tumultum arbitror Paulum hanc epistolam scripsisse, et Suetonium voluisse significare Judeos propter altercaciones de Christo expulsos a Claudio fuisse. Quumque intellexit Paulus, quod eciam tradit Suetonius, vectigalia nova atque inaudita, a C. Caligula inchoata, Ro. Imperatorem, nullo nec rerum nec hominum genere omisso cui non aliquid tributi imponeretur, exercere; ne sui fratres Romæ, molestiarum tedio forsan affecti, in dedignacionem et contemptum Romanorum magistratuum prorumpant, recusentque contumaces statutis illorum obtemperare, faciendum sibi existimavit Paulus, scribens ad illos qui Christi cultum professi sunt, ut non nihil eos doceret quomodo se gerant adversus illos Romanos et infideles principes, quibus, si Romæ vivant, non poterunt non subesse, nec omnibus illorum statutis reluctari, sed necessario dare illis aliquid quod illorum est; ut id quod suum est teneant, et *reddant,* ut jubet Salvator, *quæ sunt* Mat. xxii. *Cæsaris Cæsari, et quæ sunt Dei Deo.* Quod faciendum 21. quum animadvertit sapientissimus Paulus, hortatur illos et jubet ut sic faciant, utque nullo modo colluctentur cum

Romanis potestatibus, dentve illis occasionem stomachi et iræ, utque inter se ipsos sine discrepancia sinceram charitatem observent, sintque boni tum in se ipsis tum ad alios universos; ut bonitate in se constent, et semper bonitate, quoad possint, contrarios sibi devincant, trahantque ad bonum similitudinemque sui, ipsi autem ad malum nequaquam trahantur.

ii. 17. *sqq.* Huc spectat illud Pauli: *Nulli malum pro malo reddentes, providentes bona non tantum Deo* in vobismet ipsis, *sed coram hominibus,* illis forinsecus paganis quibuscum vivitis. *Non vosmetipsos defendentes* ab injuriis illorum infidelium, *sed date locum iræ* illorum, et habete cum omnibus pacem, et *quatenus ex vobis est, cum omnibus* omnino *servate pacem,* faciteque quoad fieri potest, ut alii quoque omnes vobiscum habeant: ultio injuriarum et vindicta nulla sit apud vos. *Quia scriptum est, Mihi vindictam, et ego retribuam, dicit Dominus.* Sed malis succurrite, et inimicos fovete, et, ad modum boni Dei, boni beneque facientes estote universis. Quæ sola est via vincendi mali faciendique ex malis bonos. Unde jubet, *Sed vince in bono malum.* Et deinde addit quæ spectant ad potenciam et autoritatem Romanorum, cui non resistendum esse dicit, quandoquidem omnia sunt ut disponit divina providencia, et manent quamdiu sinit divina voluntas.

xiii. 1. Quapropter sublimioribus illis potestatibus *subditus debet esse quisque,* ut docet Paulus; illis videlicet paganorum, penes quos tunc omnis in seculo fuit potestas; sic res regiminaque mundi disponente Deo, quæ tolleranda sunt ab hominibus, ne Dei providencia et ordinacionem rerum iniquo animo ferre videantur.

xiii. 3. Tum officium principis et gubernatoris reipublicæ tradit, et latenter docet quales debent esse qui regunt civitates; prospiciens, ut mihi videtur, prudenter, posse accidere aliquando, ut sua hæc epistola in Romanorum manus perveniat. Ita igitur loquutus est de Romanis magistratibus, ut simul eos et doceret, et eorundem favorem in Christianos conciliaret, quando admonet Christicolas non adversentur Romanis principibus, sed obediant, quandoquidem illi a Deo constituti sunt, et agunt hic in terris Dei ministerium, ut puniant malos, bonos autem et innocentes foveant et defendant. Sic facile, quum videant Christianæ religionis homines edoctos a suis magistris, ut constanter boni et innocentes sint, neminemque offendant, quumque simul audiunt talibus magistratibus[1] non nocere debere: sic, inquam, facile et hiisce verbis Pauli si forsan aliquando epistolam legerint, necesse est commoveantur plurimum, ut cum innocentibus Christianis misericorditer agant, eisque sine lesione in civitate manere concedant; quando scilicet audiunt principes non esse formidandos a bonis sed a malis, et illos Dei ministros esse, gladiumque portare ut vim faciant in improbos homines et maleficos, non in bonos et beneficos pacientesque malorum. Quia quoque hæc via est sola, ut jam sepenumero diximus, vincendi mali et quietis comparandæ; innocencia videlicet et pacientia. Ideo ammonet christicolas Romæ, pareant necessitati et ferant omnia; tum quod sic maxime vitatur ira infidelium, tum eciam potissime quod ipsa paciencia vera est fortitudo et virtus quæ perplacet Deo. Et quicquid exigitur in tributis prompte pendant, et ad ipsos questores et publicanos reverenter se gerant, et, quoad possint et liceat, cum omni humilitate et dulcedine illis satisfaciant, et[2] tanta mollicie et suavitate hominum tum vultu et gestu, tum actionibus, duri illi et acerbi infideles necessario tandem aliquantisper emoliti dulcescant. Quapropter jubet Paulus ut *tributa, timor* et *honor* illis reddatur, more et consuetudine civitatis. Quod idem sapienter apostolorum princeps Petrus asiaticis ecclesiis suadet faciendum; ad illas in epistola sic scribens: *Subjecti estote omni humanæ creaturæ propter Deum, sive regi, quasi præcellenti, sive ducibus, tanquam ab eo missis ad vindictam malefactorum, laudem vero bonorum. Quia sic est voluntas Dei, ut benefacientes obmutescere faciatis imprudencium hominum ignoranciam; quasi liberi, et non quasi velamen habentes maliciæ libertatem, sed sicut servi Dei. Omnes honorate, fraternitatem diligite; Deum timete, regem honorificate.*

Vide quam concinne unus idemque spiritus in utroque apostolo loquutus est, jussitque Christianos illos primos suæ

xiii. 7.

1 l'et. ii. 13, sqq.

---

[1] *Leg.* magistratus.   [2] *Leg.* ut.

tempestatis reges et presides et eorum leges et statuta, quam melius potuerint, non labefactata fide tollerarent. Itaque ad illos qui sunt extra civitatem Dei et hostes religionis nostræ, ut eos erga nos placemus clementesque faciamus, clementer ipsi, suppliciter et inservienter nos gerere debemus (simile enim sibi simile provocat); et tum beneficiis tum benedictis tum vultu benevolente, bonitatem et benevolenciam in nos hominum quorumquumque excitare. *Maledicimur* (describit Paulus ad Corinthios) *et benedicimus; persecutionem patimur et sustinemus; blasphemamur et obsecramus*. Sic conatus est bonus apostolus bonum bono elicere, et suo bono aliorum malum vincere. Quem nos omnes debemus imitari, sicut ille Christum, et ante omnia servare in nobismet ipsis, quisque in se et omnes in societate et ecclesia Christiana, quod ab aliis querimus; amorem videlicet mutuum et charitatem, quæ satis magna et accumulata esse non potest. Nec habet finem merementum amoris. In re enim infinita, cujusmodi est amor, quis finis reperiri potest? Quapropter jubet Paulus ut sine fine amemus. *Nemini*, inquit, *quicquam debeatis, nisi ut invicem diligatis*. In hoc enim semper oportet debitores simus, quum invicem satis magnum amorem prestare non possumus. Nam amantes mutuo conamur referre divinum amorem, qui est infinitus, et ex amore ad divinam unitatem accedere, quæ est ipsa unitas et simplicitas. Hinc illud Virgilianum: *Quis enim modus adsit amori?*

Urat ergo suus quemque amor in alium, et sine fine pergat amans, et amet sine fine. Quoniam nihil prestancius potenciusque amore est. Hic auctor bonorum est, malorum expultor, expletio legis, vinculum et firmitas humanæ societatis. Ubi enim sanctus amor regnat, ibi nulla nec injuria, nec iniquitas, nec transgressio esse potest. *Dilectio* (ait Paulus) *malum non operatur, et plenitudo legis est dilectio*. Velit Paulus christiana societas, quæ vocatur ecclesia, amore in se tota ita et ardentissime flagret, ut purus et sincerus calor amoris in se plene vigeat, tantus et tam efficax, ut eciam quosque vicinos frigidos homines extra ecclesiam, instar gliscentis ignis et efflammantis, excalefaciat, purget, extenuat, trahat, raperet in flammas et inflammatos teneat; et sic se flagranti materia indies, id est, fidelium et amantium numero, magis magisque augeat, et per totum tandem orbem terrarum se amplificet, omniaque occupet, excoquat, exciccet et ardencia igneaque faciat, ut solus in terris inque hominibus regnat ignis et ardor amoris, frigida et fluenti materia vitiorum tota consumpta. Hic est ignis quem Christus ut mittat in terram de¹ se venisse. Hic est ignis mirificus, quem *consumentem* (scilicet vicia) Paulus in epistola ad Hebreos vocat. Hic ignis est eciam id de quo Esaias ait: Quod *usque ad purum excoquit scoriam*. Et hic quidem ignis tam potens, tam magnificus, quidnam est aliud quam Deus ipse, qui est charitas, qui est *in nobis*, ut ait Joannes, et nos in ipso, qui in nobis hæc facit quæ sunt *mirabilia in oculis nostris*. Quem Deum et sanctum spiritum quamdiu in nobis tenemus, immo quamdiu ab eo continemur (continemur quamdiu nolimus arrogancia et superbia erumpere) tamdiu et sani et fortes erimus, ut et in nobis vi divini spiritus et amore uniti constemus invicti, et alios inter se odio solutos vincamus.

Luc. xxii. 49.
Heb. xii. 29.
Es. i. 25.

1 Joan. iv. 13.

Ps. cxvii. 23.

Post hæc admonet Paulus Romanos, ut ipsum tempus quo nunc sunt agnoscant, tempus diei et lucis, tempus surgendi et peregrinandi, tempus vigiliæ et laboris, tempus virtutis et bonæ actionis, tempus vitæ et leticiæ, tempus denique comparandæ salutis et felicitatis. Nam exortus est et illuxit in terras sol fidei et justiciæ Jesus Christus, et nunc dies est apud homines clarus et luculentus. Nunc potentibus Christi radiis discussæ sunt nubes malorum operum; fugatæ sunt tenebræ cecarum cogitacionum. Illustratæ sunt mentes omnium scilicet fidelium, ut jam videant quid senciant et quid agant, et quo, ad quemque finem, totum vitæ cursum dirigant; prospiciant eciam quasi ex longinquo (tam enim acer est oculus fidei) in alto monte positam urbem illam et civitatem, ad quam iter faciant, celestem videlicet Jerusalem. Quo qui, dum dies est, festinant, quique anteaquam nox occuparit omnia, quamque portæ clausæ fuerint, accesserint, recipientur intro facile et civitate donabuntur, et jure ac legibus illorum civium viventes, sempiternæ illius civitatis

Rom. xiii. 11.

---

¹ *Leg.* dicit.

fructu et felicitate perfruentur. *Agnoscamus* ergo hoc *tempus* (ut jubet Paulus) expergiscamur e somno, et spectemus quam prope adest nostra salus, quamque cicius venerit

Rom. xiii. 12.
noster salvator quam credidimus. *Abiciamus ergo* omnia *opera tenebrarum,* noctis et diaboli, opera sine virtutis lumine, et atra vicia, ac *induamus arma* et instrumenta *lucis,* fidem Deo et amorem Dei et Christi. Hiis armis resistemus tenebris, hiis instrumentis in die et luce Christo operemur, et agamus luculenta. In lumine Christi, qui nobis est sol et dies, videamus viam, et strictum callem ad urbem decernamus a via lata et trita quæ ducit ad perdicionem. Arcta enim via quæ ducit ad celum; et angustam portam, qua ingreditur, nemo cernit, nisi acies suæ mentis sole Christo irradietur, illustreturque lumine accepto at illo; quod lumen est amans fides; qua qui lucet, sub Christo in suo itinere et reditu ad paternam domum, quo quasi exul revocatur, certe a semita, tametsi stricta et fugiens communes oculos, tamen

Ps. cxviii. 105.
delirare non potest. *Lucerna* enim *pedibus ejus* (ut ait David) *erit verbum Dei, et lumen semitis ejus.* Quod quidem lumen quamdiu tenet, et lampadem a Deo accensam quamdiu inextinctam servat (quoniam, ut cecinit idem David, *tu illuminas*

Ps. xvii. 28.
lucernam meam, Domine; id est, Domine, Deus meus, illuminas tenebras meas) : quamdiu, inquam, illud spirituale lumen servat, et quasi lichenum suæ mentis accensum tenet, tamdiu profecto aberrare a via, et quo eat ignorare non potest. Quandoquidem ille spiritus illuminans non modo claro suo illustramine monstrat viam, sed preterea incedentem in via quasi post se benigniter tractat, ducitque recto meatu in plenitudinem spiritus et luminis; in quod quum viator se receperit, totus occupatus inexsaciabili luce beatus erit.

Ita lumine accepto itur in lumen, et fideli amore in veram bonitatem, et per partem in totum; quæ pars (ut docet Paulus Chorinthios) evacuabitur, quum in ipso toto et pleni-

1 Cor. xiii. 9.
tudine erimus. *Nam* inquit, *ex parte cognoscimus, et ex parte prophetamur; quum autem venerit quod perfectum est, evacuabitur quod ex parte est.* Hic parvuli sumus, tunc viri erimus; hic cognoscimus *per speculum in enigmate, tunc facie ad faciem;* hic denique *ex parte, tunc autem cognoscemus sicut cogniti sumus.* Quia tunc hoc modicum spiritus et luminis

quod nunc habemus, in plenum ac perfectum lumen promovebitur. Quo circa admonuit Paulus Thessalonicenses *ut spiritum nolint extinguere;* id est, spiritale lumen, quo hic itinerantes in patriam videant ubi suos gressus ponant. Quod si nostra improbitate extinguatur, tum miseri in tenebris nesciemus quo vadamus. Quapropter hic Paulus jubet ut induti arma lucis *in die* et Christo *honeste ambulemus,* et in diem eciam ipsum et solem Christumque eamus, relinquamusque a tergo cotidie magis magisque tenebras tenebrosasque acciones et opera noctis; uti sunt ebriosæ comessaciones, impudica cubilia, invidiosa contencio, et quicquid quod carnis petulancia et procacitas desiderat; atque sub die et luce, sub radiis solis et Christi, in cepto cursu et tota vita sancte, sobrie, temperanter, et nitide pergamus, ascendamusque et leviter et alacriter montem, *montem,* inquam, illum *sanctum* Domini, in quo nemo requiescit, nisi *qui ingreditur sine macula et operatur justiciam.*

1 Thess. v. 19.

Rom. xiii. 13.

Ps. xiv. 1.

CAP. XIV.

DEINDE vero apud Paulum est quædam admonicio et preceptum sapiens, ut in Christiana societate infirmorum in fide racio habeatur. Est enim fides, ut supra tradidimus, lux quædam spiritalis impertita humanis animis, hiis scilicet qui eliguntur ut credant Deo. Cujus participacio est varia, et unicuique, ut alibi Paulus ait, *sicut Deus divisit mensuram fidei,* ut *non plus sapiat quam oportet, sed sapiat ad sobrietatem.* Nam aliquibus est id luminis, quam fidem dicimus, ita modicum, ut ad quam plurima animus cecuciat adhuc, nec plane cernit omnia, nec admittit nec approbat quicquam facile, nisi quod crebra consuetudine et usu fuerit quasi oculis inculcatum. Quod autem fuit insolitum, nec antea visum, dura et obtusa acies non cernit quidem aperte, nec apprehendit audacter, sed cecitate diffidenciæ reformidat, et fugit, adhuc impotens et invalida ut senciat quid sit quodque, et id quod prius in usum non venerit. Itaque pro modulo suo discrecione utitur rerum et temporum, ac

Rom.xii.3.

separat distinguitque multa quæ ad vitam et mores pertinent. Nec facile quicquam agnoscit sibi consentaneum et utile, nisi racionem inveteratæ consuetudinis habuerit, quæ usu probata sibi non nocitura confidat. Alia autem ut inexperta adhuc exhorret. Nec adduci potest (ita exigua est fides) ut credat ea sine periculo se attingere posse.

Aliquibus autem tam multum est fidei lumen, ut quasi ex alto despiciunt quæ inferiora sunt, et cernunt clare omnia ac judicant, nec quicquam exhorrent ex cecitate, nec in quoquam vacillant et titubent ex infirmitate, sed forti et perspicaci visu dijudicant omnia, omniaque se aggredi et attemptare posse confidunt, presertim in hiis rebus quæ nihil ad rem pertinent; cujusmodi est cibus et potio, de quibus nunc Paulus maxime loquitur: propterea quod in Romana ecclesia, quæ partim ex Judeis partim ex gentibus constitit, nonnulla fuit altercacio, quidnam licuit cuique degustare. Judei enim ex veteri lege eorum, eis tradita a Moyse, in rata consuetudine habuerunt a multis ciborum generibus abstinere; sicut in animalibus quicquid non fuerit simul et bisulcum et ruminans; in aquaticis quicquid quod non pinnatum et squamosum fuerit; in volucribus quicquid rapacioris fuerit generis et voracioris; ac denique quicquid repens incumbit in terram, quicquidve intus in ipsa terra degit. Ab hiis sanxit Moyses omnino ut Judei se contineant.

Lev. xi. 3.

Quæ quanquam spectant ad altiorem veritatem, et monumenta dumtaxat sunt et signa eorum quæ ad animam pertinent (quod ipse quoque Moyses manifestissime declarat, quum illis sanctionibus subjungit: *Nolite contaminare animas vestras, nec tangatis quicquam eorum, ne immundi sitis; ego sum Dominus Deus vester: sancti estote sicut ego sanctus sum. Ne polluatis animas vestras in omni reptili quod movetur super terram. Ego sum Dominus qui eduxi vos de terra egipti, ut essem vobis in Deum. Sancti eritis, quia ego sanctus sum:* ita ut animæ sanctimoniam illæ figuræ et sensibiles actiones corporalisque abstinencia †quanquam† Moysis proposito spectarint) tamen, quia gens erat duræ cervicis Judaica et obtusæ aciei, in illis sensibilibus signis voluit eos assidue exercere, ut vel crebro admonerentur

Lev. xi. 43. sqq.

animas sibi mundas servant, vel ut exercitati in illis exemplis facilius tandem a magistro veritatis, quem Moyses prospexit futurum, ad veram animæ sanctitatem adducerentur. Qui veritatis magister et ille ipsa quoque veritas quum advenerit, quumque docuerit veram mundandi animi racionem, quamplurimi Judei, qui hanc disciplinam secuti sunt, quique animis emundari non recusarunt, abduci tamen a sua consuetudine et observancia in degustandis cibis, quæ longo et diuturno usu tam alte animis insederit, subito non potuerunt. Animus enim astrictus quadam angusta consuetudine latius circumspicere, et veritatem in quaque re cernere non potuit. Unde est nata diffidencia, quæ quædam est ex parvitate fidei ignorancia.

Verum certe quodque quod bona fide Deo fit, id non est contempnendum. Nec ii despiciendi sunt, qui pusillanimiter continent se a rebus in quibus nihil est periculi, modo id bona fide agunt, et suo facto Deo se placere credant; sed illorum infirmitatis miserendum est magis, et in societate molliter ac fraterniter fovendi sunt prudenti quadam consideracione, ut in melius et fortius tandem possint evadere. Unde qui sunt fortiores fide, quique arbitrantur se omnia posse, oportet valde caveant habeantque racionem imbecilitatis eorum, nec sua potestate ita abutantur ut fraternæ charitatis, et quid alii ferre possint, videantur oblivisci. Quod enim per se et simpliciter licet, idem apud omnes et omni loco et tempore non licet. Quod autem ex fide et amore et fraterna pietate fit, id nusquam nunquamque potest esse non licitum. Non tam quid nos possumus, quam quid conducat societati, unioni, et paci spectandum est; ut charitas, quæ non querit quæ sua sunt, in nobis appareat. Illi quoque si quando videant alios plusquam ipsi audent attemptare, apprehendereque plura ciborum genera quam putant ipsi se posse, non debent ex ea eorum angustia et infirmitate aliorum facta demetiri, et ex suo ipsorum sensu de aliis sentenciam ferre, dampnareque in alio quod in se ipsis dampnandum putant. Nam id perinde est ac si quispiam egrotior nolit validiorem id edere quod ipse præ infirmitate diffidit se coquere posse. Nihil in hominibus minus agendum est, quam ut alius alium ex sua ipsius potencia metiatur; magisque vitandum quam putare dampnandas opiniones omnes quæ sunt nostris dissimiles, presertim in hiisce quoque rebus, in quibus quanquam alia opinio est alia melior, tamen per se neutra mala est, modo humilitate Deo et bona fide fulciatur; cujusmodi quidem sunt esculenta et poculenta, quorum vel abstinencia vel usus neque promovent neque demovent. Quod ipse quoque Paulus testatur, ad Corinthios scribens : *Neque si manducaverimus habundamus, neque si non manducaverimus deficiemus.* *Esca* enim *nos non commendat Deo ;* id est, observancia et discretio epularum. At modus, intencio et finis certe plurimum in utramque partem potest. Qui qualis est, et quo modo quisque agit in hiis quæ indifferenter agi possunt sine periculo, non nostrum est sed solius Dei judicare, cujus servi sumus et bona fide inservientes omnia agimus. Quæ benefacta sint necne, nimirum Domini est servorum et examinare et sentenciam ferre; cujus servi sunt, quicquid sunt. Et bene maleve egeris, vivisne an moreris, ad Dominum spectat solum et approbare et improbare ; ante cujus tribunal omnes stabimus, quisque pro se suæ vitæ racionem. redditurus. Servi autem inter se ipsi alius alium nec accusabit nec condempnabit. Sed quum qui servi sunt Deo hii simul filii Dei sunt (nam Deum et Dominum et Patrem habemus, et propterea inter nos ipsi confratres sumus), ideo hæc quidem divina fraternitas exposcit ut mutuo nos quam maxime amemus, misereamur, foveamus, adjutemus, declinemus a nobis, et sepe accommodemus nos fratri, ejusque salutem magis quam nostram gloriam queramus.

In quo quum cogimur sepe id facere quod nobis non videtur optimum, persuadere nobis debemus semper id esse optimum quod ex amore proximi et charitate factum est, idque maxime placere Deo, non quod maxime nobis placet, sed quod communi utilitati et paci ecclesiæ conducit, quodque præ se fert argumentum non amoris nostri sed aliorum. Etenim Christus (ut ait Paulus) *non sibi placuit.* Itaque *quisque nostrum proximo suo placeat in bonum,* ad *edificacionem* scilicet ecclesiæ, non sibi ipsi ad destructionem; quæ superbia est quædam et approbacio tui ipsius, res odiosa Deo, et ecclesiæ perniciosa. Hinc Paulus : *Beatus,* inquit, *qui non judicat seipsum in eo quod probat*, nec effert se xiv. 22. opinione sui; quæ quanquam forsan de se factu justa est, tamen nisi animadvertas, quod potes agere, quam id societati conveniat et utile sit, quod opinaris justum erit plane iniquitas. Non ergo quod ipse probas semper effice, tametsi id per se bonum; sed id facere nunquam dubita, quod amor et imitacio Christi et charitas proximi exposcit. Cujus infirmitatem tua fortitudine non offendes, nec timidum tua audacia premes. Neque vero quod apud egrotos cavetur, quanquam id tua robustitate possis, tamen non id edas quod stomachum infirmo dedignacionemque commoveat, nec id agas semper quod tua opinione putas te posse; sed memor charitatis videas simul quid alius opinio possit capere et ferre, quidque fieri potest cum consensu et sanitate tocius corporis, id est, ecclesiæ, et cum unitate, concordia et pace. Ac semper memento, quum membrum es ecclesiastici corporis, non erumpere in aliquam opinionem tui, sed ceteris membris consentire oportere, ut totius corporis sanitas, integritas et vigor conservetur.

Sed de hac re quæ Pauli sunt verba leviter transcurramus. Inquit enim, *Infirmum in fide*, non credentem se omnia posse xiv. 1. sine periculo, *assumite* in societatem, et ejus infirmitatem ferte, et agite pie ac considerate cum eo, ut in majorem fidem et fortitudinem promoveatur. *Non in deceptacionibus cogitacionum*, non disputando et altercando cum illo. Quis enim fortis vult et debet colluctari cum infirmo, qui vires racionum ferre non potest? Immo illius modi ratiocinacio quædam dimicacio et conflictus verborum est, qui non debet esse in ecclesia. At ille infirmior in fide quisquis sit, pie, molliter et cum amore fovendus est, et cum fortioribus viribus benignis, ac dulciter et oportune trahentibus, sustinendus; non aliter atque in corpore membrum magis vitale et vigorosius bonitate naturæ, vicinum sibi membrum si egrotarit, incumbit impense et suaviter, ut id in parem sibi vigorem attrahat. Sic fides et charitas nostra qua vivimus sic luceat et ardeat in nobis, ut luculento nostro amore vivificentur magis qui vicini sunt nobis infirmi, et validiores reddantur. Quod si fieri non potest, tum ejusmodi qui sunt, benigniter et sine offensione tollantur. Est enim cujusque Christiani fovere bonum, quoad potest, et sua bonitate alius bonum vel augere prudenter vel conservare pacienter. In quo studio, vel augendi vel conservandi boni aliorum, sua ipsius bonitas maxime elucet. Fidelis autem amor est quasi luculentus calor et spiritus, quo homines, membra dominici corporis, varia imperticione varie vivificantur, ut in constructionem unius coporis conspirent contenti una et conjuncti mutuo fideli amore. In quo corpore si aliquis defectu fidei videtur languere, et sub graviore onere vacillare, ei levandum est onus, et pro modulo virium suarum misericorditer tractandus est, dummodo pro viribus contendit, et bona fide putat se placere Deo.

Rom. xiv. 2.

Alius enim credit manducare se omnia. De cibis loquitur Paulus, in quibus scrupulosius actum fuit a quibusdam non malicia sed infirmitate. Alii vero tanta fide fuerunt, et Deo in suis creaturis tantopere confisi sunt, quod fidei lumine viderint in ciborum generibus nihil esse quod exhorreant, quandoquidem omnia Dei sunt bona et munda; nec Mosaicam illam tradicionem maxime de cibis fuisse; sed quicquid ille sanxerit de cibis gustandis vitandisve, id totum figuracionem esse quandam crasso judaico populo, eorum videlicet quæ illis in mentem venirent et cogitacionem, quæque ex cogitacione per os foras proficiscerentur. Quia, ut discussor moysaicarum tenebrarum Jesus Christus ait,

Mat. xv. 11.

Non quod in os ingreditur coinquinat, sed quod egreditur. Alius igitur *credit*, id est, lumine fidei videt, manducanda esse omnia quæquunque apponuntur, sine discretione. Alius vero non tanta est fide et lumine ut videat omnia manducanda esse; et is est quem humilis consuetudo in ciborum abstinencia excecavit; cujus obfuscata mens ad huc satis magna fide non claret. Ideo ejusmodi infirmus *olus manducet;* id est, id quod coquere et digerere potest; et id faciat quod arbitratur se posse, eatenusque progrediatur audendo quatenus sua se fides extendit. Nec pergat ultra, ne excurrens ambitum suæ lucis in tenebras incidat, id quod pecca-

Rom. xiv. 23.

tum est; quia *omne quod non est ex fide peccatum est,* sicuti quod non est in luce in tenebris est.

Et quia Paulus utitur translacione sumpta a corpore egrotante et infirmo, cui olus, aut quicquid ejusmodi coctu facile exhibetur (nam olus omnis herba est, cujus foliis et caule in edulium utimur, quod fervifactum vel imbecilior stomachus non dedignatur), est animadvertendum, uti stomachus vel ventriculus ille in quem cibi recepti coquuntur, se habet in corpore, ita mens se habet in hominis spiritu. Et ut illic concoccio fit lucente calore, ita quod venit in mente retinetur, et in bonum animi alimentum vertitur, quasi rem coquente fideli amore; qui vigor est animi, quique quanto magis deficit, eo animus est in aggrediendo quodquunque minus audax et efficax. Quapropter, ut qui onerant stomachum crapula laborant, sic qui supra fidem aliquid attemptant, quasi cruditatem inducunt animo, unde morbus et animi pernicies nascatur; quod quidem peccatum est, et onus premens ex diffidencia, quæ animi quasi obscura et inefficax frigiditas est, ex defectu fidei et amoris. Nemo igitur plus attemptet quam credit se sine periculo posse, ne si diffidencia agat, ipsa diffidencia peccet.

Is qui manducat, non manducantem non spernat insolenter xiv. 3. et superbe. *Nec ille qui non manducat* et infirmior est, *manducantem* et fortiorem fide *non judicet,* nec dampnet suo judicio, existimans illum male agere, quia videt illum id quod ipse non audet agere; quod fortitudinis est, in quam traxit illum Deus, in quaque eadem potest illum sustinere. Ita latenter significat infirmis, fortitudinis esse discrecionem non ponere in cibis; ut illi imitentur.

Deus enim illum fortiorem *assumpsit;* attraxit in illam fortitudinem. *Tu quis es qui judicas alienum?* audaciorem xiv. 4. in cibis gustandis, quem judicare domini est. *Nam domino suo aut stat aut cadit:* manet in illa fortitudine sua, vel ab illa decidit. *Stabit autem.* At *stabit,* inquit Paulus, id est, perseverabit in ea magna fide, ut credat in cibis nihil immundum, non suis quidem viribus sed gracia sustinente. *Quia potens est Deus statuere illum.*

Hoc proprium est Pauli semper meliora sperare. Nec ab re quidem; quando cum magna charitate, cujusmodi in Paulo fuit, semper conjungitur magna spes, et in quaque re expectacio meliorum. Simul hic latenter probat illam fidem qua creditur nihil commune, quam id credere significat esse *stare;* et tales credentes staturos; et illam stationem a Deo;

ut infirmiores agnoscant id quod illi faciant esse ex imbecilitate. Quia sunt gradus fidei, et alius credit omni tempore et ex omnibus edendum. Hoc est quod ait Paulus:

Rom. xiv. 5.

Alius judicat omnem diem. In alta specula positus videt omnia. Et paulo post: *Qui sapit diem, domino sapit.* Judicare enim omnem diem, et diem sapere, est in fidei luce videre omnia, et credere et habere sapienciam et rerum et temporum. Sicut contra qui discernit et *judicat inter diem et diem,* et angustia fidei nequit omne tempus cernere, is aliqua ex parte ignorat res et tempora : quapropter nonnullis diffidit. Alius autem amplitudine fidei spectat omnia. *Ita quisque suo sensu abundat* et judicio.

Hic vide ne id quod dicit : *Alius judicat inter diem et diem,* sit dictum in Judeos, qui a lege data a Moyse existimarunt observanciam in cibis habendam, cujusmodi non fuit antea ;

Gen. ix. 3. quia post diluvium Noe dictum fuit: *Omne quod movetur et vivit erit vobis in cibum.* Moyses autem, ut in Levitico scri-

Lev. xi. 46. bitur : *Ista,* inquit, *est lex animancium, volucrum et omnis animæ viventis quæ movetur in aqua, et reptat in terra, ut differencias noveritis mundi et immundi, et sciatis quid comedere et respuere debeatis.*

Hæc recordantes, Judei voluerunt tempus legis a tempore ante legem distinguere, et discrecionem moysaicam servantes in cibis *inter diem,* id est, tempus ante legem, *et diem,* id est, tempus post legem datam, *judicare,* et suum tempus separare a tempore gentilium, qui in omni tempore ad cibos indifferenter se habuerunt. Suum tempus et diem voluerunt esse a lege moysaica, quo a reliquo mundo, tanquam ab immundis, exempti fuerint, et prescripcione legum seclusi a consuetudine hominum et more communi, ut ex omnibus quasi illi soli, quibusdam abstinenciis et peculiaribus ritubus, mundi et sancti essent. Qui ergo *judicaverunt diem,* et tempus peculiaris abstinenciæ, *a die* et tempore communis esus, Judei fuerunt infirmiores. Ad illos spectat id : *Alius autem judicat omnem diem.* Itaque non absurde ille locus Pauli mihi videtur sic posse exponi: scilicet, *Alius,* Judeus infirmior adhuc, inclusus angustia legis moisaicæ, *judicat* et discernit *inter diem,* id est, tempus suæ abstinenciæ, *et diem,* id est, tempus gentilium et vulgaris degustacionis. *Alius autem judicat* et sentit *omnem diem* et tempus communiter esse edendi. Is ex gentibus est, vel Judeus aliquis, qui claustra legis moysaicæ magna fide ruperit, exieritque in lucem, ut latius circumspiciat omnia. *Ita quisque suo sensu abundat,* de temporibus et cibis judicans.

In quibus quum non multum est quod ad rem pertinet, quumque in utroque quod fit bona fide agentis, et ut Domino placeat, fieri possit; profecto de illis nugis non est contendendum; sed declinet se potius fortis, et consenciat infirmo, sitque infirmis infirmus; ut concordia conservetur. *Quia qui sapit diem et manducat, Domino manducat; et qui non manducat nec sapit diem,* id est, qui non habet sapientiam et veram cognicionem temporis, quod videlicet in omni tempore et ex omnibus, quatenus est ex ipsis cibis, eciam ipsis Judeis sub lege, gustari est licitum (quum ipsi cibi per se immundi non sunt, tametsi certis proprietatibus immundicias significant), is manducans eciam *domino manducat*[1]*;* et uterque bona fide *agens gracias,* et sperans se placere Deo. Rom. xiv. 6.

Quamobrem cum actiones servorum, voluntates, sensus, immo ipsa eorum vita et mors, et quicquid sunt, ad dominum pertinent, non arroget sibi servus ut conservum judicet. Sed uterque pro modulo suo mutuis adjumentis domino serviat, examinatori et judici. Dominus autem est Christus, qui nos redemit sua morte, et resurrexit ut dominetur omnium, tum vivorum misericorditer ad salutem, tum mortuorum judicialiter ad dampnacionem. A conservis ergo et confratribus longe absit judicium et condempnacio; non modo ut caveat ne judicet alium, sed ne seipsum quidem. Ad Corinthios enim ait Paulus: *Sed nec me ipsum judico. Qui autem me judicat Dominus est. Itaque nolite ante tempus judicare,* et in humano die, *quoad usque veniat Dominus; qui et illuminabit abscondita tenebrarum, et manifestabit consilia cordium, et tunc erit unicuique laus a Deo.* 1 Cor. iv. 3—5.

Interea vero dum hic vivitur in ecclesia, faciendum est a quoque fratre ut cum suo fratre quoqunque fraterne et germane agat, misereatur infirmitatis, foveat, consoletur, vitet quicquid infirmum offendet, non cogitet quid possit ipse,

---

[1] *Leg.* non mand.

sed quid frater ferre possit, nec querat ostentacionem virium suarum, sed in fratrem charitatem ostendat, et una cum eo se infirmet, sicuti Deus infirmavit se nobis, *exinaniens seipsum pro nobis, formam servi suscipiens*, et quasi compaciens nobiscum, ut benigna conformitate nos in deos reformaret; qui magis quesivit lucrum nostrum quam ostentacionem sui, exemplum nobis relinquens quomodo quisque se gerat erga fratrem suum, quam pie, quam benigne, quam conformiter; ut alius alium non cum arrogancia et duritate, non cum offensione et scandalo, sed humiliter, molliter, placide et modo acceptabili reformet, et cum quodam studio salutis ejus considerate trahat ad sanitatem.

Ita Christus fecit, frater noster; cujas tota vita, facta, verba, nihil aliud est quam quoddam expressum exemplar, coram hominibus positum, quod imitentur, si illum, quo ille ascenderit, sequi velint. Ut enim bonus magister, veram vivendi racionem effinxit in seipso; ut, in ejus vitam spectantes, aperte legerent quonam modo sit hic vivendum hiisce qui post hanc vitam sine fine vivere velint. Offendit autem Christus Judeos, non quod egit ille quicquam quod eos offendat, qui fuit eis benignissimus; sed quod ille ex malicia eorum, quæ omnia vertit in malum, bono offendi voluerunt. Hinc illis vocatur *petra scandali, et lapis offensionis*, qui mali et amari dulcedinem et bonitatem ferre non potuerunt. Gentibus vero lapis *stulticiæ;* quæ stulta sua sapiencia mundana, divinæ sapienciæ inimica, veram Dei sapienciam stulticiam judicaverunt. Nam, ut malis omnia mala, ita stultis omnia stulta. Bonis vero et sapientibus, quibus est datum nosse misteria Dei, lapis ille Christus non offendens, sed bonitate delectans mirifice fuit; et simul talibus non stultum quiddam, sed revera ipsius Dei sapiencia.

Quantum ergo ex nobis est, nemini simus scandalo et offensioni; sed in omnibus nostris actionibus, tanquam scopulum fugiamus scandalum; et non quod licet nobis, sed semper quod expediat aliis, et non quod possimus ipsi, sed in omni tempore quod possit conducere societati et dominico corpori, cujus membra sumus, agamus, quamdiu cum aliis membris convenire volumus.

Et quia in ecclesia Romana altercacio fuit de cibis, quod

ipse sentit Paulus cum auctoritate interponit; et suam dat gravem sentenciam et spectandam; videlicet, quod in cibis nihil commune est in se absolute, id est, immundum. Nam quod communiter omnibus aliis a se fuerat in usu, id Judei appellaverunt immundum; nihil sentientes mundum nisi peculiariter proprium et suum. Quicquid apud gentes in usu fuerat, reputaverunt immundum id, et commune appellaverunt. Verum mira sane est vis fidei, ut noceat delictumque sit quod preter fidem fit. Et quisque ut credit, ita sibi eveniet. Et ut se habet fides in animo, ita quæ veniunt in mentem, vel ad bonum nostrum vel ad malum vertuntur.

Ideo Paulus, quanquam sciens et *confidens Domino* asseruit nihil commune per Christum, tamen adjunxit, *nisi ei qui existimat quid commune esse: illi commune est.* Qui diffidit id esse bonum, id ei malum est; non aliter quidem ac crudum id ei est quoque quod nequit coquere. Qui vult quod diffidit bonum esse facere, videtur voluntatem habere peccandi, et sponte quod ipse putat malum agere. Quod si cogatur, tunc importunitate et pondere rei gravatur valde et disturbatur. Non potest ullo modo quod diffidentes facimus nobis bonum esse, quum nobis quasi incoctum jacebit aggravans. *Si ergo* (addit) *propter cibum frater tuus contristatur, turbatur et offenditur,* quum videt te pergere latius in cibis quam ipse possit, tu qui non habes rationem fratris tui *non secundum charitatem ambulas,* nec ex amore; fratris non misereris; sed tuam audaciam, quanquam in bono per se, tamen impie jactas ad offensionem, ad scandalum, et lesionem infirmi fratris. *Noli cibo tuo,* audacia edendi, et opinione potestatis tuæ *illum* misellum *perdere pro quo Christus mortuus est,* peccatore et indigno Christo. *Non ergo blasphemetur,* obtrectetur, male dicatur, *bonum nostrum;* spiritalis vivificatio, unitas et pax fraterna. Nam *quam bonum* (inquit David) *et quam jocundum est, habitare fratres in unum.* Non, inquam, propter edulia et terrena, blasphemetur bonum, ne demus malidicis de cibis locum obtrectandi. *Non est enim regnum Dei esca* et potus: hoc est, observacione ciborum regnum Dei non acquiritur. Nec ad rem pertinet. In hiis habeatur discrecio, nec iræ. Modus enim edendi bibendive, aut delectiores epulæ, nec in cibis

Rom. xiv. 14.

Rom. xiv. 15.

Ps. cxxxii. 1.

distinccio, nec denique quicquam terrenum, promovet homines ad celum, regnumque Dei in terris acquirit; *sed* sola *justicia, pax et gaudium in spiritu sancto:* hiis queritur et comparatur et constat regnum Dei.

Et quod in hoc loco de esca et potu dicit Paulus, quod regnum Dei non sunt nec id constituunt, id idem de pecunia, possessionibus, decimis ,oblacionibus, et quicquid preterea terrenum est, verissime dici potest; videlicet, quod hæc regnum Dei non sunt, nec construunt quidem; unde misere insaniunt qui arbitrantur homines Christianos, eciam ecclesiasticos viros, de hiis contendere oportere, quasi eis constet ecclesia Christi; ignari quid vel inchoavit, vel auxit, vel conservavit ecclesiam ; ignari eciam quid quatit, disturbat, et evertit ecclesiam Christianam. Si circumspicias et accuratius animadvertas omnia, et perpendas singula, reperies nihil perniciosius accidisse ecclesiæ, quam possessiones, et appellacio mei et tui, et autoritas proprii vendicandi. Unde avaricia et pecuniæ cupiditas exorta est; qui morbus in Christiana ecclesia in tantum vigorem nunc excrevit, et tam late et per totum Christi corpus patet, eciam principalibus membris eo maxime occupatis et infectis, ut nisi Christus sui corporis misereatur, et periclitans adjuvet, non potest longe abesse certe quin necessario intereat. Sed ille novit tempus suum et opportunitatem. Et sinuntur omnia in eum finem qui divinam providenciam non latet.

Verum hæc non scribo quod nolim ecclesiam habere possessiones; aut sacerdotes decimas et oblaciones; sed ut de hujusmodi nullo modo contendant. Quia non est ecclesia decimæ et oblaciones, quod humiles et angusti quidem animi plerumque inter communicandum solent jactitare. Sed, ut ait Paulus, ecclesia *regnumque Dei* (quod ut aliquando adveniat in terras dominica oracio nos docet petere) *est justicia et pax et gaudium in spiritu sancto.* Ideo sacerdotes et pastores dominici gregis flagitare debent pocius, ut hæc ante omnia homines deciment Deo et offerant. Quid enim Deo cum melle, casio, segetibus, pecoribus, nummis? Horum tamen oblaciones non sunt omittendæ. Sed ante omnia a sacerdotibus, ut solet fieri rixosius, non exigendæ sunt. Illa prius si queras, hæc sua sponte sequentur, et eo prompcius et copiosius, quo eorum

tu minus cupidus esse videaris. *Querite primum regnum* Mat. vi.
Dei, jubet Salvator, quod *justicia, pax et gaudium in spiritu* 33.
sancto est, et hœc omnia adjicientur vobis. Quod in primis
quesitum in terris a Christo et apostolis constituit ecclesiam
et propagavit. Deinde studio et diligenciæ conservandæ
justiciæ et pacis accessit tandem paulatim multiplex possessio, non quesita a principibus ecclesiæ, sed ultro ab
hominibus ob virtutem ecclesiasticorum perspectam oblata
et data. In qua re conservanda eadem sola est racio, quæ
fuit comparandi. Quamobrem flagitacio decimarum et contencio in ecclesiastico homine nullo modo esse debet; quæ
appetentem animum terrenorum indicet, et ecclesiæ scandalum excitet, et blasphemiam Christi. Sed pocius, quod
docet Paulus Chorinthios, omnis fraus et injuria perpecienda est. In illa enim epistola ait: *Iam quidem omnino* 1 Cor. vi. 7.
*delictum est in nobis, quod inter vos judicia habetis. Quare
non magis injuriam accipitis? Quare non magis fraudem
patimini!*

Insanit et dementit ille rector ecclesiæ, ignarus sacrarum
literarum, ignarus Christi, ignarus officii sui, qui vult cum
parochianis suis de decimis et oblacionibus contendere;
pastor cum ovibus, pater cum filiis, minister Dei cum Dei
filiis et sibi confratribus; cum quibus in tanta necessitudine,
quæ omnem germanitatem superat, potius quam litiges,
quicquid in terris sit longe abjicias et contempnas. Nec
est querenda excusacio in peccatis, dicendumque te non
tuum lucrum sed rem Dei et partem ecclesiæ quérere.
Quid Dei? Quid ecclesiæ? Nec Deus noster istis munusculis delectatur, nec hujusmodi rebus, quæ a mundo habentur in pretio, ecclesia Dei constat, sed maxime in hiis
despiciendis elucet. Sed virtus, fides, charitas, justicia est,
quæ grata est oblacio in conspectu Dei. Quæ si ante omnia
in tua plebe queritas, illa alia eciam te non querente et
largius quam petas, sequentur. Sicut Salvator noster
scribis illis et phariseis dixit: *Væ vobis, scribæ et pharisei,* Mat. xxiii.
ypocritæ; qui decimatis mentam, anetum et siminum, et reli- 23.
*quistis quæ graviora sunt legis, judicium, misericordiam et
fidem.* Ita hiis procacibus et petulantibus sacerdotibus, qui
verbis confitentur Christum, factis autem negant, qui blasphemantur nomen Christi inter gentes, qui sub pretextu

religionis non Christi sed suum lucrum querunt, potest dici: Væ vobis, sacerdotali, hypocritæ; qui flagitatis decimacionem frugum, pecorum et nummorum, et quæ graviora sunt legis, justiciam, misericordiam et fidem relictam non flagitatis: hæc enim oportet populum prius facere, et illa non omittere. Quæ non omittentur proculdubio, si prima illa in plebe assequutus fueris, adeptusque es de quibus hic Paulus loquitur, justiciam, pacem, et gaudium in spiritu sancto; quarum rerum possessioni qui incumbit, is Christo placet et probatus est hominibus.

Rom. xiv. 19.
Sed redeamus ad apostolum, qui concludit: *Itaque quæ pacis sunt sectemur, et quæ edificacionis sunt invicem custodiamus.* Nec altercemus inter nos de quaque re terrena, abjectis et angustis animis; quasi ejusmodi ad Christum et ecclesiam pertineant. *Noli propter escam destruere opus Dei;* rixa et contencione, quæ est pestis et eruptio ecclesiæ,

Rom. xiv. 20. Tit. i. 15.
quod Dei opus est. *Omnia quidem sunt munda mundis;* quod est ut is in quem recipitur. Malis omnia mala, et tenebrosis tenebrosa omnia, et bonis omnia bona. *Sed malum est homini qui per offendiculum,* per sensum offensionis, *manducat.* Hoc latenter significat, qui meticulosius exhorrent certa ciborum genera, id esse ex immundicia. Quia immundum nihil, nisi immundo, in quo munda immunda sunt. Quia quodque a quoque recipitur pro natura recipientis, et receptum ejusmodi evadit quale ipsum recipiens est. *Bonum,* id est, melius est, *nec panem nec vinum gustare,* tametsi legittime fieri potest, quum ex eo offensio, scandalum et lesio sequatur. Per se enim bona et legittima non ubique et apud omnes bona sunt et legittima. Hoc quidem licet semper quod expedit et utile est aliis, quodque harmonicum

Rom. xiv. 22.
consensum in ecclesia servat. *Tu* fortior et majori fide preditus *fidem habes penes te ipsum,* et es tibi conscius te multa posse facere. At *habe* simul *coram Deo,* aperte et propalam in ecclesia cum fratribus, conjunctam cum charitate. Alioquin fides coram Deo et divino conspectui grata esse non potest. *Beatus qui non judicat*—laudat *se ipsum*—*in eo quod probat,* et putat se recte facere, sed laudem expectat a Deo, et ita agat ut a Deo laudetur.

Qui manducaverit, ille infirmior, *dampnatus est:* peccatum commisit dampnabile, qui non ex fide, sed ultra fidei terminos. Ideo quod egerit, sibi in bonum verti non potest. Sola est amans fides animi vigor qui omnia coquit, et in bonum animi alimentum convertit. Quæ si diminutior fuerit, animusque si aliqua diffidencia frigescat, tum comedens crudus evadit: quæ animi cruditas ex defectu fidei morbus et peccatum est. *Quamobrem,* addit, *omne quod non est ex fide,* sed cum diffidencia fit, *peccatum est.* Quia ipsa diffidencia nequit conceptum in bonum vertere.

CAP. XV.

HABENDA ergo est benigna racio infirmorum, et cavendum ne eis aliquod onus imponamus. Sed potius compatiamur cum ipsis, imitati Christum, qui nobiscum compati voluit, ut nos victores passionum faceret. Et ad consensum semper enitendum est; quæ sanitas est dominici corporis, et ecclesiæ salus; ut ab animis in unum conspirantibus coli possit Deus et adorari; qui finis convocatæ et congregatæ ecclesiæ est, et Cristianæ societatis. Propter quod, *suscipite invicem in honorem Dei,* pie et benigniter, *sicut Christus suscepit vos*; non contempnens sui dissimiles, nec infirmos despiciens, sed tum ex Judeis, tum ex gentibus ad se trahens. Qui tracti et constituti in Christo, mutuo se acceptare debent, et amare, ut ab amante Christo acceptati sunt; Judei veritate, gentes misericordia. Utrobique autem est et misericordia Dei et veritas. Deus enim verus et misericors est; et misericorditer verus et vere misericors. Sed quia majoribus hebreorum Deus misericorditer promisit Christum venturum, et vere tandem quod promisit prestitit, iccirco vera quadam misericordia Judei assumpti sunt ad salutem per Christum, qui eis salutem ministravit. Ideo Paulus eum vocat *ministrum circumcisionis;* id est, Judeorum circumcisorum. Et quia, non promissus gentibus, illarum tamen misertus est, ideo illos potest dici misericordi quadam veritate assumpsisse; ut in vocacione Judeorum, in misericordia notetur veritas in promisso et prestito; in accessione

xv. 7.

xv. 8.

gencium, in veritate Dei maxime spectetur misericordia; quibus nihil promissus mera misericordia se obtulit Christus. Quod quanquam prophetæ predixerint fore, tamen Deus non promisit futurum. Et qui venit ipse Christus dixit se non venisse nisi ad oves quæ perierant domus Israel.

Itaque Paulus dicit *Christum Jesum ministrum fuisse circumcisionis*, et circumcisis ministrasse salutem *propter veritatem Dei, ad confirmandas promissiones patrum;* id est, ut promissa patribus vera videantur; et Judeos adorare Deum promissa vocacione, *gentes autem Deum honorare per misericordiam Dei*. Cujus misericordiæ et David et Esaias testes sunt. Ille ait, *Letamini, gentes, cum plebe ejus*. Hic, erit *radix Jesse, et qui exurget regere gentes: in eo gentes sperabunt*. Quum itaque Deus verus et misericors tum Judeos tum gentes ad se traxit, et paterne amplexus est, profecto ipsi inter se Judei et gentes vicissim et fraterne amplecti debent, atque mutua se charitate convincire.

Deut. xxxii. 43; Es. xi. 10.

Rom. xv. 15.

Sequitur deinde apud Paulum quædam excusacio audaciæ suæ, quod ad Romanos scripsit, de quo forsan illi mirari potuerunt, et cogitare secum quidnam sit quod Paulus ad eos scripserit, qui apud illos nunquam fuerit. Poterant enim id audax facinus judicare. Ideo facti sui racionem reddit Paulus, dicens causam esse quod evangelizacio gentibus ei precipue mandata fuit, ut ubique locorum quoad potuit colligat ex gentibus evangelizando oblacionem Deo. Inter quas gentes in primis Romani fuerunt. Ideo illos, sicuti alias gentes, jure officii sui et legacionis potuit docere. Tametsi modeste dicit hic se illos non docere, sed admonere. Nam inquit: *Audacius scripsi vobis ex parte, tanquam in memoriam vos reducens.* Quod denotat, non docens ignota, sed admonens scita. Et hoc consonum est ei quod dixit in prima epistola, id est, in prima parte hujus epistolæ: *Desidero*

Rom. i. 11. *enim videre vos, ut aliquid impartiar vobis graciæ spiritalis ad confirmandos vos*. Quod denotat: Satis docti estis; sed forsan egetis fraterna admonicione et confirmacione.

Docti autem fuerunt Romani, et primum de Christo audierunt ab ipso Poncio Pilato, qui prefuit neci Christi; ex cujus literis Tiberius Cesar accepit, quam ille apud Judeos fuit mirificus; et Jesum in deos retulisset, si senatus passus esset. Sed ex apostolis Christi primus nuncium de Christo Romam attulit Barnabas, ut historia Clementis Romani testatur, ad Jacobum Jerosolomitanum episcopum missa. Qui Clemens, doctrinam Barnabæ secutus, postea Cesaream ad Petrum venit,° cui fuit a Barnaba commendatus. Tum Petrus, postquam in oriente undecem annos docens consumpserat, in Italiam et Romam venit, ubi annis xxv. consedit, annis autem ante Pauli adventum Romam circiter tredecem. A quo magno Christi apostolo eruditi et instructi Romani forsan potuerint dedignari aliquantisper a Paulo edoceri. Iccirco sapientissimus Paulus, qui voluit videri nihil inconsiderate agere, reddit causam scriptæ epistolæ, et eum dicit esse mandatum sibi officium, et impositum onus a Christo, ut ubivis gencium, quoad possit, adjutet incrementum fidei. *Grecis et barbaris,* inquit in prima parte hujus epistolæ, *sapientibus et insipientibus debitor sum : ita (quod in me) promptum est et vobis, qui Romæ estis, evangelizare.* Quod quum diu cupivit facere presens et non potuit, absens quantum licuit idem attemptavit : *Ut aliquem fructum habeat in illis sicut in ceteris gentibus.* Nam *a Jerusalem per circuitum usque ad Illiricum* propagavit evangelium Christi non suis viribus, sed Dei gracia ; non aliorum vestigia sequens, sede alia itinera capiens, et ad ea loca veniens in quibus antea non nominatus fuit Christus ; ut, quemadmodum Esaias predixit, *Qui non audierint de illo intelligant.* Rom. i. 14.

Rom. xv. 19.

Es. lii. 15.

Ea longa et diversa paragracione provinciarum imperii non potuit, sicut habuit diu ante in mente, Romam proficisci, sed post revisam hierosolimam, quo erat nunc iturus, partim ut rerum a se gestarum illic racionem redderet. Nam id erat celebre institutum in prima ecclesia, ut Clemens tradit, ut quisque Jacobo hierosolimæ actæ provinciæ racionem redderet. Partim eciam illuc contendit, ut fratres fame laborantes et pressos, collecta elemosina ex Macedonia et Achaia relevaret. Sevit enim tum fames gravius ; quam futuram Antiochiæ predixit Agabus. Item hierosolomitani Christiani odio habiti ab omnibus, et a Judeis ab omni commoditate exclusi, extrema necessitate astricti fuerunt. Illis, ut sibi fuit mandatum ab apostolis, Paulus voluit succurrere. Et inter predicandum in Macedonia et Grecia, quum multam hominum liberalitatem commovisset, quicquid collatum fuerit, communem illam graciam voluit ipse hierosolimam deferre. Quo facto habuit in proposito per Italiam in Hispaniam proficisci. Illuc autem aliquando venerit nec ne, non intelligo. Tametsi Ivo Carnotensis episcopus, vir non indoctus, iñ cronicis ab eo editis, Paulum in Hispaniam profectum asserit, relictis in Gallia Areletæ Trophemo, et Viennæ Crescente; qui in illis locis Christi divinitatem denunciarent. Verum secundo Neronis anno, priusquam Romam venerat, ad duodecim annos supervixit, et versus occidentem profectus est. At quousque perexit, ex nulla gravi auctoritate queo asserere; nisi audiamus quod Io. Chrysostomus scribit in libro de laudibus Pauli, omelia ultima, in qua illum in Hispaniam profectum tradit.

Quum autem dixerat Macedoniam et Achaiam re ipsa et in effectu ostendisse liberalitatem in succursum pauperum, tum subjunxit Paulus, *Placuit* enim *eis, et debitores sunt eorum,* pro spiritualibus scilicet *carnalia* (id est, quæ sunt necessaria victui) *ministrare*. Sed animadvertendum est quod dicit, *Placuit*. Quod quidem dicit ut ostendat debita posse exigi ; eaque solvere et prestare hominibus placet ; illa videlicet debita quæ in elimosinis sunt, quæ exhibeantur in victum et vestitum hominum spiritualium ; quæ quantum hominibus datoribus dare placet, accipi potest. Qui quanquam debent sustinere spirituales, tamen ab illis plus exigere non debemus quam eis dare placet. Melius enim esset non darent, quam inviti darent, propterea quod quicquid †quod† non est voluntarium in ecclesia perniciosum est. Exhortandi igitur sunt homines, non tam ut darent, quam ut sponte darent. Elicienda est dulci doctrina prompta voluntas, non acerba exaccione extorquenda pecunia nomine decimarum et oblacionum. Decimas enim et oblaciones non flagitavit Paulus, sed solum liberalitatem hominum spontaneam, et hoc duntaxat ad pauperum levandam necessitatem. Ad Timotheum scribit: *Habentes* autem *alimenta, et quibus tegamur, hiis contenti sumus. Radix omnium malorum est cupiditas.* Ideo admonuit illum ut fugeret rerum appeticionem, quæ vocatur avaricia; et *sectetur justiciam, pietatem, fidem, charitatem, pacienciam, mansuetudinem.*

Similiter hac nostra tempestate admonendi sunt sacerdotes, ut eadem sectentur, utque hæc exemplo sui in suos parochianos transfundant, faciantque illos, exemplo dato in seipsis, justos, pios, mansuetos, fideles, pacientes, charitate plenos ; et tum facile liberalitas quam exposcunt sequetur certe eciam copiosius quam velint, si ipsi non plus cupiunt quam debent. Si non solum verbis sed eciam tua ipsius vita docueris homines bonitatem imitari, tunc certe, te vel tacente, quantum tuæ vitæ erit necessarium conferetur ; quo plus cur exigamus, ex doctrina Christi non video quidem. Paulus eciam ipse ab ultro conferentibus noluit accipere, sed pocius laboravit manibus, scenofactoria arte victum queritans ; ne vel suspicionem avariciæ daret, vel evangelio scandalum faceret. Aliis autem, maxime hierosolomitanis fratribus, exegit victui necessaria; quatenus homines sua sponte dare voluerint ; quos docuit debere suppeditare quæ sunt necessaria corpori illis, a quibus acceperint quæ sunt saluti animæ necessaria.

Deinde petit a Romanis ut precentur Deum pro se, jam ituro hierosolimam in medios hostes Christiani nominis, ut ab inimicis tutam profectionem et fratribus gratam habeat. Quod revera precatu fuit necessarium. Quoniam obtigit Paulo illa ultima sua profectio hierosolimam minime tuta, cum statim illic acceptus ab infidelibus Judeis mille modis jactatus fuit, sicut Agabus propheta ei dixit fore. Sed ille homo magno animo, fide et amore Christi, fuit *paratus non solum ligari, sed eciam pro nomine Jesu Christi emori hierosolimæ.* Qui quum venerit hierosolimam, fratribus gratus et acceptus, Jacobo illic et senatui Christiano quid in Christianismo egerit totum ordine retulit. Ab illis ei imperatum fuit, ut more et ritu Judeorum se purgaret in templo diebus septem, raso capite et factis oblacionibus. [In]de crimine ei objecto quod suasit Judeis ut filios suos non circumcidant, significans circumcisionem post Christum nihil ad rem pertinere (at vero hierosolimæ apud Judeos perrexit circumcisio cum Christianitate in genere Judeorum) ; ex templo arreptus fuit a Judeis infidelibus, et tractus ad necem ; quam non vitasset, nisi Lysias Claudius, tribunus cohortis, eum e manibus Judeorum erupuisset ; quem egre defendit contra

Rom. xv. 30.

Act. xxi. 13.

Act. xxi. 26.

insidias et impetum Judeorum. In carcere tunc Paulus au-
divit a Domino: *Constans esto*. *Sicut enim testificatus es
me in hierusalem, sic te et Romæ oportet testificari*.

Act. xxiii. 11.

A tribuno missus fuit Paulus ad Felicem, profectum tunc
Siriæ et Judeæ ; in cujus custodia Cesariæ biennium mansit.
Tum relictus Portio Festo, qui imperante Nerone Felici
successit, ab eo, postquam se apud Agrippam regem defendit, missus Romam vinctus venit; ubi biennium transegit
libera custodia. Supervixit deinde annis decem, quo tempore putatur in Hyspaniam ivisse; quod Joannes Chrisosto-
mus, in libro de laudibus Pauli, et post illum Carnotensis
episcopus Ivo tradit. Quod si fecerit, tum reversus postea
Romam anno a Christi passione xxxvi^{to}, Neronis imperii
anno terciodecimo, in prima Christianorum persecucione
tandem necatus fuit. Quadriennio autem antequam Romam
venerat, et anno suæ predicacionis xx^{o} videtur hanc epistolam
ad Romanos scripsisse. Nam in collectione elemosinarum
ex Macedonia et Grecia, et profectione hierosolimam, et
conflictu cum Judeis, et denique itineracione Romam, videntur quatuor anni transiise. Itaque Romam tandem
venit, fratribus illic gratissimus, ad quos non veritus est
antea scribere, quum ei fuit mandatum ut omni racione
Christi fidem exaugeret.

CAP. XVI.

POSTREMO in hac epistola sunt amicorum commenda-
ciones, tum virorum tum feminarum, et salutaciones
quam amantissimæ, ex ingenti Pauli charitate profectæ.

Pheben femina videtur una cum hac epistola Romam
ivisse. Reliqui quos velit salutatos, quos aliis in locis
novit, vel Romæ manserunt, vel illic negociati sunt. Aquila
Judeus cum Prisca conjuge, quam Lucas in Apostolorum
hystoria vocat Priscellam, edicto Claudii imperatoris omnibus Judeis Roma migrantibus, Corinthum venit, et Paulum
venientem Athenis Corinthum hospitem recepit. Androni-
cum et Juliam vocat *nobiles in apostolis* ; unde constat omnes

xvi. 7.

missos evangelizatum merito apostolos vocari. Reliquos deinde quos salvere jubet apostolus, intelligamus insignes fuisse vel virtute vel operibus ; quos sua commemoracione et laude voluit Paulus in virtute sustinere. Recordacio enim et laus divinorum hominum ad virtutem vel currentes incitat. Jubet deinde *invicem sancte dissuavientur*, et amplexu amoris constent, caveantque a falsis et seductoribus, seminatoribus discordiarum, et scrupulos injicientes, blando sermone mestantes homines simpliciores, non Christi sed suum lucrum querentes, non inservientes Deo sed ventri. Postremo admonet, *sapientes in bono sint, et in malos simplices*, sciantque bene cogitare et agere, non male. Quod scire, videlicet malum agere, nescire est.

Ultimo loco optat eis graciam, quæ causa est effectrix, autrix, conservatrix omnium bonorum, quæ vel sunt vel esse possunt in hominibus. Cujus graciæ munere diximus scribentes in hanc epistolam quicquid bene diximus. Quod velim lector boni consulat, beneque de nobis sensiat, qui de Paulo voluimus bene sentire, conatique sumus, quoad potuimus, divina gracia adjuti, veros illius sensus exprimere. Quod quam fecimus haud scimus sane. Voluntatem tamen habuimus maximam faciendi.

Finis argumenti in Epistolam Pauli ad Romanos.

Oxoniæ.

APPENDIX.

(On a work supposed to be Dean Colet's.)

THERE is extant, among the Gale MSS. in the Library of Trinity College, Cambridge, a volume (marked O. 4. 44) " very clearly written on fine vellum, in the Italian hand of Queen Elizabeth's time," the contents of which have been generally believed to be the work of Dean Colet. Mr. Seebohm in his *Oxford Reformers* (2nd ed. p. 33 *n.*), was the first to call this opinion in question; and as the matter is one of some interest, not only in its bearing on the present Lectures, but as affecting our general estimate of Colet's writings, I will endeavour to examine the evidence for and against. I must first express my great obligation to the Librarian of Trinity, T. Aldis Wright, Esq., for furnishing me with a description of the MS., and to Mr. Seebohm, for the loan of his carefully-made transcript of it.

The first page of the volume is filled with detached apophthegms, some of which are beautiful and striking; as, "Sine alios accendere candelas in igne tuo, et abs te discere sapientiam." On the second begins a uniform series of abstracts of all St. Paul's Epistles in order, ending on p. 93. But the peculiar circumstance is, that the order is reversed; the series going regularly backwards from *Hebrews* to *Romans*. On p. 93 begins a much fuller commentary, a course of homilies, in fact, on the First Epistle of St. Peter; and some extracts from the first Chapter of *Romans*, on p. 120, complete the work. On the fly-leaf is the following note, in the handwriting of its former owner, the learned Dr. Thomas Gale:—

" Videtur esse opus Joannis Coleti Decani S^{ti} Pauli Lond :
" Multa hic plane eadem sunt cum iis quæ scripsit manu sua Coletus, in libro qui servatur in Capitulari domo Ecclesiæ S^{ti} Pauli : atque adeo hæc sunt quasi secundæ curæ.

"Multa hic parum emendata scribuntur, quo vitio Coletus laborabat. Ea subinde, notantur, et corriguntur.

" Ordo Epistolarum S^{ti} Pauli non est idem hic, qui est in illo altero libro manu Coleti scripto.

" T. G."

It will be seen from this, that Dr. Gale declared many parts of this composition to be "clearly the same" with what was found in a MS. of Colet's own writing, preserved in the Chapter House at St. Paul's. Unfortunately, the MS. thus referred to is no longer discoverable. But when we take into account the high authority, on such a point, of the Editor of *Historiæ Britannicæ Scriptores*, who was himself also a Prebendary of St. Paul's, his statement carries the greatest possible weight.

Mr. Seebohm's argument against the genuineness of the Gale MS. rested on the fact, that certain coincidences were observable between it and the *Annotationes* of Erasmus; in particular, the remarks on *Penula* (2 Tim. iv. 13), *Antichristus* (2 Thess. ii.), and the note on 1 Thess. v. 12.

Now I think it will be allowed to be natural and probable, that, if the work were Colet's, we should find some traces of indebtedness here and there to the *Annotationes*. For the first edition of them appeared in 1516, three years before Colet's death. He is known to have read the work, and it would be only reasonable that he should incorporate in his abstracts of the Epistles some of the explanations it contained. The question then becomes: can anything be found in the Gale MS., manifestly taken from an edition later than Colet's death, and not in the previous ones?

Mr. Seebohm has detected what appears to be an instance of this; but I think it is so extremely slight, as not to admit of any conclusion being based upon it. The instance is, that in the note on *Penula*, above-mentioned, the author of the MS. has "quo tegebatur ab *imbribus*," while the editions of 1516 and 1519 have " quo tegimur ab *hymbribus*," that of 1522, " quo tegimur ab *imbribus*." In other words, the spelling of *imbribus*, in the MS., agrees with the edition of 1522, not with either of the two published before Colet's death.

As evidence on the other side, I have set down, in parallel columns, a few of the more striking expressions in which a resemblance is found between the language of the MS. and that of this present work. The general cast of the language cannot be conveyed by any such fragmentary extracts; but it has left a very strong impression on my own mind that the MS. contains Dean Colet's writings.

APPENDIX. 231

Trin. Coll. MS. "O. 4. 44."

" Itaque mactetis corpora vestra, id est, *pecuinas affectiones.*" p. 91.

" Ardentes charitate inter eos *qui frigent malitia.*" p. 92.

" Ut semper in hoc *caliginoso* mundo vivatis." p. 102.

" Gratia potentior est quam peccatum ; et plus potest gratia ad salvationem, quam peccatum ad damnationem." p. 88.

" Quare Deum in Jesu sic amantem redamemus." p. 90.

" Regatis eos pastoraliter, et pascatis regaliter." p. 116.

" Purgatio, illuminatio, perfectio." p. 5.

Colet on the " Romans."

" Mactacio illa pecoris significat *pecuinas appeticiones* in corpore enecari oportere." p. 177.

" Benignitate vestra calefacietis *algentes malicia.*" p. 196.
" Calor amoris . . . *frigidos homines* . . . excalefaciat." p. 204.

" Mens detruditur in grave et hoc *caliginosum* corpus." p. 163.

" Credendum est longe plus posse in mundo graciam reconciliantem Deo, quam peccatum a Deo alienans." p. 142.

"Accepto amore amantem Deum redament." p. 143.

P. 69. *n.* 3.

(The key-note of Colet's Treatise on the *Hierarchies* : passingly alluded to, p. 198.)

It may be added, in explanation of the fact that the MS. is in a hand of Queen Elizabeth's time, that Archbishop Parker, who obtained others of Colet's papers, may probably have had the present series transcribed. Bale tells us in what state many of Colet's manuscripts were found at his death, " divaricatis pagellis, in secretissimo suæ bibliothecæ loco." If the sheets were thus scattered loosely about, it is easy to understand how, in the Elizabethan transcript, the order might have got reversed. Colet himself, in his will, speaks of " Abbreviations," as part of his literary remains ; and nothing yet found would so well answer the description.

Should the homiletic commentary on 1 Peter ever see the

light, it will not detract, I think, from Colet's fame, if he be admitted the author. The one who could utter such words as the following, deserves to prove Dean Colet:—"Conjunx conjugem aspiciat sanctis oculis, tanquam sororem in Christo. Angelus, ut ita dicam, angelum intueatur. Angelus cum angelo habitet, amator angelicæ castitatis."

INDEX.

∗∗ *The Roman numerals refer to the pages of the Introduction.*

ALEXANDER Dolensis, xv.
Anathema, 33.
Aquinas, Thomas, 124 *n*.
Aristeas, 60.
Aristotle, xvii, xxvii, 28 *n*, 76 *n*, 78 *n*.
Augustine, quoted, 36, 65, 78 *n*, 113 *n*.

Bacon, Lord, quoted, 73 *n*, 81 *n*, 87 *n*, 111 *n*.
Baptism, ancient mode of, 20 *n*.
Baptista Mantuanus, xiii, 33, 42 *n*, 49 *n*.
Bengel, quoted, 28 *n*.

Cape, discovery of the, xii.
Chaucer, quoted, 100 *n*.
Chrysostom, quoted, 53 *n*, 109 *n*., 128, 130.
Circumcision, 7.
Clemens Romanus, 126.
Clementines, the, 126 *n*.
COLET, DEAN, early life of, xi; age of, xi *n*; maxims of, xiv, 229; Platonism introduced by, xiv, xix; return of, from Italy, xxi; academic degrees of, xxv; Platonic character of his Lectures, xxvi; circumstances of their delivery, 87 *n*; previous Lectures of, on 1 Corinthians, 90 *n*; as a Persecutor? xxxvi *n*; as a Reformer, xxxviii; not Augustinian, xxxix; his love for order, xl; connection of, with physicians, 18 *n*; opinion of Ficino, 32; admiration of, for St. Paul, 57 *n*; resumes his Lectures, 57; peculiarity of style, 69 *n*; his chronology, 94; Letters on Genesis, 105 *n*; supposed work of, 229.
Collet, John, apophthegms of, 68 *n*, 69 *n*.
Columbus, xii.

Day, interpretation of the word, 113.
Divinity Lectures, xx.
Duns, John Scotus, xviii; his Latinity, xxii; his *Quæstiones*, xxiii.

Epistolæ obscurorum virorum, xvi, 50 *n*.
Erasmus, his account of studies at Cambridge, xv; unfair estimate of, xli; quoted, xxxix *n*, 39 *n*, 48 *n*, 77 *n*, 113 *n*, 119 *n*, 220 *n*.
Evil, only to be conquered by good, 86, 93.

Faith, and Reason, 44, 83; Hope and Charity, 67.

INDEX.

Ficino, Marsiglio, xxix, xxxv *n*, 16 *n*, 26 *n*, 28 *n*, 29, 61 *n*, 76 *n*, 78 *n*, 79 *n*, 93 *n*.
Fleming, Bishop, xxxvii.
Foreknowledge, God's, 5, 6 *n*.
Form, and Matter, xxvi, xxvii, 20 *n*, 43 *n*, 46 *n*, 81 *n*.

Grace, power of, 10.; nature of, 12.
Grammar, xxxvii.
Gratius, Ortuinus, his *Fasciculus*, 119 *n*.

Heptaplus, the, xxxii.
Hierarchies of Dionysius, the, xxv, 67 *n*, 78 *n*, 90, 100 *n*.
Holt, John, xvi.

Israel, meaning of, 39.
Ivo, Bishop of Chartres, 95 *n*, 125 *n*, 127, 130.

Jerome, quoted, 6 *n*, 34, 38 *n*, 39 *n*, 48 *n*, 113 *n*.
Johnson, Dr., his opinion of Mirandola, xxxv *n*.

Kyderminster, Richard, xxxvi.

Law, the Mosaic, 17.
Logic, at the Universities, xviii.
Logicalia Parva, xvii, xxix.
Longland, Bishop, xxxv.
Love of God, better than knowledge, 31.
Luther, xiii, xxxviii, xl *n*, xli.

Margaret, Lady, Divinity Professorships of, xx.
Members, in Body, 71, 81.
Milk Street, xxv *n*.
Mirandola, Pico della, xxxii, 5 *n*, 27 *n*, 73 *n*, 75 *n*, 76 *n*.

More, Sir Thomas, at Oxford, xviii; lectures on Augustine, xxv; his opinion of logical studies, xxix; translates Mirandola, xxxv; his change of views, xxxviii *n*.

Nero, Emperor, 95.

Origen, quoted, 5 *n*, 6 *n*, 15 *n*, 53 *n*, 54, 110 *n*, 113 *n*.
Oxford, logical studies at, xix; Divinity Lectures at, xx.

Paul, St., Colet's admiration for, 57 *n*.
Pearson, Bishop, quoted, 34 *n*, 94 *n*, 125 *n*.
Phantasia, 69 *n*, 76 *n*, 79 *n*.
Pico, *see* Mirandola.
Pilati *Acta*, 125 *n*.
Pius, Albertus, xix, xxviii *n*.
Plato, xxvi, xxvii, 69 *n*, 74.
Plotinus, xxvi, xxx, 16.
Predestination, xxxix, 37, 38 *n*, 41.

Quodlibets, what, xxiii.

Reform, xl.
Robertson, Thomas, xxxvii.
Romans, Epistle to the, date of, 94 *n*, 130.
Rome, authorities in, 91, 98.

Sacrifices, significance of, 61.
Schoolmen, the, estimate of, xxiv.
Scotists, the, Colet's opinion of, xxii.
Scotus, John Erigena, 62 *n*.
Sin, no second atonement for, 14.
Stafford, George, xxvi.
Suetonius, quoted, 95.

INDEX.

Tataretus, or Tartaretus, Petrus, xviii.
Tertullian, quoted, 125 *n*.
Theologia Platonica, xxx, 29.
Tithes, disputes about, 118, 119 *n*, 120, 128.
Timæus, the, xxviii, 74.

University, early studies in the, xiv.
Urceus, Codrus, xix, 76 *n*.

Virgil, quoted, 100.

Vulgate, readings of the, 21 *n*, 23 *n*, 35 *n*, 39 *n*, 48 *n*, 50 *n*, 65 *n*, 79 *n*, 96 *n*, 105 *n*, 108 *n*, 109 *n*, 110 *n*, 112 *n*, 113 *n*, 117 *n*, 121 *n*, 122 *n*, 123 *n*.

Winchcombe, Abbot of, xxxvi, 57 *n*.
Wycliffe, version of, quoted, 49 *n*.
Wylsford, Edmund, xxi.

THE END.